Aptitude Revisited

APTITUDE

REVISITED

Rethinking Math and Science
Education for America's
Next Century

DAVID E. DREW

THE JOHNS HOPKINS UNIVERSITY PRESS
Baltimore and London

05 04 03 02 01 00 99 98 97 96   54321

The Johns Hopkins University Press
2715 North Charles Street
Baltimore, Maryland 21218-4319
The Johns Hopkins Press Ltd., London

Library of Congress Cataloging-in-Publication Data will be
found at the end of this book.
A catalog record for this book is available from the
British Library.

ISBN 0-8018-5143-2

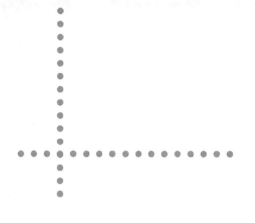

For Rebekah

Contents

Preface

The process of preparing this book has been one of discovery. I set out to write a book about science education but soon realized that mathematics education is more centrally linked to the educational and occupational achievement of young people. Ultimately, I recognized that I was writing a book about power in America. The people least likely to study mathematics and science in our society are those who have the least power, especially poor people, people of color, and women. However, in the postindustrial age, science and technology have assumed center stage. Those who fail to obtain an adequate background in these subjects in elementary school, junior high school, and high school will be at a competitive disadvantage in higher education and in the work world.

Our current expectations about who will successfully study science and mathematics are based on erroneous assumptions, totally at variance with the educational research literature. Until we correct this misapprehension about who can succeed in mathematics and science and begin educating *all* young people, the gap between the haves and the have-nots in our society will continue to widen.

Our schools are not getting the job done even for affluent White male students. If there were any doubt about this proposition, a review of the performance of American youngsters, even the top 1 percent, in international assessments of mathematics and science achievement would quickly dispel it. Unlike many, I don't believe that American schools have deteriorated during the past quarter-century. I believe the data show clearly that the problems have existed for a long time. The resources available to solve these problems include dedicated, hard-working, capable teachers who labor mightily every day to deliver a quality education to their students; parents who want the best for their children; and most important, the students themselves.

The final draft of this book was in press before the publication of Richard J. Herrnstein and Charles Murray's controversial book *The Bell Curve: Intelligence and Class Structure in American Life* (New York: Free Press, 1994). Although I was unaware of the arguments to be made by Herrnstein and Murray, my book can be viewed as a response to, and rejection of, their case. I refer the reader specifically to the section "Power and the Concept of Intelligence" in chapter 5 in my book, the research findings about the outstanding performance of African Americans and other minority students in calculus reported in chapter 6, and additional observations about the misuse of intelligence tests in the conclusion.

I believe Herrnstein and Murray have drawn the wrong conclusions from the data. But worse than that, they have asked the wrong question. Instead of asking what differences might be used to exclude some groups of people from education, wealth, and status, we should be asking how we can educate all youngsters so that they can compete in an increasingly technological economy.

The idea for this book evolved from research I have conducted about science, technology, and education, with a focus on human resources, since the late 1960s. Several principles have guided my writing:

—Usually, social scientists opt to add a highly specialized study to the literature. More attempts to synthesize and integrate the literature are needed.

—Some of the most important findings in educational research are buried, for all practical purposes, in a literature that is difficult for other scholars to use and virtually impossible for the general public to discover. This fugitive literature includes technical reports from research organizations and doctoral dissertations. Those who have access to this literature have an obligation to communicate it to wider audiences.

—Too frequently, important educational findings are published in professional journals but never translated into educational practice. Part of the blame for this lies with the researchers, who should communicate the implications of their findings to policymakers and practitioners.

Every book is shaped by the experiences of the author. As a social scientist, I have tried to review the data about mathematics and science education objectively. As a sociologist, I have focused upon the implications of the data for the distribution of status, prestige, and power in our society. As a professor, I have found that my own teaching experiences confirmed the importance of some of these research findings and led me to question others. Finally, as an adult with varied life experiences, I bring strong opinions about the importance of excellence, determination, persistence, and hard work in achieving any objective, whether personal, educational, or professional.

Preparation of this book was supported in part by a grant from the Kluge Foundation. John Kluge gave a $1 million grant to the Education program at the Claremont Graduate School for a study of ways to improve American schools in an increasingly diverse, multicultural society. This grant was facilitated by Ross Barrett, a member of the Education program's Board of Visitors. An advisory panel of consultants made up largely of present and former graduate students with particular expertise in mathematics and science education met frequently with me during preparation of the first draft, which they reviewed for me. These consultants included Martin Bonsangue, John Eichinger, Yolanda Ingles, Diana Kelly, Diane Morrison, Douglas Robinson, Daniel Solorzano, Lisa Wolf, and Audrey Yamagata-Noji, as well as my faculty colleague Philip Dreyer. In addition, early drafts profited from comments and constructive criticisms offered by Belle Drew, Gene Graham, Kenneth C. Green, Roger Rasmussen, Dudley Rauch, and Jill Tronvig. The development of my ideas also was facilitated by many lunchtime conversations with Sandy Astin and Philip Dreyer. Hedley Burrell, Bonnie Busenberg, Norman Drew, Diana Kelly, Roland Moses, Jack Schuster, and Joe Weeres forwarded books, articles, and papers that they suspected (usually correctly) I had not seen and would find useful.

Some of the text in this book appeared previously in publications of which I was the author or co-author: *Strengthening Academic Science* (New York: Praeger, 1985); "Class, Race, and Science Education," in *Class, Culture, and Race in American Schools: A Handbook*, ed. Stanley W. Rothstein (Westport, Conn.: Greenwood, 1995), 55–72; "Mathematics, Science, and Urban Education," in *Handbook of Schooling in Urban America*, ed. Stanley W. Rothstein (Westport, Conn.: Greenwood, 1993), 297–315; "How Undergraduates Experience Science Education," chapter 8 in A. Astin and H. S. Astin, *Undergraduate Science Education: The Impact of Different College Environments on the Educational Pipeline in the Sciences* (Los Angeles: Higher Education Research Institute, UCLA, 1992); Martin V. Bonsangue and David E. Drew, "Long-Term Effectiveness of the Calculus Workshop Model" (report to the National Science

Foundation, Apr. 1992); David E. Drew and Jill Anne Tronvig, *Assessing the Quality of National Data about Academic Scientists* (report to the National Science Foundation, June 1988).

My notes register my indebtedness to the works of others, permission to quote from which I here gratefully acknowledge.

Teresa Wilborn typed the manuscript and prepared and verified the tables and footnote citations. My editor at the Johns Hopkins University Press, Jackie Wehmueller, reviewed early drafts of the manuscript and guided me through the publication process. Joanne Allen was the copy editor, and the index was prepared by Gordon Brumm.

I am hopeful that any errors that remain can be blamed on one of the above people!

This book is dedicated to my daughter Rebekah, who soon will be completing high school and entering the adult world. I want to express my appreciation for the grace with which she handled the delays and disruptions in her life caused by this writing project. For one thing, she will once again be able to listen to Aerosmith at the usual ear-splitting decibel level.

Aptitude Revisited

INTRODUCTION

Problems and Solutions

> And I learned the greatest gift of all. The saddest thing in life is
> wasted talent. . . . And the choices that you make will shape your life
> forever.　　　　Colagero, in *A Bronx Tale,* by Chazz Palminteri

Compared with students in other countries, American students receive a mediocre education in mathematics and science. This is particularly disturbing because the analytical skills acquired in science education are vital for workers in the emerging international economy. As the information age has replaced the industrial age, science and technology have assumed a central importance.

Furthermore, the have-nots in American society—the poor, the disadvantaged, and people of color—are severely underrepresented in classrooms where mathematics and science are taught. Science education not only is vital for an increasingly technological society but also has become a vehicle through which the inequalities of our society are perpetuated and exacerbated. If current trends continue, the seemingly innocuous area of science education will dramatically widen the gap between the haves and the have-nots, the elite and the excluded, in the United States. In fact, the research reported in this volume strongly suggests that mathematics is the crucial filter determining access to many prestigious, respected, and lucrative careers.

Improving mathematics and science education, and more specifically increasing access to mathematics and science education, is essential for our national economic competitiveness. It can also be the catalyst for the social mobility of individuals and groups who have been outside the mainstream of the American economy. I argue in this book that every person is well advised to obtain extensive, thorough, and rigorous training in mathematics and science.

The key factors that determine who receives mathematics and science education—and, thus, who has access to wealth and power in our society and our economy—are sociological and psychological. They are not matters of curriculum, innate ability, or school funding. More to the point, the data indicate that millions of people are erroneously discouraged from studying mathematics and science, especially the former, because of false assumptions about who has the ability to master these subjects. These assumptions become self-fulfilling expectations, which ultimately undermine the self-concept of female students, impoverished students, and students of color. Sometimes these erroneous assumptions are held by teachers or parents with the best of intentions. But the resulting impact on self-concepts, aspirations, and achievement are destructive and pernicious. If a person has been persuaded not to pursue his or her dream career as a result of being told, "You would need to study math, and, let's face it, you're no good at that," then that person has suffered two injustices. The first is the establishment of an unjustified barrier to his or her professional aspirations. The second is the untenable damage done to his or her self-concept.

The fact is that most people can master the subject matter of mathematics, even calculus, and other scientific fields. The first and most important step for the student is to recognize this and not let himself or herself be ruled out of the game before it starts.

Research in a range of disciplines has suggested solutions to these problems. The disciplines include educational research (e.g., studies about cooperative learning), cognitive psychology (e.g., studies about the impact of self-esteem and self-efficacy), sociology (e.g., studies about the links between reference group interactions and achievement), multivariate statistics (e.g., examination of the assumptions underlying factor analysis and intelligence testing), and the history of science (e.g., identification of powerful insights that have come from "unlikely" people).

The single most important change required involves a national consciousness raising. Teachers, parents, and the students themselves must recognize that virtually every child has the capacity to master mathematics and science and should be taught these subjects. This is true for females as well as for males, for poverty-stricken students as well as those from more affluent backgrounds, and for persons of every ethnicity. Beyond consciousness raising, the research results provide guidance as to how the reform of science education can proceed most effectively.

Training in technical fields is essential for providing highly skilled labor for industry as well as professionals to conduct the research and development that fuel America's economic competitiveness. Most Americans take U.S. leadership in science for granted. The list of discoveries and inventions by Americans—from Benjamin Franklin's kite-flying experiment about electricity, to Edison's pioneering research, to the Manhattan Project—is awesome. However, there is a very real danger that we may lose our status as scientific leaders just as we lost our number-one status in the international automobile market. In his best-selling book *The Rise and Fall of the Great Powers,* Paul Kennedy argues that the United States, like many prior world powers, may be on an inevitable downswing, and he suggests that continued high-quality scientific research and development are vital components of our strength.[1] But we have neglected the educational programs that drive the system.

Extensive education is being done by business and industry because neither professionals nor skilled workers arrive on the job with sufficient training. There is a growing body of evidence about the inability of high school graduates to meet industry's need for workers because they have so few basic skills. For example, a young person who once needed to learn how to operate a lathe now will find himself or herself being asked to operate computer-aided machinery.

In addition, our universities are not providing students with sufficient scientific literacy and training. University scientists conduct research and teach within increasingly compartmentalized specialties. Most university science education is designed by specialists trained in the 1960s. Moreover, as has been suggested, it is easier to reorganize a graveyard then to reorganize a university department.

It is not too late to turn this situation around. A key factor is the quality of teachers we attract to our elementary and secondary schools. In addition, the barriers that have prevented women, the poor, and underrepresented minorities from participating fully in technical careers must be confronted. I argue that the fulcrum on which science education pivots, the subject that dissuades many young people from technical careers, is mathematics.

Problems

The Declining Technological Competitiveness
of American Workers

According to David Goodstein, vice provost and professor of physics and applied physics at the California Institute of Technology,

> Those engines of research are fueled by foreign graduate students, from around the world, and particularly from the Pacific rim. The role that Greece once served for the Roman Empire, and that Europe served for the prewar America, America is now serving for our friends from across the ocean. We are the source of culture and learning, at least in physics. Historians may or may not ultimately conclude that this was the era in which the torch of world leadership was passed from us to other hands. But there is no denying the fact that, at least in physics education, we are now playing the role traditionally reserved for the world leader of the previous era. There is a crucial difference, however. If we do start turning out too few American students for all those jobs we hear about, the foreign students will stay here and take them. That's why I'm not so worried about that part of the problem.[2]

I recently interviewed an experienced technical writer with a major computer firm in Silicon Valley. When I asked her about the skills of the technical staffers, she replied that she was the only American and that the other fourteen members of the technical staff were engineers from other countries. She added that her work group was not unusual. Most of the software engineers in Silicon Valley have green cards. They move there from such countries as India, Taiwan, and Korea. One of her friends, a Korean, recently bought a new car from a dealer in California who specializes in Korean customers. Her friend explained that this dealer knows what optional features Koreans prefer in an automobile. The dealership is thriving because there are so many engineers and programmers from Korea working in Silicon Valley.

Substantial numbers of the graduate students in science, mathematics, and engineering in the United States are international students. According to an article in a National Academy of Sciences journal, while more than 90 percent of undergraduates in engineering were U.S. citizens, only 45 percent of new Ph.D.'s in engineering were U.S. citizens. Since about 4 percent of these new Ph.D.'s were naturalized citizens, only 40 percent were indigenous citizens who had attended American elementary and secondary schools.[3]

I do not believe that the presence of international students in our Ph.D.

programs is in itself a problem. I agree with Harvard professor Sheldon Glashow, a Nobel prize winner in physics, who said,

We import them. We import them from Iran, we import them from Turkey, and Taiwan, from whatever countries we can find. They stay in this country—more than half of them stay in this country—they take all the good jobs. And I'm not attacking this, this is not a problem. This is the solution. These new Americans who are a vital part of America today and are the technological backbone of the country are the solution. Our people can't hack it.[4]

For many decades, naturalized citizens have been among the top scientists in America. We have only to think of the influx of highly productive scientists and engineers who escaped from Nazi Germany to illustrate this. The present influx of graduate students, including those recent immigrants from Southeast Asia, may indeed become the technological backbone of our nation's scientific and industrial effort. But our own science education is in trouble if the future of our national research enterprise becomes dependent upon the vicissitudes of immigration legislation. If new immigration laws should discourage these foreign scientists from remaining in our country after completing their education, the implications for national research and development could be devastating. What is really disturbing is Professor Glashow's last comment, "Our people can't hack it." He's right.

Frank Layden, former coach of the Utah Jazz, experienced great frustration with one player's inability to learn a new basketball maneuver despite extensive practice. Finally, he said to the player, "We've been working on this every night for weeks. Yet you still can't seem to get it. Frankly, I can't decide if your problem is ignorance or apathy." The player glared at him and replied, "I don't know and I don't care." Our young people don't know enough about mathematics and science and most of them don't care.

During the mid-1980s the International Association for the Evaluation of Educational Achievement (IEA) conducted a study of science achievement by elementary and high school students in seventeen countries.[5] Ten-year-olds in America were about in the middle of the pack when compared with ten-year-olds from countries like Australia, Finland, Hong Kong, Hungary, Japan, the Philippines, Poland, Sweden, and Thailand. American fourteen-year-olds tied for fourteenth place among the seventeen countries. Our high school seniors, tested separately in biology, chemistry, and physics, came in dead last, or close to it, depending on the discipline. The authors of this international study said about the United States that "for a technologically advanced country, it would appear that a re-examination of how science is presented and studied is required."[6]

The number of students who find science interesting seems to shrink as they progress through the school system. R. E. Yager and J. E. Penick presented data to illustrate this point and concluded that "the more years our students enroll in science courses, the less they like it. Obviously, if one of our goals is for students to enjoy science and feel successful at it, we should quit teaching science in third grade. Or perhaps we should try teaching it differently."[7]

Science Teachers from Kindergarten through College

If we are to improve the education of science students, we must improve the selection and education of science teachers. The power to change the dismal statistics about the declining number of students who believe that science is interesting or fun or exciting lies with the teacher. John Eichinger, a researcher and former junior high school science teacher, commented that "honest curiosity, fallibility, and enthusiasm are the science teacher's most powerful tools."[8]

Good teaching involves knowing what methods are effective. However, despite considerable evidence about the value of laboratory and field experience, a national study by the Educational Testing Service found:

- Only 35 percent of the seventh graders and 53 percent of the eleventh graders reported working with other students on science experiments at least on a weekly basis.
- Over half of the third graders and more than 80 percent of the seventh and eleventh graders reported *never* going on field trips with their science class.
- Sixty percent of the seventh graders and 41 percent of the eleventh graders said they *never* had to write up the results of science experiments.[9]

One explanation for the poor performance of U.S. students, according to Iris Weiss, is the decline during the past decade in the percentage of time teachers devote to hands-on work as opposed to lectures. She also observed that while many high school science and mathematics teachers have a science degree, their major was often in a different science field than the one they presently are teaching.[10]

Role models are important for elementary and secondary school students. I once heard Senator John Glenn give a vivid description of how his interest in science was stimulated by a high school teacher who invited Glenn to join him and his family on a summer vacation trip. Senator Glenn described with great enthusiasm how he saw steel being made in Pittsburgh and how they visited Niagara Falls, where he watched the generators in awe. Obviously, curriculum is very important in science education. And, obviously, we go to great lengths to teach people how to be good teachers. But we must think carefully about how we can draw more talented and committed young people into careers as science teachers.

At the college level, students planning careers in science need to see and learn from professors who are excellent research role models. Instead, they read about increasing reported instances of scientific fraud. More to the point, they rarely are taught by instructors who are actively engaged in research and can model this process for them.

Many undergraduates at large universities are taught by teaching assistants. Recall that about half the graduate students in many science and engineering disciplines are international students. Many foreign students do not have a full command of English. Many are from countries with a language and culture quite different from those of their American students.[11] For example, they may have repressive views about appropriate roles for women in society.

A more pernicious reason for the lack of good role models has to do with the stark contrast between the distribution of federal funds and the distribution of talented academic scientists. In my book *Strengthening Academic Science* I discussed how this disparity has damaged the productivity of a generation of young researchers.[12] For many years now, federal funds for university research have been concentrated in a few institutions. Every year, roughly half the federal support for basic research in many disciplines is awarded to the top twenty universities. But the data I reported suggest that the top young researchers may not be at the top twenty institutions. Because of the demography of the academic world in the past two decades, in particular the "tenure logjam," because of which many leading institutions had virtually no job openings for years, the most talented new Ph.D.'s from the best departments who chose academic careers have taken jobs in second- and third-tier institutions. Thus, the best young physicists from Harvard, Berkeley, and Michigan have not been taking jobs at similar institutions, but at schools like the University of Arkansas and North Dakota State University.

In my book, I reported analyses of surveys of sixty thousand scientists and hundreds of interviews with scientists and administrators. The data revealed that the continued concentration of federal science funds may be destroying the potential productivity of these brilliant young scientists at second- and third-tier universities. Furthermore, these new Ph.D.'s then are unable to demonstrate to undergraduates what the research process looks like. And, of course, they are unable to engage undergraduates directly as participants in that research process. College students who hear young professors talk about the excitement of research but note that those same professors are not conducting much research are less likely to choose careers as scientists.

This situation is made more serious by the fact that there are vast numbers of students, many of them highly capable potential scientists, enrolled at these universities. While some of the recent literature about future scientists focuses on the Ivy League and elite research universities and some discusses the Antioch- or Claremont-type selective liberal arts colleges, the fact is that there are far more students enrolled in the large state universities. Thousands more of our young people are attending schools like Montana State, Kansas State, and the University of Missouri than are attending schools like Harvard, Stanford, and Oberlin.

Mathematics Is the Filter

Consider the following widely held beliefs about mathematics: "Americans are better at math than people from other countries, except Asians." "Now that we have calculators and computers, nobody (except scientists) needs to learn mathematics." "Most women can't do math." Each of these statements is false, but each is a myth that has become embedded in American culture. In a ranking of things that most Americans hate, fear, and detest, mathematics rates right up there with taxes and politicians.

Mathematician John Allen Paulos has argued that Americans suffer from what he calls "innumeracy," the inability to deal with numbers and mathematics, a deficiency he describes as parallel to illiteracy. He observes that "unlike other failings which are hidden, mathematical illiteracy is often flaunted: 'I can't even balance my checkbook,' 'I'm a people person, not a numbers person' or 'I always hated math.' Part of the reason for this perverse pride in mathematical ignorance is that its consequences are not usually as obvious as are those of other weakness."[13] Even people who like mathematics often won't admit it. We've all met the die-hard sports fan who "hates mathematics" but can tell you down to the third decimal place what a baseball player's batting and slugging averages will be if he gets extra-base hits in his next two times at bat. Data reported in chapter 3, from a series of international studies conducted during the past quarter-century, consistently reveal that U.S. students perform poorly on tests of mathematics achievement.

Research is revealing that mastery of mathematics may be the single factor most related to an individual's success in college and beyond. Furthermore, virtually everyone can learn advanced mathematical concepts, even those who start late. The negative attitudes about mathematics achievement are based on incorrect assumptions about who can learn this subject.

Avoidance of mathematics is the hidden factor that explains a surprising percentage of the career decisions made by young people. There are people who want to be doctors and dentists but choose other careers so that they will not have to take mathematics in college. An academic counselor at a large technical university who works with students transferring from community colleges reports that she repeatedly is told, "I'd like to major in ——, but I can't do math so I'm going to become a teacher instead." Think of the introduction those future teachers' students will have to the joys of arithmetic and mathematics.

A recent College Board study about success on the Scholastic Aptitude Test (SAT) and in college concluded that the key factor was mathematics. In fact, according to Donald Stewart, president of the College Board, "Math is the gatekeeper for success in college."

The "Strange" Concept of Aptitude

Several years ago I was talking with a colleague who is a mathematics professor in China. He made a very telling point. He noted that virtually everybody in China learns advanced mathematics, while only a few do so in the United States. He said that in China it is assumed that everyone can master advanced concepts, and everyone is expected to do so. He said that in America we have this "strange concept of aptitude."

Our approach to teaching depends upon whether we assume that (1) virtually everyone can master the material and the challenge is to present it in a manner that allows them to do so or (2) the material is tough and only a few of the best and brightest will be able to learn it. Put another way, the question is whether mathematics is an abundant resource that can be used to empower most people in our society or a scarce resource to be doled out only to the most able. Most mathematics teachers embrace the second philosophy.

Aptitude and intelligence tests are most useful in situations where access to resources, for example, admission to college, must be limited only to a few and a legitimate basis for identifying those people is needed. (Of course, the test should be free of gender, ethnic, and economic biases.) But these tests are not needed in situations where the resources are not scarce.

Furthermore, the widespread use of such tests can be extremely destructive if they send a message—an incorrect message—to those who are not selected that they are incapable of learning the material. When this happens a device that was created to allocate scarce resources has become the instrument that destroys the self-image and aspirations of many students.

Even when our educational system works for Anglo, middle-class, male children, it discourages females, poor people, and people of color from careers in science, mathematics, and engineering. In recent years more than half of the Ph.D.s awarded nationally in engineering went to foreign students. The percentages awarded to women, African Americans, and Latinos were dismally low. The silver lining around this particular cloud is that these previously neglected students represent a large source of very capable future scientists and technical workers.

Contributing to the problem are the attitudes and expectations held by some teachers about the capabilities of girls and minority students. I teach about multivariate statistical analysis in our Ph.D. program at the Claremont Graduate School. I have encountered many students, especially women and students of color, who feared mathematics and were sure they could not do it. (Most graduate students dread statistics and put it off as long as possible.) Virtually all of these students discovered that they were capable of understanding and conducting sophisticated statistical analyses like hierarchical multiple regression. In conversation, I often find that such negative self-images go back to an elementary school teacher with a sexist or racist attitude, a person who thought that "girls can't do math" and managed to traumatize students, who now must be convinced about their real ability. Sheila Tobias has articulated and studied the concept of "math anxiety" and has shown how and why this affliction is particularly prevalent among women.[14]

Through the 1988 movie *Stand and Deliver,* many people have become aware of the extraordinary accomplishments of Jaime Escalante, the mathematics teacher at Garfield High School in East Los Angeles who successfully prepared many Latino and other students from poor families to take the Educational Testing Service Advanced Placement test in calculus. The most important message from this experience is not that Jaime Escalante is an extraordinary and successful teacher, although this certainly is true, but that many poor, minority high school students, whom most educators might have considered incapable of mastering calculus, did just that when they were taught by a very creative instructor.

It is disturbing that many teachers erroneously believe that certain kinds of students cannot do mathematics. This becomes tragic when the students themselves incorporate those devastating myths into their self-concepts and then lower their aspirations, thereby shortchanging what they can do with their lives.

There is a fascinating book called *The Experts Speak* that is devoted totally to incorrect predictions made by experts about people in sports, politics, literature, the arts, and entertainment. To cite one example, after viewing one young man's screen test, a movie executive summed him up as follows: "short, balding, can't act, dances a little."[15] He was writing about Fred Astaire. We are all lucky Mr. Astaire didn't lower his aspirations.

Without question, the best information available about college students comes from the Cooperative Institutional Research Program (CIRP), conducted by UCLA's Higher Education Research Institute (HERI). The program has collected substantial data about more than seven million college freshmen during the past twenty-five years. The data include information about freshmen majors and career aspirations. Plotted over a twenty-five-year period, the percentage of freshmen choosing mathematics dropped precipitously. Mathematics is not attracting students. In part, this is because many mathematics professors take the attitude that they'll see who's tough enough to survive and flunk the rest out.

In recent analyses I conducted with the CIRP data I examined mathematical self-concepts, specifically, the percentage of students who rated themselves as being in the top 10 percent of college students in terms of their mathematics ability. The results are both fascinating and disturbing. Among Anglos 24 percent of the men thought they were in the top 10 percent, whereas only 10 percent of the women placed themselves there. Among African Americans 14 percent of the men and 8 percent of the women thought they were in the top 10 percent; and among Chicanos, 28 percent of the men and 8 percent of women. Finally, among Asians 40 percent of the men and 24 percent of the women thought they were in the top 10 percent. In further analyses, which are discussed in chapter 4, I related these self-assessments to an actual ability measure. The findings about the mathematical self-concepts of women were particularly disturbing.

Solutions

During the past decade many task force reports and studies have detailed what is wrong with American education. The first, and the most widely quoted, was *A Nation at Risk*.[16] Also, a number of curriculum and educational reform initiatives have been launched. Because of the fundamentally decentralized nature of American schooling, few reform movements aimed at the schools are likely to have a massive impact. Key policy decisions are made in thousands of separate school districts. However, several efforts in science education should be highlighted.

Project 2061 (named for the year Halley's comet next returns to Earth) is a massive, long-term effort sponsored by the American Association for the Advancement of Science (AAAS). A preliminary report, *Science for All Americans*, has been widely disseminated and discussed.[17] Another large project, sponsored by the National Science Teachers Association and titled Scope, Sequence, and Coordination, is being implemented more rapidly. Curriculum reform presently is under way in California, Iowa, and Texas. These two efforts, along with a parallel effort in mathematics education spearheaded by the National Council of Teachers of Mathematics, share certain themes: less memorization, greater emphasis on hands-on activities, a greater focus on students' questions and the ideas they bring, linking science to society's problems, and emphasizing the scientific process and how problems are solved. In addition, the Education and Human Resources Directorate (EHR) of the National Science Foundation, under the leadership of Luther Williams, is engaged in a massive funding effort aimed at dramatically increasing the participation of underrepresented students in the science and engineering pipeline.

As important as these efforts are, three changes are fundamental to the improvement of science education:

— We now know that students learn best when working in cooperative study groups with their peers.
— We need to attract the most qualified young people into teaching science and mathematics and to reward them appropriately.
— We must recognize that virtually every student, regardless of ethnicity or gender can master mathematics and science. We should expect and require them to do so.

Cooperative Study Groups

The most exciting research about how people learn mathematics was carried out by a graduate student at Berkeley. Uri Treisman, while a teaching assistant in calculus courses, observed that the African American students performed very poorly, while the Chinese students excelled.[18] He did not accept the conventional wisdom that the low achievement rates of the African American students were due to such factors as their parents' poverty or the poor schools they had attended as young children. He thought maybe it had to do with how they studied, what they studied, and with whom. So Treisman spent eighteen months observing both the Chinese and the African American students. He found that the Chinese spent longer hours studying than other students and that they frequently studied together in groups, for example, working out extra homework problems. Treisman then developed an experimental workshop in which he replicated these interaction and study patterns with the African American students. The results were astounding: the African American students went on to excel in calculus.

Treisman found that his workshop students consistently outperformed both Anglos and Asians who entered college with comparable SAT scores. A central component of the workshop approach was encouraging the students by giving them extra, advanced problems. While the African American students who participated in the workshop had been experiencing difficulties and failure in the preworkshop era, they were high school valedictorians who resented and rejected an approach based on remediation. In short, one key to Treisman's success was his focus on self-concept. The students were treated like the winners they could be, not like helpless losers.

Wait a minute, a critic might say, those African American students already were good enough to be admitted by Berkeley. Would these methods work in other colleges and universities, and would they work with students of other ethnic backgrounds? My colleague Martin Bonsangue and I received a grant from the National Science Foundation to explore these questions.[19] Bonsangue gathered data about a workshop program based on the Treisman model that has been implemented at California State Polytechnic University at Pomona. In fact, this institution has the oldest and best-established workshop program in the country. The Cal-Poly workshop results show precisely the kind of dramatic improvement that Treisman found at Berkeley. More specifically, the calculus achievement of Latino workshop students improved dramatically. Furthermore, in addition to assessing performance in the calculus course itself, Bonsangue was able to measure longitudinal effects. Once again, he found dramatic positive effects associated with workshop participation. For example, participants were significantly less likely to drop out of advanced calculus courses and science, mathematics, and engineering majors.

Teaching and the Curriculum

Given that part of the problem may be the kinds of science and mathematics teachers students encounter in their elementary and secondary education and that part of the solution may be better teacher recruitment and training, other data from the CIRP might be of some interest. These data suggest that most undergraduates planning teaching careers these days are education majors. But the data indicate that this was not true twenty years ago. In other words, fifteen or twenty years ago a high school student was much more likely to be taught by a young teacher who had majored in mathematics and physics in college. Today the same student might well have a teacher who has had more coursework in education than in mathematics and physics.

There clearly has been a decline in the quality of science and mathematics teachers as a side effect of the women's movement. Happily, increased career opportunities for women during the past two decades have meant that intelligent young women no longer are constrained to careers in teaching, nursing, and one or two other fields. The result is that the educational system has lost the "hidden subsidy" it enjoyed when so many bright young women chose teaching.

The most effective teaching does not take place when a mechanical model is employed. Learning involves the active engagement by the learner. He or she must incorporate the new material, and this means linking the new material to the existing body of knowledge, based on both experience and prior learning, that the student brings to the classroom. This makes it all the more important that teachers at both the precollege and college levels find ways to connect to the frame of reference in the student's mind. In my experience, the method that seems most promising is the frequent use of metaphors or stories.

The instructor must learn about the students' frame of reference to improve the quality and effectiveness of his or her teaching. *The benefits of doing this are reciprocal.* Scientific research, theorizing, and model-building are enriched, and may be transformed, if we learn more about the cultural perspectives previously underrepresented groups bring to the table.

Changing Expectations

The research by Treisman and Bonsangue and work at Harvard by Richard Light have revealed pretty clearly what works in college instruction.[20] There is evidence that these findings also apply at the precollege level. Robert Reich has observed that in America's best classrooms,

instead of individual achievement and competition, the focus is on group learning. Students learn to articulate, clarify, and then restate for one another how they identify and find answers. They learn how to seek and accept criticism from peers, solicit help, and give credit to others. They also learn to negotiate—to explain their own needs, to discern what others need and view things from others' perspectives, and to discover mutually beneficial resolutions. This is an ideal preparation for lifetimes of symbolic-analytic teamwork.[21]

Students learn more effectively when they engage in a dialogue with other students (and with their instructors). They also learn more when they are expected to excel, when they are not approached as being in need of remediation. Almost thirty years ago, in 1966, some Coleman Report findings about self-efficacy foreshadowed these results.[22] At the time, the study by James Coleman and his associates was the largest social science study ever conducted. Self-esteem and self-efficacy are central to educational achievement and the development of meaningful educational and career aspirations. *In mathematics and science, and, for that matter, in every educational enterprise, we should use a talent development model rather than a model of exclusion.* Furthermore, these workshop group studies remind us that learning is a social and psychological process, not a mechanical one.

Equity 2000, an intervention project of the College Board, is attempting to increase the percentage of minority students who go to college. The project, which will impact more than two hundred thousand students, brings together local educators and national experts. Since research has shown the links between mathematics attainment and college attendance, the focus is on mathematics instruction and on encouraging more young people to take more mathematics. An important component of this intervention effort is educating instructors about the capacities of young people from minority backgrounds to master mathematics. In that regard, results from the first year of the project are instructive. According to the College

Board, the percentage of students that the teachers believed were capable of passing algebra or geometry increased dramatically, tripling in the case of geometry. In the pilot city of Fort Worth, Texas, the number of students who took algebra increased 36 percent during a single year.[23]

A novel approach to examining how teacher expectations may affect student achievement was taken by Robert Rosenthal and Lenore Jacobson.[24] They randomly selected some students who had not performed particularly well on aptitude tests. They next told the teachers of these students that, in fact, these young people were potential geniuses whose extraordinary talents were not revealed on intelligence tests. The students' performance in school improved dramatically. The teachers were more inclined to answer their questions, to interpret their questions as intelligent, and to spend time working with the students. Perhaps the perception that these students were bright affected the subjective component of the teachers' grading process. In any case, these "average" students excelled when their teachers thought they could.

Conclusions

Our mathematics and science education programs are not getting the job done. We can turn this situation around if we provide incentives to recruit outstanding young people into teaching, if we rethink the curriculum, and if we stop discouraging able students by expecting them to fail.

This book addresses each of these issues in detail. Chapters 1 through 4 present the problems in mathematics and science education. Chapter 1 includes a discussion of the links between education, technological productivity, and economic development. The dependence of a high-tech economy upon the education of scientists and skilled workers is explained. Chapter 2 discusses the appalling lack of scientific literacy in the American public, as profiled in national surveys. It is important for citizens to understand how to make decisions and to comprehend the fundamentals of statistical reasoning. Chapter 3 presents a critical evaluation and review of the international assessments of the science capabilities of elementary and high school students. It seems clear that our young people perform dismally when compared with students from a wide spectrum of countries. Chapter 4 focuses on the college student: What kinds of students choose majors and careers in science? Which students defect from such choices while in college? What factors are associated with student satisfaction with, enthusiasm about, and career aspirations in science?

Chapters 5 through 7 present solutions to the problems presented in chapters 1 through 4. Chapter 5 focuses on the extraordinary hidden talent in groups that are underrepresented in the study of mathematics and science—women, poor people, and people of color. Uri Treisman's groundbreaking research at the University of California at Berkeley is discussed further in chapter 6. Recent research by Martin Bonsangue at Cal-Poly Ponoma and Richard Light's study of Harvard undergraduates reinforce and extend the Berkeley findings. A new approach to teaching mathematics and statistics that builds upon the frame of reference the students bring with them is presented in chapter 7. National curriculum reform efforts in mathematics and science education are reviewed, as are the human resources development programs of the National Science Foundation. The Conclusion reprises the findings and recommendations that emerged from this investigation. Several inspiring success stories are related.

In this book I attempt to show how science education is tied to success in a high-tech workplace. Moreover, mathematics education from kindergarten through twelfth grade may be more closely linked to subsequent educational and career achievement. Both mathematics and science education will provide a mechanism for social mobility, for achieving wealth, status, and power in twenty-first-century America.

Science occurs in a social context. Just as Heisenberg discovered that the behavior of subatomic particles cannot be described in isolation, independent of the observer, so scientific research and development can and should not be conducted independent of the society that will interpret and apply the findings. Our scientific theories, hypotheses, and interpretations will be strengthened if the research is conducted and informed by people with differing world-views and cultural perspectives. Furthermore, science, which has contributed so much to the quality of our lives and promises to contribute even more in the near future, also represents potential threats to our world, dangers that must be controlled. An informed citizenry, capable of making sound judgments, will be needed to set the boundaries for science so that we can continue to reap its rewards.

PART I

The Problems

ONE

Technological Training and Economic Competitiveness

In 1988 Motorola conducted a study that showed that a Japanese student can be moved into the workplace at an employer cost of $0.47, while an American student's transition costs the employer $226. This is primarily due, says Motorola, to the emphasis on statistics and applied diagnostics in Japanese schools.

Building a Quality Workforce

We have made the transition from an industrial economy to a postindustrial or information-based economy. Furthermore, we are entering an era characterized by a global marketplace, in which workers from the United States will compete for jobs against skilled workers from countries with powerful educational systems. Each of these factors has implications for the education American students receive in science and mathematics. Each is examined in this chapter.

Competing in a Global, High-Tech Economy

Peter Drucker has produced many books and articles about management and about economic, social, and historical forces and change. Drucker begins his volume *The New Realities* by noting that "sometime between 1965 and 1973 we passed over . . . a divide and entered the next century. We passed out of creeds, commitments, and alignments that had shaped politics for a century or two."[1] Spotlighting an important trend, Drucker notes that "the shift to knowledge and education as the passport to good jobs and career opportunities means, above all, a shift from a society in which business was the main avenue of advancement to a society in which business is only one of the available opportunities and no longer a distinct one." Society's center of gravity, he observes, "is shifting to a new group—the knowledge worker—who has new values and expectations" (174–75).

In this book and elsewhere, Peter Drucker has chronicled the rise and fall of the blue-collar worker. Farming once dominated the American economy, but early in this century the farming sector began a decline that has never leveled off. Similarly, blue-collar factory workers provided the labor that fueled the Industrial Revolution; their decline, which began more recently, has been swifter. Blue-collar assembly-line work still creates most of the products we buy, but increasingly the assembly work is being done in countries where labor costs are considerably diminished (and where the actual work, incidentally, usually is done by impoverished young women, usually women of color). According to Drucker, "If any phenomenon can compare to the rise of the blue-collar, mass-production worker in this century, it's the fall of the blue-collar, mass-production worker. From now on, everyone needs a sheepskin."[2]

In his book *The Work of Nations: Preparing Ourselves for Twenty-first Century Capitalism*, Robert Reich describes the emerging global economy and how it is reshaping discussions of America's competitiveness. "The competitiveness of Americans in this global market," he notes, "is coming to depend, not on the fortunes of any American corporation or on American industry, but on the functions that Americans perform—the value they add—within the global economy."[3]

Reich then argues that an economic analysis of jobs and productivity cannot be based on the traditional Census Bureau classification of jobs, a taxonomy that is inherently linked to the old industrial occupational structures. In its place, he defines and discusses three emerging categories of work. The first two are routine production services (which include most of the traditional blue-collar, assembly-line jobs as well as repetitive work in today's service and information industries) and in-person services (also routine jobs but performed on a person-to-person basis and requiring that the worker interact with others pleasantly and courteously).

The third and most important category, according to Reich, is symbolic-analytic services, which Reich describes as "all the problem solving, problem identifying, and strategic brokering activities . . . the manipulation of symbols—data, words, oral and visual representation" (177).

Symbolic analysts may be scientists and engineers, but they may also be public relations executives, investment bankers, lawyers, real estate developers, management information specialists, organizational development specialists, systems analysts, architects, writers and editors, or musicians. Of symbolic analysts, Reich notes that they "often work alone or in small teams, which may be connected to larger organizations,including worldwide webs. *Teamwork is often critical.* Since neither problems nor solutions can be defined in advance, frequent and informal conversations help ensure that insights and discoveries are put to their best uses and subjected to quick, critical evaluation" (179, emphasis added).

Reich goes on to argue that despite the ills that have befallen American education, many American children—he estimates 15 to 20 percent—are being well educated for symbolic analytic work. He cites as evidence the excellent American university system, the willingness of affluent, symbolic analytic workers to provide such resources as private schools and educational toys for their children, and the more amorphous, but real, educational experiences acquired through social interaction with other children and adults from the same economic background. The question, of course, is whether 15–20 percent is enough.

"Japan's greatest educational success," Reich argues, "has been to assure that even its slowest learners achieve a relatively high level of proficiency" (228). Consider, too, that "the software engineer from Belmont, Mass., working on a contract for Siemens, which is financed out of Tokyo, the routine coding of which will be done in Bulgaria, the hardware for which will be assembled in Mexico, is a true citizen of the global economy."[4] Again, we must ask, are we doing enough, and are we doing enough for enough?

The skills required by Reich's symbolic analyst are echoed in the American Library Association's definition of information literacy.

To be information literate, a person must be able to recognize when information is needed and have the ability to locate, evaluate and use effectively the needed information. . . . Ultimately, information-literate people are those who have learned how to learn. They know how to learn because they know how knowledge is organized, how to find information, and how to use information in such a way that others can learn from them. They are people prepared for lifelong learning, because they can always find the information needed for any task or decision at hand.[5]

When Americans think about their economic competitors, they think first about Japan. The key phrase for Paul Tsongas's short-lived presidential campaign was "The cold war is over and Japan won." The clearest indicator of the shifting economic fortunes of the United States and Japan has been the automobile industry. In *The Reckoning,* David Halberstam provides a thorough history of the decades in which the American automobile industry faltered and the Japanese automobile industry soared.[6] Halberstam's search for the clue to these shifting economic fortunes focuses in part on education. He notes that the Japanese had a national commitment to economic success.

The dream of Japanese greatness through military power had proved a false and destructive one. The ashes of that dream were all around them. There had to be another path. Quickly a consensus evolved: Japan was so limited in size and natural resources, so vulnerable—as seen at Hiroshima and Nagasaki—to modern weaponry, that it could become strong only if it focused all of its energies on commerce and completely avoided military solutions. (270–71)

One of the most significant decisions made by the Japanese establishment was to strengthen education generally and engineering education in particular. Halberstam quotes historian Frank Gibney, who stated that Japan's educational system was "the key that winds the watch" (276). In Japanese society, social mobility was encouraged, the objective being a well-educated meritocracy.

The status of an elementary school teacher in a village was, in the post-war years, far greater than that of a teacher in a comparable American small town. The educational system was critical to the rise of modern Japan: it crystallized, legitimized, and modernized values already existing. It removed a great deal of potential class resentment on the part of the poor, *and it provided Japan with an extraordinarily well qualified, proud, amenable, and ambitious working class.* If modern post-war Japan was perhaps the world's most efficient distribution system, in which remarkably little was wasted, in human, material, or capital terms, then a vital part of it was the educational system: it supplied the nation with the right number of workers, the right number of engineers, and the right number of managers for every need of a modern society. But, equally important, *it brought to the poorest homes the sense that there were better possibilities for the children.* (276–77, emphasis added)

Halberstam notes that psychological testing performed during the 1950s revealed that the Japanese viewed education as vital to success. "The values of these Japanese workers in the fifties and sixties were like the values which had been passed on to the children of American immigrants, values that these Americans, in their affluence, were no longer so successfully passing on to their own offspring" (277). In Japan, engineering education was expanded, and scholarships were available for interested students.[7] The Japanese elite wanted to flood the factories with well-trained, capable engineers. "They might work on something tiny, perhaps a task a good deal smaller than what they had dreamed of while they were students," says Halberstam, "but the cumulative effect of so many talented engineers working on so many small things would be incalculable" (278).

Similar initiatives have proven valuable in other nations as well. As Paul Dehart Hurd observes, the Soviet Union, East Germany, the People's Republic of China, and Japan all have demonstrated "that it is possible to redirect an educational system and to do so in a comparatively short time. In the 1940s these countries were either devastated by a war, losers in a war, or engaged in a civil revolution," but since then their educational policies have emphasized the importance of science and mathematics to economic and cultural progress. "Knowledge of and about science and technology is considered a national resource," he writes, "and all citizens have a 'moral' responsibility to improve their knowledge of the sciences so they may better the welfare of the state. *In China science education policies are written into the constitution of the People's Republic.*"[8]

The U.S. economy will require workers with increasingly greater skills. Sue Berryman, director of the National Center on Education and Employment, offers a description of the kinds of changes that have taken place within one industry.

In the insurance industry, computerization has caused five jobs to be folded into one, known as a claims adjuster. The job occupant is less an order taker than an advisory analyst. He or she has to have good communication skills and be able to help diagnose the customer's needs through an analytic series of questions and answers. The person needs less specific and splintered knowledge—the ability to understand multiple arrays of information, the rules governing them, and the relationships between arrays. He or she also needs to be able to frame answers to less standardized requests. Insurance companies used to hire high school dropouts or graduates for the five jobs. They now hire individuals with at least two years of college for the restructured claims adjuster jobs.[9]

Computers and the Information Economy

The most pervasive new technology in the emerging information society is the computer. The obvious advantages of word processors are sending the typewriter to the same junkyard as the icebox. Teachers using instructional software are creating an exciting learning environment that accelerates mastery, encourages creativity, and individualizes instruction. Archaeologists have even used computer-based pattern recognition algorithms to decipher previously obscure text in partially damaged ancient religious scrolls, algorithms that were developed, incidentally, by the Defense Department for use in such theological pursuits as detecting missile launchers in satellite photographs. Computer-based techniques have been used by scholars to determine the authorship of the disputed *Federalist Papers*. And the field of artificial intelligence has recast epistemological inquiry about the nature of thought.

What does all this mean for the young student who is trying to plan a career or for the middle-aged worker who feels that his or her solid occupational foundations are crumbling? The occupational mosaic certainly is changing rapidly, and for most people the development of some computer literacy (a frequently abused term) is valuable, if not essential. Who should specialize in computer fields? Who will become the new "computer elite"? Should parents encourage their children to move toward a career in computers?

Research about these issues by Mary Poplin, Robert Gable, and myself yielded the Computer Aptitude, Literacy, and Interest Profile (CALIP), a psychometric instrument that was distributed to many school districts, corporations, and other organizations from 1984 to 1991. In the manual that accompanied the test, we expressed the hope that this examination would reveal that many more students could master and enjoy computers than previously had been assumed. The test was created in the early 1980s, when many people assumed that only a few people could work with computers successfully. Our research and experience with the application of this test helped me to recognize the limitations of aptitude tests, particularly as they are used and interpreted by many educators.

The jury is still out on whether computers will increase social mobility or increase the gap between the haves and the have-nots in our society. On the one hand, microcomputers are found much more frequently in affluent homes. On the other, instructors are discovering that some minority students who were failing conventional subjects thrive when they use computers. Some then adapt their new skills to other areas of curriculum. A few of these students not only master computers but through the experience acquire social status and the ability to instruct others. However, this growth experience requires a supportive environment.

Computer-based education in poor schools is in deep trouble. Inner-city and rural school districts rarely have the skills or funds to maintain their machines. These districts lack the training and social support to use computers effectively. In most cases, computers simply perpetuate a two-tier system of education for rich and poor. Educators, experts, and politicians agree that the U.S. urgently needs high-quality computer-based learning. Yet in the effort to survive amid budget cuts and social decay, poor schools tend to use computers so rigidly and ineptly as to repel students. Poor schools create refugees from technology. . . . There is a widespread tendency to use computers only to teach basic skills in poor schools, but to provide rich discovery environments in affluent schools. . . . As literacy has come to mean more than the ability to read and write, a generation of young people is losing its franchise on independence and its shot at a better life in the information age.[10]

To paraphrase what the psychologist Ebbinghaus said about his profession, computer technology has a long past but a short history. In other words, people have been computing and making logical decisions since the beginning of human intelligence, but since the first modern digital computer was built in the 1940s the changes in the technology and associated occupations have been explosive. As recently as twenty years ago those who worked with computers were a relatively well-defined group engaged in an esoteric art. Times have changed.

Perhaps the evolving technology itself will create new and different occupations within the information industry. An analogy might be useful. Modern telecommunications began with Marconi's invention of the telegraph. There was a period late in the nineteenth century when an esoteric occupational specialty built around this technology, that of the telegraph operator, thrived. These specialists had to learn how to send and receive Morse code signals very rapidly. Eventually the telegraph gave way to the telephone. Now almost anyone can communicate via telephone simply by picking up a receiver and dialing a number. This is the future of computer applications. Computers and the associated software will become more and more "user-friendly"; that is, the equipment will become more internally sophisticated, so that users will need fewer instructions. These days, people who have no understanding of the logic of programming are able to use computers for a variety of tasks.

Many vendors and others who advocate a computer on every desk have little awareness of the history that preceded the explosion of microcomputers. Take the case of Gutenberg. We often hear rhetoric about how computers present the opportunity for an information revolution that parallels what Gutenberg accomplished with the printing press. Two frequently cited books about information and communication are Anthony Smith's *Goodbye Gutenberg* and Marshall McLuhan's *Gutenberg Galaxy*.[11] Vendors sometimes push this Gutenberg comparison too far. This is ironic because Gutenberg died penniless, living on a dole from one of his investors, a classic example of technological success and financial frustration.

Consider next a historical example of scientific success but technological frustration. Theoretical work by Charles Babbage in nineteenth-century Britain paved the way for the technological opportunities we enjoy today. Babbage was a brilliant Renaissance man whose creativity was unbounded. His pioneering work in the mathematical area of operations research included research for the British Post Office that led to something we now take for granted, that a letter going to any part of the country requires the same postage. He was an inventor, designing the "cow catcher" on railroads, for example. More to the point, he envisioned a device like a computer. After designing a "difference machine," he developed plans for a more sophisticated "analytical engine." Then he tried to build them.

His collaborator in these efforts was his lover, Ada Lovelace (a daughter of Lord Byron), who, fortuitously, was brilliant and wealthy. Because of her intellectual contributions, above and beyond her financial contributions, some consider her the world's first programmer. The U.S. Defense Department acknowledged this in naming a programming language after her. Despite Babbage and Lovelace's combined capabilities and their lack of concern about cost, however, the technology simply was not feasible in nineteenth-century Britain.

Thirty years ago I worked full-time as a professional programmer at the Harvard University Computer Center. I wrote application programs in FORTRAN, which at that time was considered a "user-oriented" language, on Harvard's most powerful computer, an IBM 7090, a machine that serviced virtually the entire university. At the time, we contrasted this sleek electronic device with the Mark I, arguably the world's first computer. The Mark I had been developed by a Harvard physicist, Howard Aiken, who worked in collaboration with IBM engineers in the 1940s. A part of the Mark I, a huge, slow-moving machine that consisted largely of electromechanical relays, was maintained in the Computer Center lobby to underscore the contrast. The cost of the 7090 reached six figures even in the early 1960s. Today, a desktop microcomputer has much greater capacity and power. But while the technology has changed, many of the issues about learning and applying it have remained the same.

Computer technology is changing both the kinds of information available to policymakers in business, education, and government and the kinds of decisions they are called upon to make. Many of today's managers are conversant with a spectrum of computer-based, decision-making aids, including, for example, simulation and linear programming. Successful executives are not intimidated by technology, nor do they ignore it; they harness it and use it to reach their organizational objectives.

Some years ago I conducted a workshop for senior corporation executives about the potential applications of computers. I pointed to a large machine and explained proudly that it could carry out five hundred thousand calculations per second. A distinguished-looking gentleman raised his hand and said, "I am just an old country boy (he was a senior officer of a large corporation), and I don't know much about computers, but . . . I figure if that computer can do five hundred thousand calculations a second, it can make five hundred thousand mistakes a second." That man was unlikely to misapply computers in the management of his business.

Displaced Workers: What Happens to the Worker with 1955 Skills in 1995?

In the second half of the twentieth century, the smokestack industries are being replaced by service-oriented, information-processing businesses. These changes have created massive educational needs for both workers and executives.

While I was in college, I worked in a machine shop next to an old, skilled European craftsman who ridiculed those of us who operated lathes. If that proud craftsman is alive today, he must be shaking his head in wonder at the precision of industrial products effortlessly turned out by the current computer-based machinery. (Insiders call this CAD/CAM, computer-aided design / computer-aided machining, or CNC, computerized numerical control machining.)

Traditionally, machinists manually adjusted levers and dials, following an engineer's blueprint. Modern machinists using CNC machines still follow blueprints, but they set the machines using a symbolic programming language. "What is important about systems such as these is that they depart in significant ways from the traditional systems of knowledge that reflect accumulated production wisdom. They are content-free, formal, closed conceptual systems that have many of the characteristics of 'school' subjects, such as mathematics or grammar."[12]

Blue-collar workers who find themselves unemployed when manufacturing industries are replaced by information-processing firms or when an auto plant is moved from, say, Southern California to South Korea have been labeled "displaced workers." A vivid example of automation's threat to skilled workers is provided by the newspaper business. Setting type used to be a challenging craft, difficult to master. Now it is done easily with computers.

In that machine shop both the craftsman and I were supervised by a foreman who knew considerably less about the manufacturing process than the old man (but considerably more than I did). In a kind of reverse apprenticeship, the craftsman quietly and graciously carried out an informal educational program for his supervisor about how the machinery could be pushed for maximum productivity. Informal training was, and remains, a major component of worker learning.

Many displaced workers now have alternative learning options. Some companies provide formal training programs in the new technology. Some displaced workers are "retro-fitted" through occupational training at their local community college. And a new organizational form has been emerging in the American economy: organizations that link industry with college training programs.

Consider materials requirements planning (MRP). It has been suggested that while U.S. companies measure their inventory needs in weeks, Japanese companies measure theirs in minutes. An oversupply of key components can tie up capital, while an insufficient supply can slow or halt the production process. Modern companies implement inventory control through computer-based MRP systems. These systems require skilled operators, and some successful programs have trained such operators. Such programs are needed because many companies choose the correct hardware and software but fail to implement the MRP systems successfully because of inadequate worker training and skills.

Jobs and Skills That Will Be Needed in the New Economy

In an article containing projections developed by the U.S. Department of Labor, Shelby Davis notes that "increased demand for health services from a growing and aging population will spur employment growth for radiologic technologists, medical record technicians, surgical technologists, and EEG technologists. In fact, jobs for health technologists and technicians are expected to account for almost half of all new technician jobs. Employment of computer programmers also will continue to grow rapidly, as more and more organizations use computers."[13]

Table 1.1, from a table in *Outlook 2000,* a publication of the U.S. Department of Labor Bureau of Labor Statistics, shows the projected percentage change in employment for selected occupations between 1988 and 2000, as well as the percentage of Whites, African Americans, and Latinos employed in each occupation in 1988. The information in the table reinforces the necessity for good mathematics and science education. One should also note the higher percentage of African Americans and Latinos in the "service occupations."

According to another Department of Labor publication, companies from different industries in different locations report appalling deficiencies in the skills of entry-level workers. The percentage of applicants for positions as tellers at the Chemical Bank of New York who passed a basic mathematics test fell from 70 percent in 1983 to 55 percent four years later. Participants in a Massachusetts state job program read, on average, at a fourth-grade level. Five years earlier, participants had read at a ninth-grade level.[14]

The results from a 1990 survey of businesses in the state of Washington support the conclusions of Department of Labor analyses and, in fact, suggest that those conclusions may be understated! Questionnaires were returned by 4,200 employers representing roughly 10 percent of the state's work force. According to an article entitled "Training Today: More Signs of Skills Shortage," "nearly one-third say they are generally dissatisfied with their employees' basic skills (such as reading, writing and arithmetic) and technical skills."[15]

Because of the low skill levels of American workers, New York Life now has its health insurance claims processed in Ireland.[16] Banks, which have computerized and expanded services, now find that they need more sophisticated employees. Fewer entry-level tellers and clerks are needed. The ATM machine is a ubiquitous symbol of automation and the displaced worker.

I should note that not everyone believes that high-tech jobs will proliferate in the American economy. For example, the Commission on the Skills of the American Work Force issued a report criticizing the findings and recommendations of the Department of Labor report.[17] The commission specifically questioned whether there would be tremendous growth in complex jobs requiring higher-level skills. Their report raises the specter that many students who master science and mathematics skills may not be able to find jobs that match those skills. However, even if the report's pessimistic projections prove correct, these students will be much more

Table 1.1

Projected Percentage Change in Employment for Selected Occupations, 1988–2000, and Employment of Whites, African Americans, and Latinos, 1988

Occupation	% change, 1988–2000	% Whites	% African Americans	% Latinos
All occupations	15	87	10	7
Executive, administrative, and managerial occupations	22	92	6	4
Professional specialty occupations	24	89	7	3
Engineers	25	90	4	3
Computer, mathematical, and operations research analysts	52	86	7	3
Natural scientists	19	90	3	3
Health diagnosing workers	24	88	3	4
Health assessment workers	38	87	8	3
Teachers, college	3	89	4	4
Teachers, except college	18	89	9	4
Lawyers and judges	30	96	2	2
Other professional workers	23	90	8	4
Technicians and related support occupations	32	86	9	4
Health technicians and technologists	34	81	14	4
Engineering and scientific technicians	22	89	7	5
All other technicians	39	88	7	4
Marketing and sales occupations	20	91	6	5
Administrative support occupations, including clerical	12	86	11	6
Clerical supervisors and managers	12	85	14	6
Computer operators and peripheral equipment operators	29	83	14	6
Secretaries, typists, and stenographers	10	89	8	5
Financial recordkeepers	1	90	6	5
Mail clerks and messengers	10	74	22	9
Other clerical	13	84	13	7
Service occupations	23	79	18	10
Private household workers	−5	76	23	17
Protective service workers	23	81	17	6
Food service workers	23	83	12	10
Health service occupations	34	69	28	6
Cleaning service workers	20	74	23	15
Personal service workers	27	85	12	8
Precision production, craft and repair occupations	10	90	8	8
Mechanics, installers, and repairers	13	91	7	8
Construction workers	16	91	7	8
Other precision construction workers	3	88	8	9
Operatives, frabicators, and laborers	1	82	15	11
Machine setters, set-up operators, operators and tenders	−3	83	15	7
Transportation and material-moving machine and vehicle operators	12	82	16	11
Helpers, laborers, and material movers	2	82	16	13
Agriculture, forestry, fishing, and related workers	−5	92	7	13

SOURCE: U.S. Department of Labor, Bureau of Labor Statistics, *Outlook 2000*, Bulletin 2352 (Washington, D.C., Apr. 1990), 63.

NOTE: Latinos can be of any race; therefore, percentage totals sometimes exceed 100 percent.

competitive in the emerging international economy. If there are no jobs for them in U.S. companies, there are likely to be jobs for them in corporations headquartered in other countries. Furthermore, even the second commission report acknowledged that the approach they described among these companies, that of "dumbing down" jobs, was myopic. If the American economy is to thrive, companies should structure their work around highly skilled positions and seek job applicants who have those skills.

In an article about the work of the Commission on the Skills of the American Work Force, Tom Gonzales observes that

> if we are to remain a country whose workers earn high wages, we will need a high-performance, high-skill work organization. This new organization is used by the best-performing companies worldwide, and it is more widespread in countries that are leading us in productivity, quality, product variety, and speed of new product introduction. The front-line workers are given more authority and responsibility for supervision, quality control, equipment maintenance, and production scheduling.[18]

This new model contrasts with the traditional industrial model that pervades the United States, the F. W. Taylor model of the organization, which, Gonzales writes, "viewed reliability, willingness to take directions, and being a steady worker as the most important traits for a front-line worker. Education was a low priority. This model was used extensively by individuals such as Henry Ford and provided a systematic way to mass-produce goods with a large population of low-skilled workers. The managers did the thinking, and technology provided the productivity gains that were made from the 1940s through the 1960s" (28).

In an article reviewing and synthesizing the current literature about learning for the workplace, Berryman concludes:

> Although surveys of innovative organizations of work are weak reeds, analyses of the total U.S. occupational structure and of changes in the wage returns to different education groups for the U.S. economy reveal the national effect of changes in the American economy on skill requirements. These analyses both suggest an increasing demand for skill. Higher skill occupations have grown and are projected to grow at rates greater than their share of the total occupational structure. Returns to a college degree have increased, and these increases have been attributed analytically primarily to increased demand for skill.[19]

Training for High-Tech Jobs

A few years ago, an individual who provides remedial training for industrial employees was approached by a company that makes floor and roof trusses about training its employees. The company was experiencing a period of rapid growth. "They had hired a large number of new workers, who were having difficulty with the math skills necessary to produce the trusses," this person recalled. "One of the carpenters who had been with the company for a long time explained the problem to me this way: 'Some of us can do this because we learned to do math as apprentices, but these new people learned math in school.' "[20] This story is but one of many that could be told about the U.S. educational system's deficiencies when it comes to preparing workers for U.S. industry, deficiencies that have had, and will continue to have, a deleterious effect on our economic competitiveness.

Anthony Carnevale, Leila Gainer, and Ann Meltzer, the authors of a 1991 book, *Workplace Basics: The Essential Skills Employers Want,* note that employers are increasingly focusing on how sophisticated their employees' computational abilities are. They explain that "the reason for this is simple—technology requires it." "Ironically," they add, "as occupational skill-level requirements climb, higher educational dropout rates and worsening worker deficiencies in computational skills are appearing. . . . Employers already are complaining of their workers' computational skill deficiencies, particularly those evidenced by miscalculations of decimals and fractions, resulting in expensive production errors."[21]

John Rigden, director of physics programs at the American Institute of Physics, also has remarked on this development. Knowing how to operate a drill press is not enough, he says.

To survive, the new employee has to have a firm grounding in math and science and a range of analytic and problem-solving skills.

Consider skilled trades such as carpenter, plumber, pipe fitter, electrician, tool-and-die maker and model maker. At General Motors Corp., a carpenter now is required to know algebra and geometry. A GM plumber needs algebra, geometry and physics; an electrician needs algebra, trigonometry and physics; and a tool-and-die maker, model maker or machine repairman needs algebra, geometry, trigonometry and physics. These requirements are a harbinger of things elsewhere.[22]

Charles Mitchell, who has written an account of the experiences of his company, Parker Bertea Aerospace Group, manufacturers of complex aircraft components, described how shocked he and his associates were when their employees performed very poorly on some of the mathematics items on a simple, twenty-item test designed to measure mathematics and verbal skills. When they observed their employees more closely to find out how the work was getting done, they discovered that "in almost every work group there happened to be a person who was good at math, and the other employees took advantage of that talent. When calculations were required, they asked the experts to check their results. In effect, these experts were carrying the other people. Often the knowledgeable individual was the supervisor, but not always." In two situations in which a senior technician who had been his group's mathematics expert retired, "the supervisor was at a complete loss when it came to helping his crew work through problems involving shop math." Mitchell notes that "the real difficulty with college courses is that they are aimed at a broad audience. They are not specific enough to be recognizably usable, and they rarely offer examples that are typical of a machine shop."[23]

With respect to workers' knowledge of statistics, Brian Joyner, a quality-control consultant who works with Fortune 500 companies, says that it is difficult to overestimate the problem and that "it's just as bad in the executive suites as it is on the factory floor." According to Joyner, every week managers get data that fall within normal ranges of error, but because they don't understand the concept of variation, "they end up reacting to noise instead of statistically significant information."[24]

In the view of Carnevale, Gainer, and Meltzer,

the serious problems lie in workers' inability to determine which computational algorithm(s) to apply to a particular job problem or to recognize errors resulting from inappropriate applications because they do not understand why specific computations should be used. Neither time-consuming skill drills nor the use of calculators is an effective remedy because, while either can correct the problem of computational errors, neither helps a person understand which computation is needed to solve an on-the-job problem. The most effective way to reach the skills and strategies that will equip workers to solve mathematics problems in the workplace is through the use of contextual materials that simulate job situations.[25]

Mathematics educators differentiate between elementary skills (adding, subtracting, multiplying, and dividing), intermediate skills (manipulating rational numbers, percentages, and fractions), and advanced skills (factoring, mathematical reasoning, solving linear equations, and applying calculus). All of these have been found to be relevant to skilled work in industry. Carnevale and his co-authors cite several programs, including a massive in-house educational effort initiated by Delco Products, a division of General Motors, that attempt to educate workers in computational skill areas where they are deficient.

A 1990 survey of the twelve hundred largest U.S. corporations conducted by the National Alliance of Business (NAB) reported that 72 percent of executives thought that the mathematics skills of new employees had worsened during the past five years. As William Kolberg, president of the NAB stated, "We have abandoned the millions of kids who don't plan to attend college. Somewhere along the way, we lost respect for the skills we now so desperately need in our factories and on the front lines of our service industries."[26] Kolberg noted that about 82 million U.S. jobs do not require a college degree, and filling those jobs may become impossible unless the educational system is changed. Only 36 percent of the respondents in the NAB survey expressed satisfaction with the competence of new hires. Mathematical "competence" was defined as the ability to use mathematics at above the fifth-grade level.

To understand how competence may be played out in the workplace, we may consider that until recently disc jockeys and other radio announcers had to learn how to repair transmitters and other electronic equipment before they could be licensed. While they were rarely called upon to demonstrate those skills on the job, the theory was that an announcer in a remote, rural radio station might have to go outside and fix the antenna or some other piece of equipment. Paul Kelly, a professor and former announcer, remembers going through this training process and being taught trigonometry and calculus as they relate to the diagnosis and repair of problems in electronic equipment. However, he didn't realize until after the fact that these mathematical techniques could be labeled trigonometry and calculus. He was expected to learn them, and he did. This was made easier because the educational process was embedded in a job-relevant context, in which he could see the direct applications of this knowledge.

In a preview of his technology policy, President Bill Clinton stated,

The U.S. education system must make sure that American workers have the requisite skills. The focus should be not only on the top American students who measure up to world-class standards, but also on average and disadvantaged students. It must also take into account the need to upgrade workers' skills and help people make the difficult transition from repetitive, low-skill jobs to the demands of a flexible, high-skill workplace. Unlike Germany, the United States does not have a sophisticated vocational education program, and unlike Japan, U.S. firms do not have a strong incentive to invest in the training and retraining of their workers. We need more of both, geared to meet the needs of the mobile U.S. workforce.[27]

One of Peter Drucker's "new realities" is that "an economy in which knowledge is becoming the true capital and the premier wealth-producing resource makes new and stringent demands on the schools for educational performance and educational responsibility."[28] He adds that the new responsibilities will include giving students a real understanding of technology and teaching them how to learn. In other words, what they learn is less important than learning how to learn. In words that foreshadow research results from Berkeley, Cal Poly-Pomona, and Harvard (presented in chapter 6), Drucker observes:

> We do know, however, how people learn how to learn. In fact, we have known it for two thousand years. The first and wisest writer on raising small children, the great Greek biographer and historian Plutarch, spelled it out in a charming little book, Paidea *(Raising Children)*, in the first century of the Christian era. All it requires is to make learners achieve. All it requires is to focus on the strengths and talents of learners so that they excel in whatever it is they do well. Any teacher of young artists—musicians, actors, painters—knows this. So does any teacher of young athletes. But schools do not do it. They focus instead on a learner's weaknesses. (236–37)

As detailed in this chapter, during the latter part of this century the economy of the United States has undergone a transformation equivalent in magnitude to the industrial revolution of the nineteenth century. This has been the transition from an industrially based economy to an economy based on technology and information, with computers playing a central role. While an industrially based economy could function effectively with front-line workers who had few technical skills, a high-tech economy depends upon workers' analytical skills. We in the United States have been slower to realize this than some of our economic competitors, most notably Japan. Many workers who prepared for the smokestack world of the mid-twentieth century may find themselves displaced by well-trained, mathematically literate symbolic analysts. These economic forces provide compelling reasons for transforming and revitalizing the mathematics and science education provided in our nation's schools.

TWO

Scientific Literacy

At least part of the motivation for any book is anger, and this book is no exception. I'm distressed by a society which depends so completely on mathematics and science and yet seems so indifferent to the innumeracy and scientific illiteracy of so many of its citizens; with a military that spends more than one quarter of a trillion dollars each year on ever smarter weapons for ever more poorly educated soldiers; and with the media, which invariably become obsessed with this hostage on an airliner, or that baby who has fallen into a well, and seem insufficiently passionate when it comes to addressing problems such as urban crime, environmental deterioration, or poverty.

John Allen Paulos, *Innumeracy*

In an increasingly complex, technology-based world adults are faced with bewildering decisions about their personal life as well as their positions and votes on public policy issues. Should a young woman undergo a mammogram? Is it worth spending the extra money for optional airbags or antilock brakes in a new automobile? Should your house be tested for radon, or is this just another media scare? How important is it to avoid fettuccini Alfredo, which has been reported to contain huge levels of fat and cholesterol? Should the United States invest billions of dollars in a supercollider or in space stations? Are nuclear plants safe, efficient sources of much-needed energy or dangerous, poorly managed sources of contamination, pollution, and destruction? Educational preparation to confront questions like these usually is described by the term *scientific literacy.*

Science and the Citizen: A Case Study

When the history of science in the twentieth century is written, an unlikely figure, Alfred Vellucci of Cambridge, Massachusetts, may assume heroic proportions. The efforts of Cambridge citizens and politicians, spearheaded by Vellucci, to review and assure reasonable precautions in recombinant DNA research being done at Harvard started a domino effect that led to new National Institutes of Health (NIH) standards. Furthermore, the recombinant DNA debate has become a model for how such science policy decisions can be made in the future.

As in many university towns, city politics in Cambridge, Massachusetts, reflect a town-gown split. During the 1960s the Cambridge city council was divided almost evenly between representatives of Harvard and MIT on the one hand and representatives of the city's blue-collar working people on the other. More frequently than not, the key vote belonged to Alfred Vellucci. He repeatedly gave outlandish speeches ridiculing Harvard, which endeared him to many of the townspeople of Cambridge. However, rumor had it that on the key votes he quietly supported the universities. His rhetorical and political skills combined to make him arguably the most powerful man in Cambridge at that time. In his speeches he proposed, at one time or another, that

—Harvard formally be requested to move from Cambridge to Waltham, Massachusetts;
—Widener Library (one of the world's great libraries) be converted into a public restroom;
—the famous Harvard Yard be paved and converted into a public parking lot.

By the 1970s Alfred Vellucci had become mayor of Cambridge. In the mid-seventies, biological scientists were poised to launch new investigations into recombinant DNA, research that offered the possibility of incredible intellectual and human payoffs. The Harvard biology department, led by Nobel laureate James Watson, was, of course, at the cutting edge of this research. Expressing concern that the DNA research would create "monsters that would crawl over the wall from Harvard and attack the good citizens of Cambridge," Vellucci called hearings to examine the potential threats posed by the research. Nobel laureates and other leading scientists dutifully appeared to discuss the potential value of their research. Vellucci appointed a citizen court to review the evidence.

In an article about this citizen court and its implications, Sheldon Krimsky, a member of the citizen review panel, asks, "At what point does public accountability for the goals, the funding mechanisms, the research programs, the operations and applications of science begin to threaten the vitality of scientific institutions or impede their potential for authentic progress? Where does the balance lie between freedom of inquiry and the public's role in science policy?"[1] He notes that several options had been available to the city:

Since the debate was primarily between members of the academic fraternity, the Council could have thrown it back to the universities. But the universities had already had their hearings and failed to resolve the conflict. The Council could have referred the issue back to the federal authorities, requesting assurances that the community was in no danger. Or they could have placed a ban on the research until national legislation was passed covering all sectors of the society and assuring full compliance with the National Environmental Policy Act. Perhaps the most difficult option was the one the city chose, namely, to tackle the problem head on. (38)

The hearings lasted three months. Numerous experts were cross-examined by the citizen panel. In terms of educational background, the members of the review panel ranged from two who had only completed high school to one with a master's degree in engineering, a medical doctor, and one with a doctorate in philosophy. The director of the NIH participated in an open-line telephone conversation with the review panel. The panel was wrestling with technical questions such as whether it is true that "E.coli.K12 cannot be transformed into a pathogen" (41). The board's final report, which was supported unanimously by the city council, took a position "somewhere between the status quo and banning the research outright, with a strong emphasis on laboratory monitoring, public disclosure and broad participation in decisions of risk assessment" (42).

The term *scientific literacy* is frequently invoked, but, unfortunately, it usually is not defined precisely. Most policy discussions about scientific literacy employ or imply one of the following (overlapping) connotations of the term:

— the knowledge about science held by members of the general public who have gone through the school system;
— knowledge that will be used by high school graduates and others in their work;
— knowledge of science that will be used by those who choose to specialize in technical careers in science, mathematics, or engineering.

In this chapter I focus on the first connotation, the knowledge and critical reasoning skills educated citizens bring to personal and political decisions that involve science and technology. I argue *(a)* that scientific literacy is vital to our society and *(b)* that the level of scientific literacy of our students and graduates is dismal.

Placing Science in a Broader Social Context

Consider the role of science and scientists in a democratic society. Science and the scientific method have transformed our world in wondrous ways, especially since the Renaissance. But science and technology also pose threats. Albert Einstein contributed brilliant insights about physics that yielded the horror of atomic weapons as a direct application. Perhaps no technology has had the impact on American society that the automobile has had, yet it brought with it unparalleled levels of pollution. (Ironically, when the automobile was first introduced, it was heralded because it would mean an end to pollution, i.e., the widespread despoiling of the environment with horse manure.) Insecticides are perfected to facilitate the production of delicious fruit, but the same spray that protects the orchards is found to be associated with an increase in birth defects among children born to women who live nearby. Some theories about the origins of the AIDS epidemic have attributed it either to scientific research gone awry (recombinant DNA research) or to failed technologies (faulty World Health Organization inoculation programs for other illnesses).

Does the average citizen have a right to contribute to policy development about science and technology? This question raises the larger question of the role of science and scientists in a democratic society.

One can align the most respected philosophers and theorists in the history of Western civilization into one of two camps: *(a)* those who believe that experts or authoritarian leaders should or would make society's decisions and *(b)* and those who believe that all citizens should participate in such decisions. Perhaps the most enlightened presentation of the first viewpoint is found in Plato's *Republic*. Plato argues that societal decision making should be in the hands of carefully selected philosopher-kings, people whose special intelligence and training qualify them to make better decisions. Hobbes also can be placed in this camp, since he argues that in a brutal world societies will be ruled by the powerful and that idealistic statements to the contrary are naive. Into this camp fall most of history's authoritarian and autocratic leaders, many of whom used the above arguments to justify their position.

The second viewpoint was articulated by Aristotle, Locke, and Jefferson, among others. The recurring theme in their arguments is that each individual has the right to contribute to societal decisions that will affect him or her. Of course, the representative form of government we enjoy in the United States is based on this premise. Despite distortions in the original concepts set forth by the Founding Fathers (including the development of mass media technology, political ads, and "spin doctors"), we still have a system of government that, ultimately, gives considerable power to the individual citizen.

One development the Founding Fathers were in no position to anticipate was the scientific revolution. However, Jefferson, then secretary of the treasury, recognized the importance of science and took time from his other duties to test new inventions. Indeed, while there is a long history of federal concern about science, the government did not enter the science business in a big way until after World War II.

Federal expenditures for scientific research have been commonplace since World War II and the spectacular technical success of the Manhattan Project. Shortly after the war, in 1945, the case for continued government support of basic scientific research was made by Vannevar Bush, then director of the Office of Scientific Research and Development (OSRD), and others. The major science organization to grow out of this federal concern was the National Science Foundation (NSF). Through the NSF and various government departments and agencies, federal monies were channeled into universities for research and development activities. In the late 1950s, with the voyage of Sputnik, science education became a national priority. That period spawned a wide array of measures in support of science education, the National Defense Education Act being a prime example.

By the 1960s universities were highly affluent, and their scientific activities and others were being generously underwritten by the government. The period was so comfortable that someone then observed that if the Edsel Division of Ford had been an academic department, it would still be in existence. Expansion and growth were widely held objectives for universities and for science in general. (Times have changed. Both universities and science have been in difficult financial straits since the beginning of the 1970s.)

The tremendous acceleration of the growth of science following World

War II forced a reconsideration of the role of the scientist. The issues were presented and analyzed in a probing, thoughtful book by Don Price called *The Scientific Estate*.[2] Employing the medieval concept of estates, Price traces how scientists and other experts have acquired power and influence in the federal government and explores what this concentration of power in the hands of experts means for a democratic society.

Certainly, experts and other scientists are ubiquitous in the federal government. For example, not infrequently in our country's recent history the president's national security adviser has exercised considerable power in the area of foreign policy. Perhaps the most visible example was Henry Kissinger. The national security adviser is not an elected official, but is appointed by the president because of his or her expertise.

Another example of the influence of experts is the huge research and development industry that focuses on policy analysis. When their daily newspaper reports findings of a government study released by the Department of Transportation, or Housing and Urban Development, or Education, few citizens realize that almost certainly the study was done externally, under contract, by a private group of experts. There are many nonprofit corporations and profit-making firms that exist entirely on the basis of such "soft money," that is, grants and contracts from the federal government. Some of the better-known examples are the Rand Corporation, the Battelle Research Institute, and Abt Associates. While it is now somewhat dated, James Dickson's portrait of the research and development world, *Think Tanks,* is an accurate and entertaining description of these organizations.[3]

Some observers have argued that the proliferation of such firms means that experts have supplanted elected officials as the decision makers in our government and that this poses a threat to our democracy. A compelling (though I believe exaggerated) presentation of this point of view is the Nader Organization's book *The Shadow Government*.[4] In contrast, others have argued that all of this research and development funding and activity is useless, since government decision makers commission the studies and then ignore them when it is time to make policy decisions. The truth, I believe, lies somewhere in between. Perhaps it is most useful to explore the conditions under which policy analyses actually affect decisions.

Not surprisingly, policymakers are puzzled by conflicting findings. Frequently, administrative policy is developed without the benefit of solid information; or, worse, flawed research affects policy, while good research goes unnoticed. A fundamental problem is that policymakers and researchers come from entirely different worlds and look at things from totally different perspectives. It is like the apocryphal story of the blind men and the elephant, in short, a case of two cultures colliding. This is the kind of issue that anthropologists have studied among primitive tribes, and, not surprisingly, some anthropologists have examined this one. H. Russell Bernard reported a study of "eight areas of value conflict between the subcultures of basic science and policy making." He quotes a scientist as saying, "People in Washington ask us for the wrong advice. They want us to solve problems that creep up on them but they never ask a scientist if the questions they ask are important ones. So all we ever get asked to do is bail the bastards out of some political crisis."[5]

Unfortunately, research often is used to justify a position previously reached. Furthermore, a book or an article that concentrates on establishing a single idea, particularly if the idea is controversial, will be listened to more than a carefully reasoned wide-ranging research study. In 1965 Daniel Patrick Moynihan, then assistant secretary of labor, published a report on Black Americans. His conclusion was that many highly publicized minority problems, such as unemployment and housing, were by-products of a fundamental breakdown in the African American family, caused by the absence of a father figure. This report influenced President Lyndon Johnson (who drew upon it in a Howard University commencement address and convened a White House conference) and provoked much debate. Its critics noted that the monograph essentially contained persuasive arguments for one theory and was not an objective study.[6] Some felt that Moynihan's selection and presentation of data and previous research finds were biased in favor of his dramatic hypothesis. Admittedly, subsequent events have supported Moynihan's theory.

Unfortunately, some scientists contribute to the research-policy gap. Harold Orlans, a Washington authority on this communication failure, criticized such "imperialistic" social scientists: "Anything that comes out of their mouths, or drips from their pens, is equated, as though all their comments were equally valid and scientific statements about society. In fact, the average citizen may know more about a given subject than Margaret Mead."[7]

Definitions of Scientific Literacy

Noting that language choices and definitions reflect ideologies, Gerard Fourez has analyzed the implicit and explicit differences between the definitions of scientific literacy in four major reports on science education: (1) *Science for All Americans,* the Phase I report of Project 2061; (2) "Science Objectives: 1990 Assessment," published by the National Assessment of Educational Progress; (3) "Science and Technology Education for the Elementary Years," prepared by the National Center for Improving Science Education; and (4) "Science for Ages 5–16," a report from the Wales, United Kingdom, Department of Education in Science.[8] Fourez observes that

Each document has its own idiosyncratic definition of scientific literacy, stated either explicitly or implicitly. The choice of definition has implications for both the way the curriculum is subsequently developed and for achieving the desired outcome with respect to the way students will live their individual and collective lives. . . . Each report advocates that all children understand the nature of science. But each report focuses on a different aspect of understanding, thus reflecting past and present debates between epistemologists and philosophers of science. (91)

Fourez adds that when *Science for All Americans* discusses observation, it "does not acknowledge the many studies that emphasize how observation is always an *interpretation* which depends on accepted theories, context, and ideas." He says that "interpretation seems to be a source of biases that scientists try to avoid. It is never seen as the foundation of every kind of observation" (95).

The reports differ also in the linkages they describe between science and technology. (In a table entitled "Contrasting Ideologies of Science and Technology," reproduced here as table 2.1, Fourez summarizes the ideological implications of the different definitions of scientific literacy articulated in these four reports.) "Questions never occur with respect to the *natural world,*" he observes, "but with respect to a *culturally filled world.* To state it approximately, the notion of the natural world, as we use it today, is an abstraction invented culturally in the sixteenth and seventeenth centuries. " Fourez concludes that scientific literacy involves both knowledge and power. "To put it bluntly, scientific literacy is not simply a disinterested business; power, money, autonomy, and status are all at stake" (106).

Anthropologist Benjamin Whorf described how the language we learn shapes how we perceive the world and *what we can think*. He observed, first, that some languages make finer distinctions than others. For example, the Eskimos have a number of words describing different kinds of snow, and the Chinese have a number of words describing different kinds of rice. More importantly, different languages embody different notions of

Table 2.1

Contrasting Ideologies of Science and Technology

Science begins with observations.	Science begins with questions.
Science starts with an observation, non-biased, if possible.	Science originates in contextual ideas and theories.
Science is disciplinary, cumulative, and results-centered.	Science originates in contextual questions.
Science is defined by method.	Science is a historical human process and unique event.
The world is an organized universe with one basic set of rules.	We construct theories and ideas to organize the world from our context.
The universe has one universal rationality.	Rationality is related to human points of view and projects.
There is only one scientific method.	There is a diversity of methods related to contexts and objectives.
Science and technology are clearly distinct.	Science can be seen as an intellectual technology.
Technologies resemble tools that can be used or not.	Technologies are social as well as material systems.
Technology is applied science.	Technology is an intellectual knowledge system by itself.
Scientified theories are *discovered* whereas technologies are invented.	People invent scientific models as well as technologies.

SOURCE: G. Fourez, "Scientific Literacy, Societal Choices, and Ideologies," in *Scientific Literacy*, ed. A. Champagne, B. Levitts, and B. Calinger (Washington, D.C.: AAAS, 1989), 98.

the nature of reality. The notions of space and time in the Hopi language are strikingly different from those in English. Similarly, each definition of scientific literacy, if widely adopted, has implications for what should be taught, how it should be taught, and who can learn it under what circumstances.[9]

Whorf's theory is doubly relevant to the ideas presented in this book. I argue in chapter 5 that students from different cultural backgrounds not only should be included in the educational process but can make unique, invaluable contributions as scientists. Also, creative scientists need to be able to view phenomena from new perspectives. In his seminal volume *The Structure of Scientific Revolutions*, Thomas Kuhn suggests that scientific knowledge accumulates in small, incremental steps under an existing paradigm or theory until someone (like Einstein) proposes a new paradigm that totally realigns our view of the world.[10] People whose earliest views of the world were shaped by languages other than English may be in a much better position to view scientific problems from different perspectives and to provide creative theories, hypotheses, and, possibly, paradigms. *Viewed from this perspective, a student who enters school speaking English as a second language may have an advantage, not a disadvantage, as a budding young scientist.*

The real challenge is to find the right balance with respect to the number and kinds of different cultural perspectives students bring to the classroom. If the world-views are too divergent, it will be increasingly difficult to introduce science by providing examples that build on a common basis of knowledge and experience. But for too long the problem has been the opposite. Virtually all the students in our classrooms have had the same language and knowledge base. Those who move on to become scientists have a limited foundation in terms of the diversity and complexity of their language and experience from which to draw creative solutions to scientific problems.

Ezra Shahn cites C. P. Snow's well-known book *The Two Cultures,* in which Snow argues that even people who are otherwise well educated—in the arts and the humanities—are scientifically illiterate.[11] Snow suggests that if such a person were to learn only one item of scientific information, it should be the second law of thermodynamics. But, Shahn observes that five years and ten reprints later Snow seemed to have changed his mind. "Instead of 'entropy,' he decided that the one crucial concept that should be in the working vocabulary of every non-scientist should be what he referred to as 'molecular biology'" (43). Shahn suggests that in addition to noting the existence of two cultures, Snow has shown, perhaps inadvertently, "that science literacy cannot be based on, or scientific illiteracy remedied by, the acquisition of a specific body of knowledge" (43).

Noting that the history of science is filled with conclusions we have now discarded as wrong, Shahn observes:

The way in which we choose to interpret observations is to a large extent determined by a world-view that exists prior to the act of observation or the attempt at analysis. In a formal sense this world-view is our metaphysics, or more generally our meta-science. . . .

More recently, we are told that the difficulty in accepting the conclusion that DNA was the carrier of genetic information lay partly in the strong belief that the variety of nucleic acids was inadequate to the tasks: compared to proteins they are just too "simple." The "simplicity" was in a naive concept (from today's vantage point) that complexity of task required complexity of structure. The insight that overcame this block was the realization that information for structural complexity could be carried in coded form. (45)

Science's Twenty Greatest Hits

In their widely discussed book *Science Matters: Achieving Science Literacy*, Robert Hazen and James Trefil suggest that most university scientists are so specialized that they cannot teach general science courses to undergraduates.[12] According to Robert Pool, Hazen and Trefil charge that "this scientific illiteracy among scientists lies at the heart of the problems with undergraduate science education—a system that apparently produces large numbers of adults who believe in astrology, don't believe in evolution, and can't remember whether the earth goes around the sun or vice versa."[13] Hazen and Trefil identify a university reward structure that advances faculty who publish extensively in a highly specialized field, whether or not they teach well, as a prime cause of this problem. Incidentally, they argue that "most scientists will basically agree on the most important and fundamental ideas underlying all of science" (267). In fact, they propose twenty such great ideas of science, the key points of which are presented below:

"Science's Top 20 Greatest Hits"
1. The universe is regular and predictable.
2. One set of laws describes all motion.
3. Energy is conserved.
4. Energy always goes from more useful to less useful forms.
5. Electricity and magnetism are two aspects of the same force.
6. Everything is made of atoms.
7. Everything—particles, energy, the rate of electron spin—comes in discrete units, and you can't measure anything without changing it.
8. Atoms are bound together by electron "glue."
9. The way a material behaves depends on how its atoms are arranged.
10. Nuclear energy comes from the conversion of mass.
11. Everything is really made of quarks and leptons.
12. Stars live and die like everything else.
13. The universe was born at a specific time in the past, and it has been expanding ever since.
14. Every observer sees the same laws of nature.
15. The surface of the earth is constantly changing, and no feature on the earth is permanent.
16. Everything on the earth operates in cycles.

17. All living things are made from cells, the chemical factories of life.
18. All life is based on the same genetic code.
19. All forms of life evolved by natural selection.
20. All life is connected.[14]

After Hazen and Trefil published their list, the journal *Science* invited readers to comment.[15] One hundred ninety-nine replies were faxed to the journal. Most applauded the idea of presenting science for nonscientists and attempting to specify the most important ideas. But many suggested additions, modifications, and deletions to the list. Many felt that the list, created by a physicist and a geophysicist, did not contain enough accomplishments and concepts from mathematics and biology. In fact, Hazen and Trefil had omitted mathematics entirely. Among the suggested additions was, "Equations can describe the universe, the concept of mathematical proofs, and some elements of probability and statistics" (1308). Others noted that the list focused strictly on content and did not include reference to the scientific method and the scientific processes.

In a provocative article titled "Why My Kids Hate Science," Hazen says that the working scientists are to blame for the scientific literacy crisis in America. Too often they sacrifice general education for their own specialized interests. He says that the reason why children have not been taught the basics in science is that most university scientists at the top of the educational hierarchy are interested in teaching only future scientists. Those scientists see science education as a process that "weeds out and casts aside the unworthy. It's not surprising that scientists have guided science education in this way. All the good things in academic life—tenure, promotion, salary, prestige—hinge on one's reputation in specialized research. Educators focus on teaching advanced courses to students who are willing to run the laboratory. Time devoted to teaching, or even reading, general science is time wasted."[16]

In his book *Scientific Literacy and the Myth of the Scientific Method*, Henry Bauer, a chemist, suggests that

Instead of making one or another science a required part of everyone's education in college, courses in STS [science, technology, and society] ought to be a part of everyone's education. Of course, some science—and more than now—ought to be taught at school: children should learn not only about the birds, the bees, and the flowers but a little also about the galaxies and the stars, and about the substances that they encounter and use and of which they are themselves made. *A great deal of that can be done within the framework of stories,* more like natural history than molecular biology.[17]

He concludes by saying that thinking of scientific literacy as learning STS is not only sensible but "eminently practical" as well.

Mathematical Illiteracy

In a book that has become a national bestseller, John Allen Paulos argues that Americans are afflicted with mathematical illiteracy, which he labels *innumeracy*.

Innumeracy, an inability to deal comfortably with the fundamental notions of number and chance, plagues far too many otherwise knowledgeable citizens. The same people who cringe when words such as "imply" and "infer" are confused react without a trace of embarrassment to even the most egregious of numerical solecisms. I remember once listening to someone at a party drone on about the difference between "continually" and "continuously." Later that evening we were watching the news, and the TV weathercaster announced that there was a fifty percent chance of rain for Saturday and a fifty percent chance for Sunday, and concluded that there was therefore a 100 percent chance of rain that weekend. The remark went right by the self-styled grammarian, and even after I explained the mistake to him, he wasn't nearly as indignant as he would have been had the weathercaster left a dangling participle.[18]

Paulos laments that "in a society where genetic engineering, laser technology, and micro-chip circuits are daily adding to our understanding of the world . . . a significant portion of our adult population still believes in Tarot cards, channeling mediums, and crystal power" (5).

Paulos observes that many people have trouble processing large numbers; they regard millions, billions, and trillions as more or less interchangeable. As a consequence, many people misperceive risks and opportunities. He notes that most people feel comfortable driving even though roughly as many Americans die on the highways each year in automobile accidents as died during the entire Vietnam War. Americans sometimes hesitate to travel abroad for fear of being killed or injured by a terrorist attack. This fear is heightened immediately after a terrorist attack. According to Paulos, the probability of being killed by terrorists while traveling abroad is considerably less than that of choking to death, drowning, dying in a bicycle or car crash, or smoking. "The number of deaths due to smoking," notes Paulos, "is roughly the equivalent of three fully loaded jumbo jets crashing each and every day of the year, more than 300,000 Americans annually" (111).

In the 1960s I taught short, noncredit courses on FORTRAN programing for Harvard University faculty, staff, and students. I searched for a way to describe how fast the modern new digital computers could process information. Ultimately, it is the computer's speed that makes it so powerful and allows it to appear intelligent. The computers I dealt with then could carry out some calculations in a few millionths of a second. But how could I introduce the concept of a millionth of a second so that students could differentiate, for example, a millionth of a second from a thousandth? I suggested that they envision a hypothetical planet where each millionth of a second on earth was equal to a full second in time. On such a planet the parallel to a full second on earth would be eleven days!

A political commentator with a vast radio audience repeatedly announced that his program attracts twenty-five thousand new listeners every minute. On occasion he expressed this growth rate as four hundred new listeners each second. Those two numbers are consistent with each other but inconsistent with reality, as some simple multiplications will illustrate. Twenty-five thousand new listeners every minute adds up to 1.5 million new listeners each hour. This man broadcasts three hours a day, five days a week. This means that he is claiming 22.5 million new listeners every week. At that rate, he would attract the entire population of the United States—every man, woman, and child—in less than three months!

Combinatorial problems can be especially confusing, as an example given by Paulos illustrates: "A sportswriter once recommended in print that a baseball manager should play every possible combination of his twenty-five-member team for one game to find the nine that play best together. There are various ways to interpret this suggestion, but in all of them the number of games is so large that the players would be long dead before the games were completed" (25).

Commenting on our educational system Paulos observes that too little attention is given to mathematical skills that have practical value, for example, inductive reasoning and making reasonable estimates, or to pleasurable ways to learn these skills, for example, puzzles, games and riddles. "If mathematics is important (and it certainly is)," says Paulos, "then so is mathematics education. Mathematicians who don't deign to communicate their subject to a wider audience are a little like multimillionaires who don't contribute anything to charity. Given the relatively low salaries of many mathematicians, both failings might be overcome if multimillionaires supported mathematicians who wrote for a popular audience. (Just a thought)" (107–8).

Thomas Jefferson and Scientific Literacy

Paul DeHart Hurd is arguably the single most influential person in the United States today with respect to science education reform. Writing about the historical and philosophical foundations of the notions of science literacy, he notes that Thomas Jefferson believed that science and mathematics education was crucial to the development of a new nation. Jefferson invited the French minister of agriculture, DuPont de Nemours, a medical doctor, to review education in the United States. Dr. de Nemours agreed that science and mathematics were important and lamented that there were no textbooks in the United States on these subjects.

What ensued is instructive in light of today's problems. Jefferson asked Congress for ten thousand dollars to write a science textbook for each grade level relating science and mathematics to the welfare of the nation. Congress refused to grant the money, saying that jurisdiction over church and schools belonged to the local communities.[19]

"In terms of relating science and technology to human affairs, and social and economic progress," says Hurd, "we are about at the same place we were 200 years ago or even 400 years ago. If we had been successful in relating science to the welfare of the individual and the common good, there would have been no need for the report called *A Nation at Risk* and the 300 national reports that have emerged since, in which various citizen groups, organizations, and single purpose groups have vented their wrath on education in the United States" (2).

Now consider the conclusion from a study of science education in five other nations:

Japan, West Germany, East Germany, China, and the Soviet Union each have an explicit, unambiguous, and strong national commitment to science education. Each has a policy calling for every student to receive a thorough grounding in mathematics and the sciences. Each is strenuously engaged in improving its ability to implement that policy. And each believes that its future—its economy, its security, its status in the world, its attractiveness as a human society—will be strongly influenced by its success in doing so. . . . *As a nation,* the United States displays no comparable commitment. That it is essential to make such a commitment is . . . the most important lesson to be learned from this study.[20]

Hurd reserves particularly harsh criticism for conventional laboratory instruction, saying that whatever its value in the past may have been, "it now offers little more than simple routines with preprogrammed answers on which all students are expected to agree; a non-conforming observation is a wrong answer. We will never know how many discoveries have been thrown in the wastebasket because they didn't agree with the answer book." Nothing, he says, conveys as false an image of science as does the conventional laboratory experiment performed in schools.[21]

In a summary of the literature about critical thinking, Kathleen Hart cites research showing that students who verbalize or talk a problem through are more likely to acquire problem-solving skills.[22] Statistics courses have been more successful than logic courses in teaching reasoning skills. Laboratory courses that emphasize the acquisition of problem-solving skills generally succeed. Hart notes that research has identified student discussion and interaction as a key component in learning to solve problems.

How Much Do Americans Know about Science?

Jon Miller, the director of the National Longitudinal Study of American Youth, has written extensively on the subject of scientific literacy. He has developed a three-dimensional definition of literacy, embracing *(a)* content, *(b)* process, and *(c)* significance. His own research has indicated that only about *5 percent* of American adults can meet a minimal definition of scientific literacy. Miller reminds us that literacy is a minimum threshold measure, not a continuous scale. Thus, literacy and nonliteracy constitute a dichotomous distinction. Does the person possess minimal knowledge or skills?[23]

Miller has constructed tests and conducted surveys tapping each of the three dimensions of scientific literacy. The following are examples of items used in the assessment of whether a person understands basic scientific terms and concepts:

The oxygen we breathe comes from plants. True or False?
Electrons are smaller than atoms. True or False?
Human beings, as we know them today, developed from earlier species of animals. True or False?
The earliest human beings lived at the same time as the dinosaurs. True or False?
The speed of light is faster than the speed of sound. True or False?

Sample items from Miller's scale assessing whether a person understands the impact of science and technology on his or her daily life include:

Radioactive milk can be made safe by boiling it. True or False?
Antibiotics kill viruses as well as bacteria. True or False?
Eating animal fat is a major cause of heart disease. True or False?

According to Miller's scientific literacy survey, 21 percent of adult Americans think the sun goes around the earth, 17 percent think the earth goes around the sun once a day, and 20 percent think that atoms are smaller than electrons.

Educating those who will not be scientists about science can be both challenging and rewarding. Nobel laureate Leon Lederman, reflecting on his recent experiences at the University of Chicago, where he has chosen to teach nonscience majors, said that "in some sense they were a special challenge. . . . You wanted them to get excited about physics, to remember certain things later on. There are plenty of guys to teach physics majors or chemistry majors. But to reach kids who are going to be the TV journalists, the newspaper editors, literate citizens, Congressmen, and all those things—there are fewer of us to do that."[24]

THREE

"Don't Know Much about Science Books"
Elementary and Secondary Education

> Reasons given by Japanese teachers for low achievement of their mathematics classes tended to be internalized—the teachers accepted much of the responsibility themselves. U.S. teachers, on the other hand, tended to cite external causes, such as lack of student ability, for their students' low achievement.
>
> C. McKnight et al., *The Underachieving Curriculum*

For a period following World War II most Americans viewed their country as first in everything. They had led the free world to victory over the Axis powers. They had developed the most awesome weapon in the history of the planet using a technology that could also be harnessed for peaceful applications. The U.S. economy was a dominant force on the international scene. Americans were better educated and had better universities. It seemed that everyone wanted to copy American culture: the Japanese loved baseball, and the Soviets claimed that they had invented it. American movie stars such as Marilyn Monroe and James Dean had fans in Thailand, Australia, Argentina, and France.

Times have changed. Most Americans now question whether the United States can compete economically with many European and Asian nations such as Germany and Japan. Virtually everyone in America believes that Japan makes better cars than the United States, a particularly disturbing realization since the automobile had been the heart of the American industrial machine. Reading Studs Terkel's book *Working*, an oral history that profiles the American worker, one is struck by the pervasiveness of work involving the construction and maintenance of the automobile, including such subsidiary industries as car renting.[1]

Our postwar view of America's preeminence probably was too rosy. And our current pessimism about America's decline and vulnerability to Japanese economic domination almost certainly is a pessimistic exaggeration. So there are questions in need of answer: Where do we stand on science and mathematics education? Can our children compete internationally?

In international assessments of mathematics and science achievement over the past twenty-five years, U.S. students have consistently performed poorly. These studies, listed in the order in which they are discussed below, include international assessments of science and mathematics achievement (1991, 1980s, 1960s and 1970s) and studies comparing the achievement of students in the United States, Japan, and Taiwan conducted in 1980 and 1990. One of the findings that emerge from these assessments is that fewer students study advanced science and mathematics in the Unites States than do in most other countries. This chapter concludes with data from the Educational Testing Service describing who does study science and the results of research about student attitudes and experiences in high school science.

The 1991 International Assessment

In the introduction to the most recent international achievement assessment, the authors observe:

Some might say that a study that compares the United States with Slovenia or England with Sao Paulo Brazil, is inappropriate or irrelevant. Indeed, education is, in fact, imbedded in each society and culture, and performance should not be studied or described without considering the important differences from country to country. The life of a thirteen-year-old in a rural Chinese community is very different from that of his or her peer growing up in a middle-class Paris apartment. And yet, these two young citizens may well meet in the global marketplace twenty years from now. And if they do, chances are they will rely on the mathematics and science they learned in this decade to succeed in the complex business and technological environment of 2012.[2]

In this study the mathematics and science achievement of 9-year-olds was assessed in fourteen countries, and that of 13-year-olds was assessed in twenty countries. The total sample size was 175,000. I focus on the

Table 3.1
*Results of the Science
Achievement Test, 1991*

Country	Average % correct
Korea	78
Taiwan	76
Switzerland[a]	74
Hungary	73
Soviet Union[b]	71
Slovenia	70
Emilia-Romagna, Italy	70
Israel[c]	70
Canada	69
France	69
Scotland	68
Spain[d]	68
United States	67
Ireland	63
Jordan	57

SOURCE: A. E. Lapointe, N. A. Mead, and J. M. Askew, *Learning Science,* report no. 22-CAEP-02 (Princeton, N.J., Educational Testing Service, 1992).
[a]Fifteen cantons.
[b]Russian-speaking schools in 14 republics.
[c]Hebrew-speaking schools.
[d]Spanish-speaking schools except in Catalonia.

results for 13-year-olds, who took a seventy-six-item mathematics test and a seventy-two-item science test. One important conclusion from the science study is that "the highest achieving countries with the exception of Taiwan do not practice ability grouping within science classes at age thirteen."[3]

Table 3.1 summarizes the results from the 1991 international science assessment for 13-year-olds. The findings from the United States are not encouraging: U.S. students scored below those from every other country that sampled a comprehensive population except Ireland and Jordan.[4] Among the countries scoring higher than the United States were Spain and Slovenia.

The results of the 1991 international mathematics assessment are shown in table 3.2. U.S. students performed below those from all the other assessed countries except Jordan. Upon reviewing the results from these international assessments, President George Bush and the nation's governors set a goal: that the United States would become number one in the world in mathematics and science by the year 2000.[5]

Results published by the National Assessment of Educational Progress

Table 3.2
*Results of the Mathematics
Achievement Test, 1991*

Country	Average % correct
Korea	73
Taiwan	73
Switzerland[a]	71
Hungary	70
Soviet Union[b]	68
Slovenia	64
Emilia-Romagna, Italy	64
Israel[c]	63
Canada	62
France	61
Scotland	61
Spain[d]	57
United States	55
Ireland	55
Jordan	40

SOURCE: A. E. Lapointe, N. A. Mead, and J. M. Askew, *Learning Mathematics,* report no. 22-CAEP-01 (Princeton, N.J., Educational Testing Service, 1992).
[a]Fifteen cantons.
[b]Russian-speaking schools in 14 republics.
[c]Hebrew-speaking schools.
[d]Spanish-speaking schools except in Catalonia.

in 1994 showed some slight improvement in science proficiency. This may reflect the reform efforts described in part 2 of this book. Yet, after reviewing the full range of results from this most recent study, Mark Musick, president of the Southern Regional Education Board, commented, "While the trend is up in science and math—which is heartening—'up' doesn't seem to be very high. . . . Virtually all thirteen- and seventeen-year-olds can read, write, add, subtract and count their change. But as one moves up the scale toward slightly more complicated tasks, student success falls off rapidly."[6]

The 1980s International Assessments

Perhaps the most widely publicized assessment was conducted by the International Association for the Evaluation of Educational Achievement. Its preliminary report, *Science Achievement in Seventeen Countries,* changed many Americans' perception of the U.S. educational system.[7]

This IEA study was conducted between 1983 and 1986 in Australia,

English-speaking Canada, England, Finland, Hong Kong, Hungary, Italy, Japan, Korea, the Netherlands, Norway, the Philippines, Poland, Singapore, Sweden, Thailand, and the United States. Separate assessments were conducted of students at three levels: 10-year-olds (typically grade four or five), 14-year-olds (typically grade eight or nine), and students in the final year of secondary school (typically grade twelve). While the 10- and 14-year-olds took a general test of science competence, the students tested during their final year of secondary school were assessed separately in biology, chemistry, and physics. All told, 220,848 students from 9,808 schools participated in the assessment. Table 3.3 summarizes the results of these assessments.

Note that as the age level increases, the U.S. students move from the middle of the pack to close to the bottom or dead last, depending on the subject. The IEA researchers note that between an earlier survey in 1970 and this survey, "the United States has dropped from seventh out of seventeen countries to third from bottom" (2). With respect to the 14-year-olds in England, Hong Kong, Italy, Singapore, and the United States, they state that "the lowest scoring children were scoring at chance level, indicating that from the test's point of view, they were *scientifically illiterate*" (4, emphasis added). And they add that students in grade nine in the United States had about the same level of achievement as students in grade seven in Japan and Korea (68). At all levels, male students scored higher than females, and the difference was greater for 14-year-olds than for 10-year-olds.

Noting that in some countries, including the United States, there is high variability among schools, while in other countries it doesn't matter much which school a student attends, the authors computed the percentage of schools in each country that scored below the lowest school in the highest-scoring country. In the United States, for example, 38 percent of the schools attended by 10-year-olds had mean scores that fell below that of the worst school in Japan, which was the leading country. Among the 14-year-olds the top-scoring country was Hungary, and 30 percent of U.S. schools had mean scores below that of the worst school in Hungary. For students in the last year of secondary school, three countries tied for first place in chemistry, and 48 percent of U.S. schools scored below the worst schools in those countries. Hong Kong was the top country in physics, and 89 percent of U.S. schools did more poorly than the worst school in Hong Kong. Finally, *98 percent* of U.S. schools scored below the worst school in Singapore, which was the top country in biology.

Table 3.3
Rank Order of Countries for Achievement at each Age Level, Mid-1980s

Country	Population 1	Population 2	Population 3 Biology	Chemistry	Physics	Nonscience students
Australia	9	10	9	6	8	4
Canada (English-speaking)	6	4	11	12	11	8
England	12	11	2	2	2	2
Finland	3	5	7	13	12	—
Hong Kong	13	16	5	1	1	—
Hungary	5	1	3	5	3	1
Italy	7	11	12	10	13	7
Japan	1	2	10	4	4	3
Korea	1	7	—	—	—	—
Netherlands	—	3	—	—	—	—
Norway	10	9	6	8	6	5
Philippines	15	17	—	—	—	—
Poland	11	7	4	7	7	—
Singapore	13	14	1	3	5	6
Sweden	4	6	8	9	10	—
Thailand	—	14	—	—	—	—
United States	8	14	13	11	9	—
Total	15	17	13	13	13	8

SOURCE: International Association for the Evaluation of Educational Achievement, *Science Achievement in Seventeen Countries: A Preliminary Report* (New York: Pergamon, 1988), 3.
NOTE: Data were collected between 1983 and 1986.

John Eichinger and others have presented methodological criticisms of the IEA study (see the discussion below). The major objections are (1) that the samples are not comparable because the United States, in particular, retains a higher percentage of students in school in the senior year than do other countries and (2) that the tests inadvertently favor small countries with highly centralized curricula.

The IEA researchers provide detailed data about the sampling at each age level. Examination of the data reveals that virtually 100 percent of the children aged 10 and 14 were in school in each country. In the senior year, 90 percent of U.S. students were in school, while the percentages for the other countries were considerably lower, for example, 71 percent for Canada, 20 for England and Hong Kong, 18 percent for Hungary, 63 percent for Japan, and 17 percent for Singapore.[8]

With respect to the second criticism, the IEA researchers emphasize that these are international tests.

They are not tests based on the curriculum of one educational system with the expectation that other systems use those tests regardless of how much overlap the first system's curriculum has with other systems' curricula. Indeed, the development of all instruments was a collaborative effort involving all educational systems in the study at that time. This is essential for the validity of the cross-national comparisons that are made. A common curriculum grid was developed using the curricula of all systems participating in the study: Items were provided by all systems for the measurement of particular cells in the grid; any new item was trialled in at least five different systems.[9]

The percentages of U.S. students who were studying biology (6%), chemistry (1%), and physics (1%) in the senior year—the group that actually was tested—are considerably lower, for the most part, than the percentages in other countries. Conversely, the percentage of U.S. students who did not study science in their senior year, 66 percent, is higher than that for any other country that reported data. Furthermore, while the correlation between achievement in the three science tests and the proportion of a country's age group studying that subject were negative, there were some exceptions: "For example, Sweden, Norway, and Hong Kong with fifteen percent, fifteen percent and fourteen percent of an age group achieve at a higher level in chemistry than the United States with only one percent of an age group in advanced placement chemistry" (13).

Sample Items from the International Science Assessment

The statistical results from this study about the performance of American students are disturbing. The problems are highlighted when we examine the results for some sample items presented in the appendix to the IEA report. A sample item from the test for population 1 (10-year-olds) reads as follows:

The sun is the only body in our solar system that gives off large amounts of light and heat. Why can we see the moon?
  a. It is reflecting light from the sun.
  b. It is without an atmosphere.
  c. It is a star.
  d. It is the biggest object in the solar system.
  e. It is nearer the Earth than the Sun.

The correct answer is *(a)*. Sixty-six percent of American 10-year-olds chose this answer; 19 percent chose *(e)*. On this particular item American students ranked fifth out of fifteen. The countries scoring higher were Finland (68%), Hungary (68%), Japan (66%), and Sweden (70%). Poland had the lowest score on this item, with only 41 percent of students choosing the correct answer.

This item was repeated in the test for population 2 (14-year-olds), on which the percentage of U.S. students correctly choosing *(a)* increased to seventy. However, the relative position of the United States slipped, as more countries than before exceeded that score. These countries were: Australia (slightly higher), Canada (73%), Finland (83%), Hong Kong (77%), Hungary (95%), Japan (71%), the Netherlands (74%), the Philippines (72%), Poland (72%), Singapore (89%), and Sweden (86%). Among the seventeen countries that participated in the assessment of population 2, on this item the United States placed twelfth. The countries that performed more poorly than the United States were England (53%), Italy (62%), Korea (63%), Norway (68%), and Thailand (60%).

The following item was administered to students in populations 1 and 2:

Paint applied to an iron surface prevents the iron from rusting. Which *one* of the following provides the best reason?
   a. it prevents nitrogen from coming in contact with the iron.
   b. it reacts chemically with the iron.
   c. it prevents carbon dioxide from coming in contact with the iron.
   d. it makes the surface of the iron smoother.
   e. it prevents oxygen and moisture from coming in contact with the iron. (106)

The correct answer, *e*, was selected by 46 percent of American 10-year-olds. The percentage of correct responses varied from a high of 70 percent for Finland to a low of 32 percent for Singapore. The United States placed above only four countries: England, the Philippines, Hong Kong, and Singapore. When this item was given to students in population 2, the U.S. score was 66 percent correct. However, American students surpassed only those from the Philippines, with only 51 percent giving the correct answer. Among 14-year-olds, those from Hungary performed best on this item, with 91 percent giving the correct answer.

It has been argued that many apparently superior educational systems in other countries, for example, Japan, require a considerable amount of memorization, while the American educational system continues to place a high priority on creativity, cognitive flexibility, and the ability to interpret complex information. In this regard, the data from an item administered to population 3 that required interpretation, not merely feeding back memorized information, are fascinating:

In order to obtain two crops in one growing season a farmer planted some seeds which he had harvested the previous week but the seeds failed to germinate. What can be concluded from this observation?

a. The farmer did not provide the right conditions for germination.
b. The seeds needed a longer period of maturation.
c. The farmer had not removed inhibiting substances.
d. The seeds required a period of low temperature.
e. The data are inadequate for a conclusion to be reached.

The correct answer is *(e);* it was selected by 53 percent of students from the United States. Singapore scored considerably higher (66%). The only other country whose students scored higher than the American students was England, with 55 percent, only marginally higher than the American score. Particularly low scores were earned by the students from Finland (22%), Hungary (23%), Italy (27%), and Norway (28%).[10]

Parallel to the IEA international assessment in science was an IEA international assessment in mathematics during the 1981–82 school year. Five topics were included: arithmetic, algebra, geometry, statistics, and measurement. According to the project report, *The Underachieving Curriculum,* among students in the eighth grade, Japan scored ahead of all other countries on all five topics. U.S. students were a little above average in calculation, a little below average in problem solving, about average in algebra, and far below average in geometry. Twelfth-grade students were assessed on six topics: number systems, sets and relations, algebra, geometry, elementary functions and calculus, and probability and statistics. For this age group Hong Kong students scored above those from other countries in each topic, with Japan a close second. U.S. students in calculus (the percentage of mathematics students who take calculus in the United States is much smaller than the percentage in other countries) scored about average. American precalculus students fell far below average. "In some cases the U.S. ranked with the lower one-fourth of all countries in the study and was the lowest of the advanced industrialized countries."[11]

It should be noted that a measure of the extent of American mathematics teachers' coverage of topics on the international test was at or below the international average for most content areas. "Within the United States, coverage varied a great deal among classes. That is, marked differences in opportunities to learn mathematics were found between students" (viii). Not only is the mathematics achievement of U.S. students mediocre (at best) but, compared with students in other countries, a smaller percentage study calculus, and the percentage of students who enroll in advanced mathematics more generally is about average. This is true despite the fact that a much higher percentage of young people are in school in America than in other countries.

Surprisingly, American students did about as much homework as did students in most other countries. Also, the number of students per classroom in mathematics in Japan greatly exceeded that in the United States. For example, in the twelfth grade the average class size in Japan was forty-three students; in the United States it was twenty. The number of hours of instruction in mathematics in the eighth grade in the United States was about average; in the twelfth grade the U.S. figure was below average. However, U.S. teachers have a higher teaching load than do teachers in most other countries.

The authors of this report recommended that, "with respect to form, the excessive repetition of topics from year to year should be eliminated. A more focused organization of the subject matter, with a more intense treatment of topics, should be considered" (xii). They also recommended less repetition of arithmetic and greater inclusion of geometry, probability and statistics, and algebra in the junior high school curriculum.

In order to control for differing proportions of young people still in school and of young people still taking mathematics as high school seniors in different countries, a special analysis was made of the achievement scores in algebra of the top 1 percent and the top 5 percent. The top American students scored lower than the top students from any other country for which data were available. "That is to say, the algebra achievement of our most able students (the top one percent) was lower than that of the top one percent of any other country. The algebra achievement of our top five percent group was lower than any other country, except for Israel" (27). These samples were selected from the cohort in the last year.

In the eighth-grade population there was a close correspondence between the percentage of test items taught in a country's curriculum, an "opportunity-to-learn" measure, and the achievement test scores. The United States ranked slightly below the middle on opportunity to learn. While this was true in algebra, all countries scored relatively low on the opportunity to learn geometry.

The authors of this international assessment consider five explanations often offered for the low achievement level of American students, explanations that they label "deceptive":

1. Time for mathematics instruction differs from country to country.
2. Class size differs.
3. The United States has more comprehensive education, retaining more students in school.

4. The preparation and status of teachers differs.
5. The quality of mathematics teaching differs.

They conclude that the culprit is the curriculum. They report that their study has shown the U.S. mathematics curriculum to be underachieving "in its goals, in its strategies and in its expectations for students" (85). "The U.S. eighth grade curriculum, therefore, is much more like a curriculum of the last years of elementary school while that of Japan, and many other countries, resembles that of the first years of secondary school. At the twelfth grade level, the U.S. curriculum is much more like that of early years of secondary school while the curriculum of most other countries is more like that of beginning college level" (95).

International Assessments in the 1960s and the 1970s

Has the achievement of American students declined during the past quarter-century, or have they always scored poorly? Findings from the original IEA surveys, for which planning began in 1966, are revealing. (The original discussions by researchers from many countries about the possibility of international studies were held in 1959.) A twelve-country feasibility study had been conducted in 1962, and a study of mathematical achievement in twelve countries was published in 1967.[12] Three areas—science, literature, and reading comprehension—were studied between 1970 and 1972 (with reports published in 1973), and three more areas—English, French as a foreign language, and civic education—were studied in 1974 and 1975 (with reports published in 1976). In 1976 David Walker published a volume summarizing the results from all six subject surveys, which were conducted in twenty-one countries.[13] One year later Richard Wolf published a report about the IEA results as they related specifically to the United States.[14]

While attention following the publication of the IEA reports has focused on comparative national achievement scores, a major thrust of these investigations was to relate achievement in a given country with predictor variables such as class size, teacher qualifications, and the socioeconomic status of the student. A special focus of the science survey was whether achievement in science was related to the degree to which teaching involved investigations carried out by the students themselves. Researchers were interested both in the students' knowledge of content and in their knowledge of the scientific method. Data also were collected about the

Table 3.4

Mean Science Achievement Test Scores for Populations 1, 2, and 4, 1973

	Population 1			Population 2			Population 4			Grand total score (Populations 1, 2, 4)
	Total score	Opportunity to learn	Holding power	Total score	Opportunity to learn	Holding power	Total score	Opportunity to learn	Holding power[a]	
Maximum	40	4.00	100	80	4.00	100	60	4.00	100	66
Australia	—	—	99	24.6	2.03	99	24.7	2.57	29	26.1
Belgium (Flemish-speaking)	17.9	2.34	99	21.2	1.83	90	17.4	2.02	47	18.0
Belgium (French-speaking)	13.9	1.97	99	15.4	2.03	90	15.3	2.88	47	15.9
England	15.7	2.12	99	21.3	1.79	99	23.1	2.07	20	24.3
Federal Republic of Germany	14.9	1.67	99	23.7	1.82	94	26.9	3.15	9	28.3
Finland	17.5	2.05	99	20.5	1.51	99	19.8	2.65	21	20.8
France	—	—	99	—	—	99	18.3	2.60	29	19.0
Hungary	16.7	1.70	99	29.1	2.78	83	23.0	3.03	28	23.9
Italy	16.5	2.43	99	18.5	1.86	55	15.9	2.50	16	16.9
Japan	21.7	2.07	99	31.2	2.96	99	—	—	70	—
Netherlands	15.3	1.97	99	17.8	1.37	98	23.3	2.42	13	24.2
New Zealand	—	—	99	24.2	2.15	99	29.0	2.88	13	30.7
Scotland	14.0	1.96	99	21.4	1.90	99	23.1	2.17	17	24.3
Sweden	18.3	1.80	99	21.7	1.88	99	19.2	2.75	45	20.0
United States	17.7	2.60	99	21.6	1.98	99	13.7	2.13	75	14.1
Mean	16.7	2.06		22.3	1.99		20.9	2.56		21.9
Chile	9.1	1.96	94	9.2	1.48	71	8.8	2.69	16	9.2
India	8.5	1.73	50	7.6	1.48	25	6.0	1.85	14	6.2
Iran	4.1	—	75	7.8	—	25	10.2	—	9	10.7
Thailand	9.9	—	50	15.6	—	40	12.4	—	10	—

SOURCE: L. C. Comber and J. P. Keeves, eds., *Science Education in Nineteen Countries: An Empirical Study* (New York: John Wiley & Sons, 1973), 159.
[a]These figures for holding power depend to a considerable degree upon the way population 4 was defined in the different countries.

students' attitudes toward science and toward the teaching methods employed. Additional independent variables gathered in the research included the age, gender, and socioeconomic status of the student, as well as measures about both the school and the country's educational system.

Nineteen countries participated in the science study. However, data from four developing countries—Chile, India, Iran, and Thailand—had to be analyzed separately from data from the developed countries. "It was found that similarities in science curricula far outweighed differences and it was therefore possible to devise tests which were reasonably appropriate for all participating countries. Nevertheless, students of the developing countries found the test to be much more difficult than did their peers elsewhere."[15]

The amount of instruction, as indicated by both the number of years of study and the number of minutes per week, was strongly related to science achievement in the pre-university population. Unfortunately, in the science study there was no clear finding about the relationship between practical learning and inquiry methods, on the one hand, and science achievement, on the other. In reviewing the science achievement results in light of the different retention rates, the researchers concluded that "the different systems produce comparable proportions of high achievers, but the less selective systems produce, in addition, greater proportions of students with at least moderate achievements in science. . . . High selectivity minimizes failure, whereas low selectivity maximizes success. Somewhere between the two extremes lies a point that a particular country can afford and which fits the particular set of circumstances as well as can be judged" (236).

Table 3.4 summarizes the results from the science achievement survey. Data are presented for each participating country, with data from the four developing countries presented separately. Achievement test means are displayed for each of the three age groups. In addition, a grand total score is presented for each country, as is a measure of the "holding power," that is, the percentage of the school-age population still in school.

In population 1, the United States did reasonably well. The mean score of 17.7 places it fourth out of the twelve developed countries from which scores were obtained. In population 2 the United States ranked seventh out of the fourteen developed countries that reported data. However, by the pre-university year, that is, population 4, the United States was in last place in science out of the fourteen developed countries that reported data. The U.S. score was not substantially higher than that achieved by Thailand, one of the developing countries. The United States also ranked last out of the fourteen developed countries in the grand total score, which included some extra advanced science items administered in a carefully rotated fashion.[16]

In summary, even twenty years ago American high school seniors were performing dismally on science achievement tests in an international comparison. Therefore, today's low scores probably do not represent a substantial decline in the quality of American schools.

Note also that the holding power is higher for the United States than in other countries, indicating that a greater proportion of students were still in school for the Population 4 assessment. This factor may contribute to the dismal performance of American high school seniors on the science achievement test. What happens if we compare the best U.S. students with the best students from other countries?

Table 3.5 presents data that allow further exploration of the effect of student retention upon the achievement test scores. Mean scores for each country are produced for the top 1 percent of students in the age group as well as the top 5 percent. When we look only at the top 1 percent of the age group, the United States places ninth out of fourteen, rather than last. In short, controlling for the proportion of the population in school increased the U.S. rank from fourteenth to ninth. When we look at the top 5 percent, the United States places eighth. In short, when we control the bias introduced by differing percentages of students studying science in various countries, American high school seniors move from last place to the middle of the pack.

The field testing in the six subject surveys conducted in the early 1970s involved 258,000 students, 50,000 teachers, and 9,700 schools. Why, one might ask, did the researchers embark on such a venture? "We conceived of the world as one big educational laboratory where a great variety of practices in terms of school structure and curricula were tried out. We simply wanted to take advantage of the international variability with regard both to the outcomes of the educational systems and the factors which caused differences in those outcomes."[17]

According to the authors of the IEA report on science in nineteen countries, their inquiry took place

at a time when the nature of science education and its contribution to a general education, as distinct from a specific training, was coming under close scrutiny in many parts of the world. Traditional patterns, affecting both subject content and learning methods, were giving way to new programs, often under the stimulus of

Table 3.5

*Mean Science Achievement Test Scores for Total Sample and Equivalent
Proportions of an Age Group, 1973*

Country	% in School	Full sample	Top 1%	Top 5%
New Zealand	13	30.8	52.8	43.5
England	20	24.4	51.6	41.6
Australia	29	26.1	51.5	44.0
Scotland	17	24.4	50.7	40.6
Sweden	45	20.1	49.5	41.2
Hungary	28	24.0	48.0	39.0
Netherlands	13	24.4	47.1	37.2
Finland	21	20.8	46.0	35.7
United States	75	14.2	45.8	36.8
Federal Republic of Germany	9	28.4	45.0	35.3
France	29	19.1	40.5	33.3
Belgium (Flemish-speaking)	47	18.1	39.8	33.0
Italy	16	16.5	38.2	27.4
Belgium (French-speaking)	47	16.0	36.2	30.9
Average		22.0	45.9	37.1
Range		16.6	16.6	16.6
Chile	16	9.3	23.5	16.8
India	14	6.3	20.8	12.8
Iran	9	10.8	21.9	14.8
Thailand	10	12.5	23.2	17.4

SOURCE: Comber and Keeves, *Science Education in Nineteen Countries*, 174.

NOTE: The means reported above are derived from a slightly different number of cases than those in table 3.4.

curriculum projects organized on a vast scale and employing new curriculum reform techniques. It is fair to say that the study was made at a critical stage in the history of science teaching and the results obtained may influence considerably the direction of future progress. (17)

The authors note that in many countries science content areas are being updated rapidly and the scientific method is being introduced to students at an earlier age. "Differences between countries, and between schools within countries, are widening as a result of the different levels of importance attached to these modern trends and the pace at which changes in science curricula are being made." They point out that "probably the most significant difference between science education as practiced in different countries lies in the nature and extent of the practical experience given in the laboratory" (18).

Unfortunately, direct comparisons of the U.S. achievement scores at this pre-university-year level with those from Japan is not possible because

Japan did not participate in studies at that level. This comparison would have been fascinating for two reasons: because of the economic power of Japan, which, as noted in chapter 1, is tied to its educational philosophy, and because Japan and the United States are the countries with the highest retention rates.

Data collected during the surveys about the structure of science education in the elementary and secondary years reveal that the proportion of secondary school students studying science in the United States was relatively low compared with the proportion in such countries as Chile, Finland, Hungary, and Thailand, among others. For example, 43 percent of students in the United States took science in high school, whereas 100 percent of the students in Thailand did so. In fact, the only country that registered a lower percentage was England, whose educational system forces students to make major curriculum choices earlier in their career than in other countries.

In table 3.6, the information from the 1970 IEA science survey about the retention rate of the school systems is combined with the percentage of those in secondary school who take science. When these percentages are multiplied, a measure of the percentage of the age cohort who are studying science in school is obtained. When these new statistics for what might be called the "science holding power" are compared, the United States does

Table 3.6
Percentage of Students Studying Science, 1970

Country	Holding power (A)	% Taking science (B)	% Cohort in science (A × B)
Australia	29	79	22.9
Belgium (Flemish-speaking)	47	91	42.8
Belgium (French-speaking)	47	79	37.1
England	20	41	8.2
Federal Republic of Germany	9	97	8.7
Finland	21	73	15.3
France	29	48	13.9
Hungary	28	75	21.0
Italy	16	57	9.1
Japan	70		
Netherlands	13	68	8.8
New Zealand	13	82	10.7
Scotland	17	56	9.5
Sweden	45	45	20.3
United States	75	43	32.3

SOURCE: Adapted from Comber and Keeves, *Science Education in Nineteen Countries.*

Table 3.7
International Mathematics Assessment Results, 1965

Country	Mean Score	
	Mathematics students	Nonmathematics students
Australia	21.6	
Belgium	34.6	24.2
England	35.2	21.4
Finland	25.3	22.5
France	33.4	26.2
Germany	28.8	27.7
Israel	36.4	
Japan	31.4	25.3
Netherlands	31.9	24.7
Scotland	25.5	20.7
Sweden	27.3	12.6
United States	13.8	8.3

SOURCE: T. Husen, ed., *International Study of Achievement in Mathematics* (New York: John Wiley & Sons, 1967), 24.

not appear to be the deviant case it appears to be when one looks at the figures for holding power only: the U.S. percentage is closer to those from the other developed countries and, in fact, is only lower than the percentages for both the Belgium educational systems. (The U.S. achievement score at the pre-university level was below that of both Belgium educational systems.) Richard Wolf observed that "students in the United States performed in close accord with the amount of opportunity to learn what was being tested. *The implication here is that increased opportunity to learn specific material will lead to higher test performance.*"[18]

The results of the mathematics achievements testing done in the 1965 international assessment are summarized in table 3.7. Perhaps the most important finding is that among mathematics students the U.S. mean score of 13.8 on the seventy-item test was considerably below the nearest score among the other countries in the study (21.6, Australia). It is particularly disturbing to compare the U.S. score with the Japanese score of 31.4.

The following are among the findings of the pilot study of mathematics achievement:

—National differences in achievement were directly related to the differing emphases given to different topics.
—Class size was not related to mathematical achievement.
—The percentage of an age group still in school at the pre-university stage ranged tremendously, from 8 percent to 70 percent. Differences in achievement scores were closely related to these differences in

retention. When only the top 4 percent of the age group was considered, there was much less variation in the national averages.

—Students who were in selective schools, or tracked, did better than students in comprehensive schools when they were tested as 13-year-olds. By the time they were at the pre-university stage, the differences had evaporated.

—For 13-year-olds, mathematics achievement was associated with the status of the father's occupation, but this relationship also evaporated when students reached the pre-university stage.

Criticisms of the IEA Surveys

In a systematic, rigorous critique of the methodology of the IEA studies, Eichinger observes, "Several factors mitigate the interpretive power of the IEA report. These factors should be considered before acting upon IEA's findings, since they complicate the survey's results and weaken its conclusions."[19] He notes that different countries structure their science curricula differently, which make comparisons less meaningful. For example, American high school students study a different subject each year, while European students learn a little about each subject each year.

The key question is the degree to which the IEA study results are an artifact of the range of students allowed to study science in secondary school. Countries that weed out weaker students prior to secondary school have an advantage in international comparisons with countries that attempt to teach science to the entire adolescent population.

Eichinger also cites potential cultural biases. "For instance, students from a primarily agricultural nation might have an advantage on questions regarding the practical aspects of botany, simply by virtue of their personal experience with plants" (35). He notes that countries also vary widely in terms of sample size, response rate, and the mean ages of the national samples, and he identifies some data analysis problems.

Finally, noting that each IEA test contained very few items (twenty-four to thirty, depending upon the test) and that all items were in the multiple-choice format, Eichinger says that "it appears that the tests were not 'equally "fair" or "unfair" to all systems,' but favored countries with explicit or implicit national science curricula" (36). He cites the following statement from the IEA report: "It is clear that a school system where only ten percent of its curriculum is covered by a test cannot be expected to have a level of performance comparable to that of another system where ninety percent of the curriculum is covered" (36). Eichinger concludes that "since the test questions were based on a combination of stated or approximated national curricula, students from countries such as the U.S., which have no official or unofficial national curricular standards, may be at a disadvantage" (37). To test this notion he computed Spearman rank correlations between IEA test scores and national population and between test scores and national land area. The correlations were statistically significant and negative, suggesting that "high school students in populous countries and all three student populations in large countries tend to score lower on IEA tests" (37).

Eichinger concludes his review this way: "As a science teacher, I must ask myself the following question after reading the IEA study: Can a single twenty-four to thirty item test possibly be an accurate index to the curriculum in my classroom, in all other American science classrooms, and in the science classrooms of sixteen other countries? The degree of disagreement in my answer should be proportional to the degree of skepticism that I exercise as I interpret IEA's results" (38).

Japan and the United States Compared

In 1983 President Reagan and Prime Minister Nakasone of Japan launched a cooperative research project in which each country would study the education system of the other. The American review of Japanese education has produced two reports: *Japanese Education Today* (1987) and *Japanese Educational Productivity* (1992).[20] The more recent volume contains updated scholarly papers that focus directly on productivity.

The Japanese set aside one hour a week for moral education in elementary and lower secondary schools. There are twenty-eight moral education themes at the elementary level.

The twenty-eight themes roughly fall into six categories. The first involves the importance of order, regularity, cooperation, thoughtfulness, participation, manners, and respect for public property. The second stresses endurance, hard work, character development, and high aspirations. Such moral attributes of human life as freedom, justice, fairness, rights, duties, trust, and conviction are central concerns in the third category. The fourth examines the individual's place in groups, such as the family, the school, the nation, and the world. The fifth category focuses on harmony with and appreciation of nature and the essential need for rational, scientific attitudes toward human life, and the sixth emphasizes originality.[21]

Harold Stevenson and Karen Bartsch analyzed the content of elementary and secondary mathematics texts used in the United States and Japan. The Japanese elementary texts were much shorter than the U.S. textbooks and were concentrated in a spartan manner on the material to be learned. The American texts included much more in the way of photographs and illustrations. Noting that Japanese textbook writers appear to rely much more heavily on the teacher to augment textbook material, the authors comment, "The writers of Japanese textbooks also seek to engage the child's active participation in the development of understanding to a greater degree than American writers seem to believe is necessary or possible."[22] The Japanese texts provided much less repetition and review and did not exhibit the *spiral curriculum* common to American textbooks, a curriculum in which topics appear each year in incrementally advanced levels. According to Stevenson and Bartsch, "The emphases given to various topics in the two countries differ, but more notable than the differences are the similarities in the mathematical concepts and operations that appear in the elementary school textbooks. The major difference lies, therefore, not in the content of the curricula, but in the manner and timing in which the curricula are presented in the textbooks" (115).

Similar differences were found in secondary mathematics textbooks. For example, the American texts were longer, were filled with illustrations and graphs, and introduced abstract constructs through examples of everyday experience. Stevenson and Bartsch report that "American textbooks appear to be written so that understanding the content of the lesson is less dependent upon what happens in mathematics classes" (125).

With respect to the topics covered in secondary education, they say that

American secondary school textbooks give greater emphasis to fractions, percentages, and ratios; addition and subtraction; measurement; decimals; general geometry; and geometric triangles and angles than do the Japanese textbooks. Japanese textbooks, on the other hand, give greater emphasis to graphing functions, three-dimensional figures, equations and sets, probability and statistics, and calculus. When a differential emphasis was given to the topics in the two countries, emphasis appeared to be placed on more advanced topics in Japan than in the United States. (130)

In one study, tests of reasoning skills were given to junior high school students in Hiroshima, Japan, and North Carolina. The Japanese students consistently demonstrated better reasoning skills, for example, proportional thinking, probabilistic thinking, and combinatorial thinking, than did the American students. When an estimate was made of the Piagetian level (a measure of cognitive development) of the students, 42 percent of the Japanese students but only 13 percent of the American students were found to be working with formal operations.

For both the Japanese and the American students the authors of the study report correlations between achievement test scores and a series of items about science in school and about the students' life outside of school. The variable that correlated most highly with achievement in both fifth and ninth grade for Japanese students and in fifth grade for American students (among U.S. ninth graders it had the second highest correlation) was not a school variable but a home variable: "books in the home."[23]

In January 1993, Harold Stevenson, Chuansheng Chen, and Shin-Ying Lee reported fascinating results from a ten-year study of the mathematics achievement of Chinese, Japanese, and American children.[24] In their research they went to great lengths to test students only on material that was covered in all three countries. In 1980 they tested first and fifth graders; in 1984 they tested the first graders from the 1980 test, who were now in fifth grade; in 1990 they tested fifth graders and a sizable sample of eleventh graders (including most of those who had been first graders in the original 1980 survey). They also examined parent and teacher attitudes through both interviews and questionnaires.

At each point in time the American students consistently placed third in comparisons at each grade level. Furthermore, the American students in the longitudinal sample, who were tested in both the first and the eleventh grade, fell further below the other students in high school than they had been in elementary school. "The gap is large," reported Stevenson and his colleagues. "For example, [in the fifth grade] only 4.1 percent of the Chinese children and 10.3 percent of the Japanese children in 1990 had scores as low as those of the average American child. . . . [in the eleventh grade] only 14.5 percent of the Chinese and 8.0 percent of the Japanese students received scores below the average score of the American students" (54).

Despite a decade of journalistic reports about the poor performance of American students, the American parents were more satisfied with their children's achievement than were the Japanese or Chinese parents. In light of the arguments advanced in this book about the concept of aptitude, it is interesting to note that these researchers found that American students and parents attributed success in mathematics to innate ability, while the Chinese and Japanese attributed it to hard work.

The links between simple hard work and achievement should be underscored. In *Head to Head,* which compares the economic futures of the

United States, Europe, and Japan, Lester Thurow states that "those who worked hard in high school should be rewarded with admission to universities, whether public or private. Those who did not work should not be admitted—no matter how smart they are."[25] And consider also the following observations by economist Robert Samuelson on the subject of school reform:

The main reason that most American students don't do as well as they might, is that they don't work very hard. Yet almost all school reform proposals (including Clinton's) conveniently skip the subject of student effort, as if it didn't exist.

It is not that American students are exceptionally lazy. Our schools simply don't demand much of them, and in this, the schools merely do what the public wants.[26]

Perhaps the most surprising finding from this international comparison is that the Japanese students reported the lowest amount of stress in their lives. This stands in sharp contrast to the image of the overachieving but highly stressed and depressed Japanese high school student.

Noting that the American sample was drawn from the Minneapolis school system, the authors observe, "The low levels of achievement found in Minneapolis are especially worrisome because Minnesota students rank high among the states in mathematics achievement. . . . When problems are found in Minnesota, more severe ones might be expected to occur in many other states."[27]

In an interesting twist, these researchers also tested the students on items of general information, material not usually presented in school but rather acquired through personal experience. *The American students ranked first on this test, indicating that the cause of the low performance in mathematics lies in the schools.* "We attribute the early superiority of the American children to the greater cognitive stimulation provided by their parents, who indicated that they read more frequently to their young children, took them on more excursions, and accompanied them to more cultural events than did the Chinese or Japanese parents" (55).

Finally, these researchers found that in all three cultures boys and girls scored equally in elementary school but that by high school the achievement scores of boys were significantly higher than those of girls.

Elaborating upon the study's findings, Harold Stevenson dispels some myths about the differences between American and Japanese schools. For one thing, Asian children find school a pleasant place, not the prisonlike, excessively demanding environment that Americans picture. Noting that "American children spend most of their time at school in the classroom," Stevenson says that, in contrast, the daily routine in Asian schools offers many opportunities for social experience. There are frequent recesses, long lunch periods, and after-school activities and clubs. Such opportunities make up about one-fourth of the time spent during the eight hours at school. The school day is longer in Asia mainly because of the time devoted to these nonacademic periods. Play, social interaction and extra-curricular activity may not contribute directly to academic success, but they make school an enjoyable place. The enjoyment likely creates cooperative attitudes. (74)

A second surprise was that American teachers spend more time in the classroom each day than do Japanese and Taiwanese teachers. According to the authors of this study, "teaching is more of a group endeavor in Asia than it is in the U.S. Teachers frequently consult with one another, because, in following the national curriculum, they are all teaching the same lessons at about the same time. More experienced teachers help newer ones." American teachers, on the other hand, spend most of their time at school in their own classrooms and have few opportunities for interactions or consultation with their colleagues (75).

The Asian teachers they studied described themselves as well-informed guides, and they saw their students as "active participants in the learning process who must play an important role in producing, explaining and evaluating solutions to problems" (75). In contrast, the American teachers were more likely to see themselves as dispensers of information. Asian teachers learn their skills in the classroom under the guidance of more experienced teachers. Surprisingly, they have much less formal instruction in college about teaching methods. James Stigler and Harold Stevenson found that teachers in the United States and in Japan ask questions for different reasons. In the United States the purpose of a question is to get an answer; in Japan the purpose is to stimulate thought. In fact, Japanese teachers consider questions to be poor if they elicit immediate answers because this indicates that students were not challenged to think.[28]

An English translation of the mathematics section of the 1990 University Entrance Center Examination, a test given in Japan that parallels the mathematics SAT, was published recently by the Mathematical Association of American (MAA). Mathematicians in the United States have been staggered by the test's sophistication. Richard Askey, a University of Wisconsin mathematician, said that if college-bound students in the United State were given the Japanese exam, they "would bomb out completely."[29]

However, several factors must be considered in comparing Japanese and American students' success on college entrance examinations. Many Japanese high school students attend special cram schools. Furthermore, the last year of study at many of the most prestigious Japanese secondary schools is devoted to preparing for the test, the secondary school curriculum having been fully covered in the previous years.

It has been suggested that one reason for the superiority of the American system of higher education and its graduate schools is that American students do not reach college already exhausted from their efforts in secondary school. As S. W. Kim put it in a letter to the editor of *Science,* "Many Chinese, Korean, and Japanese students are so exhausted by the time they enter college that they want a period of respite. Their American counterparts, on the other hand, are just beginning to tighten their belts and dig in. I believe the vigor and intensity of U.S. researchers are partly due to the fact that they were not crippled during the high school years."[30]

In 1992 Ian Westbury reexamined data from the IEA Second International Mathematics Study (SIMS), conducted in the early 1980s. When he compared achievement in eighth-grade algebra classes in Japan and in the United States, he found that where the curriculum content was comparable the achievement was also comparable.[31] However, the fact remains that American students generally test at a level below students from Japan and most other countries. If the explanation indeed lies entirely in the curriculum, this is a strong argument for strengthening our curriculum. According to Westbury,

> The international data yielded by SIMS can be seen as showing, for example, that all or most junior secondary students *can* readily master the elements of algebra and that a culminating course in calculus *can* be an effective part of the high school experience for many students. It suggests, when we look at other countries' experiences, that something approaching a "mathematics for all" *can* be a realistic possibility for the junior secondary years. Moreover, it suggests that the American teacher force *does* deliver the U.S. national curriculum quite effectively—without the need for national examinations or forced animation by way of competency tests of one kind or another. (24, emphasis in the original)

In another study whose results shatter myths Americans hold about Japanese education, Lois Peak examined preschool life in Japan. She observed students and teachers in two typical private Japanese preschools and interviewed the mothers and teachers. "The first surprise is that the primary goal of preschool experience is to establish fundamental habits of daily life and to assimilate the group-oriented behavior and attitudes appropriate to social situations. Acquiring academic facts and learning-readiness skills are not major goals of Japanese preschool education."[32]

Furthermore, there is a discontinuity in Japan between the behavior expected of children in school (obedience, working well with other children) and at home, where one can have temper tantrums and be undisciplined and selfish. Another surprise is that Japanese preschools mold compliant and cooperative behavior on the part of students without a heavy emphasis on teacher discipline. Finally, Japanese schools allow periods for "play and exuberant spontaneity," which are alternated with periods of formal behavior, cooperation, and learning.

We must be very careful when trying to transpose strategies from Japan, or another country, into the educational system of the United States. These strategies and techniques are embedded in a culture. What works in Japan, because it is interwoven with the cultural fabric of that society, may not necessarily work in the United States. Dennis Laurie studied the experiences of American executives who work in Japanese companies and published the results in his book *Yankee Samurai*.[33] He expresses reservations about whether highly touted Japanese management strategies, for example, quality circles, would be successful in firms in the United States. The reason for his hesitation is that such techniques grow out of the Japanese culture, which involves different assumptions and norms from those in American culture.

Who Studies Science?

According to F. James Rutherford, the author of a major study of science education in five countries, if students are to learn a substantial amount of science, they need to put in the necessary time.

Factoring in days of instruction per year (about 180 in the United States, 210 to 220 in the other five countries), actual attendance patterns, length of school day and week, fraction of total school time allotted to science, and amount of homework assigned, it appears that American students spend one-half to one-third as much time learning science as their counterparts in the USSR and the other four countries.

He adds that "the picture is only slightly better in mathematics."[34]

David Berliner reports that international expenditure data demonstrate that the Unites States spends far less than most industrialized nations on pre-primary, primary, and secondary education. "In 1988 dollars we ranked ninth among 16 industrialized nations in per-pupil expenditures in K-12, spending 14 percent *less* than Germany, 30 percent *less* than Japan, and 51 percent *less* than Switzerland. . . . out of 16 industrialized nations, 13 of them spend a greater percent of per-capita income on K-12 education than we do."[35]

Tables 3.8 and 3.9, adapted from an Educational Testing Service report

Table 3.8
*Percentage of High School Students Taking
Algebra II, Geometry, Trigonometry, and
Calculus, in 1982, 1987, and 1990*

Gender/ethnic group	1982	1987	1990
All	.96	2.4	2.2
Male	1.2	2.9	2.5
Female	0.7	1.9	1.8
White	1.1	2.3	2.3
African American	0.2	1.2	1.1
Latino	0.5	2.2	1.5
Asian	2.5	14.5	6.5

SOURCE: Educational Testing Service, *What Americans Study: Revisited* (Princeton, N.J., 1994), 11.

entitled *What Americans Study,*[36] show the percentage of high school students who had taken advanced mathematics and science courses in 1982, 1987, and 1990. The percentages are given separately for males and females as well as for ethnic groups. The percentage of high school students taking advanced mathematics courses is very small. Clearly, the numbers are higher for males than for females and for Whites and Asians than for African Americans and Latinos. The percentages for females, African Americans, and Latinos increased from 1982 and 1987 but then dropped slightly between 1987 and 1990. For these groups, then, the most recent trend lines are in the wrong direction.

According to table 3.9, in 1990 about 19 percent of high school students had taken biology, chemistry, and physics. As in mathematics, the percentages are higher for males and for Whites and Asians; in the sciences, however, the percentages for females and for African Americans and Latinos increased during both time periods (i.e., from 1982 to 1987 and from 1987 to 1990). Those trend lines are in the right direction. Perhaps the most discouraging information in these tables is the minuscule percentage of students who take this sequence of advanced mathematics courses, regardless of gender or ethnicity. Furthermore, even the science percentages should be higher.

Student Attitudes toward Science

In a 1989 article in *Parade Magazine,* Carl Sagan said that every now and then he was "lucky enough to teach a class in kindergarten or the first

Table 3.9
*Percentage of High School Students
Taking Biology, Chemistry, and Physics,
in 1982, 1987, and 1990*

Gender/ethnic group	1982	1987	1990
All	10.5	16.8	18.9
Male	13.3	20.8	22.1
Female	8.0	12.9	16.0
White	12.1	17.9	20.7
African American	4.6	8.8	12.1
Latino	3.9	8.2	10.2
Asian	27.3	42.4	33.8

SOURCE: See table 3.8.

grade. Many of these children are curious, intellectually vigorous, ask provocative and insightful questions and exhibit great enthusiasm for science." But he said that when he talked to high school students, he found something different.

They memorize "facts." But, by and large, the joy of discovery, the life behind those facts, has gone out of them. They're worried about asking "dumb" questions; they're willing to accept inadequate answers; they don't pose follow-up questions; the room is awash with sidelong glances to judge, second-by-second, the approval of their peers. Something has happened between first and twelfth grade, and it's not just puberty.[37]

Some research suggests that the most dangerous years may be the junior high school years. Robert James and Stan Smith suggest that one reason why students may begin to lose their positive attitude toward science in these years is that the seventh grade is often the first time science is taught as a separate subject in a separate classroom. In addition, it is usually a required subject at this grade level. "Seventh grade science may be one of the earliest attempts to require students to use self-directed problem solving techniques to a greater degree than earlier grades. Perhaps this additional rigor explains the response. Since K-6 science is frequently not graded, seventh grade may be the first time students work has been evaluated."[38]

F. James Rutherford, who is the director of a major science education project of the American Association for the Advancement of Science, comments, "You have to know something is wrong when teaching something as exciting as science can result in most of us disliking it."[39]

Luanne Gogolin and Fred Swartz investigated the attitudes of 102 non-science students and 81 science students toward science, both before and after the students were exposed to a science course. Not surprisingly, science students began with a more positive attitude toward science on all six scales of the Attitude Toward Science Inventory (ATSI). The science students then took a traditional botany course, while the nonscience students took an introductory course in human anatomy and physiology that stressed relevance and high-interest activities. Following the courses, the nonscience students had a more positive view of science than they had held previously, while the science students had a less positive attitude than they had held previously. According to Gogolin and Swartz, "The results of this study and others suggest that attitudes toward science change with exposure to science, but that the direction of change may be related to the quality of that exposure."[40]

Earlier work by John Keeves suggested that the home, the school, and the peer group all affect a high school student's attitude toward science and whether he or she achieves.[41] Research by E. Lynn Talton and Ronald Simpson also identified links between science attitudes and both the family and the classroom.[42] And a study by R. Schibeci reinforced the links between home environment, school environment, and peer groups, on the one hand, and student attitudes about science and science achievement, on the other.[43] One of the most interesting findings from Schibeci's study was serendipitous and may have interesting implications for instruction: "Almost every student interviewed became more actively involved in the class shortly after the interview took place. The student appeared more at ease in the lecture hall and demonstrated increased initiative in the laboratory."[44] The interviews conducted with the students who participated in Schibeci's study reinforced the notion that both the family environment and peer relationships affect the development of attitudes toward science.

John Eichinger studied high-achieving college students' impressions about about their experiences in junior and senior high school science classes.[45] His sample consisted of 114 science and 87 nonscience undergraduates from two highly selective colleges, Harvey Mudd and Pomona. He compared the responses of the science students with those of the nonscience students and with data about noncollegiate adults reported in an earlier study by Yager and Penick.[46] According to Eichinger, "Science and non-science majors reported similar levels of science interest in grade seven and eight. The two groups differed significantly in grades 9–12, as science major interests rose, while non-science major interest remained relatively

Table 3.10

Frequency of Positive Responses to Perceptions of Science Classes, Teachers, and Value of Course Content

	Science majors		Nonscience majors		
	Junior high	High school	Junior high	High school	Yager adults[a]
Science classes are fun	57*	83*	46*	54*	2
Science classes are interesting	54*	90*	43*	72*	21
Science classes are exciting	25	46*	14*	29	29
Science classes made me feel uncomfortable	11*	10*	15*	30	31
Science classes made me feel curious	34*	81*	38*	58*	21
Science classes made me feel successful	55*	75*	36*	45*	20
Science teachers often asked questions	43*	71*	32*	59	60
Science teachers liked you to ask science questions	61*	84*	58*	82*	48
Science teachers let you give own ideas	42*	84*	38	66*	31
Science teachers really liked science	61	91*	58	89*	63
Science teachers made class exciting	20*	57*	17*	36	40
Science teacher knew a lot about science	43*	88*	44*	86*	64
Science teacher admitted to not knowing all the answers	47*	86*	39*	66*	17
Content useful in daily living	29*	65*	30*	56*	43
Content useful for further study	49*	78*	28	60*	36
Content useful in future	62*	90*	37*	58*	24

*$p < .05$, chi-square goodness of fit.

SOURCE: J. Eichinger, "High Ability College Students' Perceptions of Secondary School Science" (Ph.D diss., Claremont Graduate School, 1990), 94.

[a]Data from adults sampled by Yager and Pennick in 1984.

static" (ii). These retrospective assessments revealed that the factor that contributed most to developing student' interest in science was the personality of the teacher. Other important factors were teacher knowledge, course content, and instructional methods, especially laboratory activities, teacher demonstrations, lectures, and discussions.

Table 3.10 summarizes the frequency of positive responses in the college science majors' assessments of their junior high and high school science classes, teachers, and course content compared with the frequency of positive responses in the assessments of nonscience majors and in the earlier assessments of noncollegiate adults studied by Yager and Penick.

Eichinger compared the traits of junior high school and high school science teachers that had positively influenced college science majors to study science further. He concluded that science majors preferred teachers who were, in descending order, "knowledgeable, enthusiastic, good communicators, committed, and competent. At the bottom of the list . . . were (in ascending order) the following traits: attractive, emotional, effective disciplinarian, polite, warm, and good role model" (116–17). With regard to instructional activities, he said that science majors remembered having more computer activities and discussion in their junior high school courses, while their high school classes involved "less memorization, more teacher demonstrations, more computers, and more discussion" (134). When asked which instructional techniques they preferred, science majors said they had benefited most from, in descending order, "teacher demonstration, laboratory activities, and discussion" (136).

Eichinger observes, however, that other results from his study "suggest that science educators have not been as successful in stimulating science interest as they might wish to be" (186). He gives several examples to illustrate this point. The highly motivated science majors whom Eichinger studied revealed that "over one-half in high school, and three-fourths in junior high did not find their science classes exciting; about one-third in high school and two-thirds in junior high did not find the content useful in their daily life; and only 54 percent found junior high science classes interesting" (186).

Conclusions

The evidence appears to indicate that when the proportion of the school-age population still attending school is controlled, U.S. students perform at or just below the middle level. Furthermore, while it is difficult to estimate accurately the impact of test item bias—and the data on this vary from study to study—it is possible that this factor might increase the true U.S. ranking somewhat. However, the net result of these statistical adjustments is to upgrade the relative performance of U.S. students from disastrous to mediocre.

In the analyses conducted to estimate the effects of differing national school attendance rates, an interesting fact emerges. While the United States has a very high percentage of 18-year-olds in school relative to other countries, *the percentage of those in U.S. schools who study mathematics and science is very low!* The statistics on the relative percentage of American students who study advanced mathematics, for example, calculus, are even more disturbing.

Rutherford concluded from his study of science education in China, Japan, East Germany, West Germany, and the Soviet Union that their science education systems are characterized by the following common features:

1. An unmistakable commitment to the achievement nationwide of science and technology literacy as well as the training of students for careers in science and technology.

2. A high priority for science and mathematics instruction in all schools at all levels.

3. Direct national interest in the preparation of competent teachers of science and mathematics for the elementary and secondary grades, with quality and content of training not something to be left to local whims or to be neglected by institutions of higher education.

4. Provisions for increasing the effectiveness of teaching on a continuing basis.

5. Processes involving both teachers and scientists for ongoing curriculum development in science and mathematics.

6. Examinations and external monitoring as part of the quality control processes in science education.[47]

Dr. Margarita Calderon, a faculty member at the University of Texas at El Paso, for a number of years directed the remedial center there. Students who are having trouble in a variety of subjects, including mathematics, come to the center for tutoring. The center hires undergraduates and graduate students as tutors. In reviewing the hiring decisions made by the center over a number of years, Calderon observed that Americans were rarely hired to tutor in mathematics. Rather, mathematics tutors tended to be from Malaysia, India, and Mexico. Most of the Mexican students at the University of Texas, El Paso, come from Juarez, which is about a mile from El Paso across the Rio Grande River. While it is possible that those Mexican tutors are from the more affluent sector of Juarez, it appears that a young person who goes through the Juarez school system emerges with a much better knowledge of mathematics than the same young person would if he or she attended school in the United States, just a mile away. Another indicator of the quality of mathematics instruction in Juarez is that some of the teachers from Juarez have been providing guidance to the American teachers about mathematics instruction.

FOUR

Science and Mathematics in College

> It is an American tradition to import brainpower. But these are not
> necessarily permanent immigrants. Can we assume that the gifted
> Chinese or Korean will always take a job in Minneapolis rather than
> in Kyoto or Hamburg?
>
> Is the government going to rely once again on rhetoric and treat
> this human-resources problem the way we treat our need for VCR's,
> namely importing foreign products to meet our domestic talent
> shortage? We rely at our peril on borrowing brains.
>
> M. B. Zuckerman, "The Lost Generation"

There is no question that the United States has a superior
higher education system, arguably the best in the world. This is why many
students from other countries attend college and graduate school here. My
concern is less with how many scientists and engineers are being trained in
our colleges (although I discuss that issue below) than with the quality of
the scientific literacy being acquired. To assess this, we must look at who
studies science in college, who is dissuaded from such study, and how
science courses are presented. In addition, we need to consider the psychological and sociological factors that lead to students' satisfaction, enthusiasm, and achievement in their science courses.

Meaningful analysis of policy issues requires excellent data. For decades the best data about college students have been acquired through the
Cooperative Institutional Research Program (CIRP), developed and directed by Alexander Astin, the nation's preeminent higher education researcher. Each year this group prepares a snapshot profile of the nation's

college freshmen, based on hundreds of thousands of responses to a detailed questionnaire, the Student Information Form. Subsequent longitudinal follow-up studies make possible analyses of how the college environment affects student outcomes four years later and in the years following college graduation.

College Science Majors

Writing in *Science* magazine in 1990, R. C. Atkinson said that "the fact that the number of young people selecting science and engineering careers has not increased during a generation in which S&T [science and technology] pervades every aspect of our lives is nothing less than a scandal."[1] A major study directed by Alexander and Helen Astin drew upon the CIRP data and explored issues about defection from and recruitment to science majors; career choices of women and underrepresented minority students; and the institutional environmental factors, such as faculty interaction with students, that affect student aspirations and achievement.[2]

Astin and Astin gathered data on 27,065 students from 388 four-year colleges and universities in their freshman year (fall 1985) and again four years later. They also surveyed the faculties at most of the institutions. With respect to changes in student choice of major, the authors comment,

Between the freshman and the senior years, the percent of students majoring in fields of natural science, mathematics, and engineering (SME) declines from 28.7 to 17.4, a forty percent relative decline. Losses are greatest in the biological sciences (fifty percent decline) and engineering (forty percent decline). The net loss in the physical sciences (including mathematics) is substantially less (twenty percent decline) in part because these fields recruit substantial numbers of engineering dropouts during the undergraduate years. (1)

One of their conclusions relates directly to the arguments presented in this book about elementary and secondary education: "[the data] suggest that the numbers of students pursuing science majors and careers at the point of college entry and the numbers maintaining (and switching into) such choices during the college years could be increased if the overall level of mathematical competency in the high school population could be increased" (3).

Astin and Astin also reported that a strongly student-oriented faculty positively affected persistence in the biological sciences and research career aspirations, while a strongly research-oriented faculty negatively af-

Table 4.1

Changes in Undergraduate Major Field of Study, 1985–1989
(N = 26,306)

Field of study	% in 1985	% in 1989	% Change
Biological science	11.9	6.2	−5.7
Physical science	6.3	5.2	−1.1
Engineering	10.5	6.0	−4.5
Psychology	4.3	5.1	+0.8
Social science	6.7	10.7	+4.0
Nonscience	52.7	66.8	+14.1
Undecided	7.6	0.0	−7.6

SOURCE: A. Astin and H. S. Astin, *Undergraduate Science Education: The Impact of Different College Environments on the Educational Pipeline in the Sciences* (Los Angeles: Higher Education Research Institute, UCLA, 1992), 3–4.

fected persistence among physical science majors. They say that "this last finding can be explained in part by the tendency for strongly research-oriented faculties to rely heavily on teaching assistants in their under-graduate courses" (5). Table 4.1 summarizes the changes in undergraduates' selection of their major field.

Trends in Freshmen's Choice of a Major

In a widely discussed article in the *American Scientist,* Kenneth Green presented data from the CIRP data base on trends in college freshmen's initial choice of a major. According to Green, "The largest and oldest empirical study of higher education in the United States indicates that the nation's science resources, as represented by the students who are planning undergraduate work in the science, have suffered serious erosion over the past two decades."[3]

While interest in the sciences has declined less among women than among men, even among women there has been a substantial drop. Green notes that students' shift during the 1980s from scientific to nonscientific fields occurred mainly among B students, not among A students. "In 1988, 45.3 percent of the aspiring science and engineering majors in four-year colleges and universities reported high school grade averages of at least A-, compared to 26.3 percent for students planning other majors" (476). Interest in the sciences increased among students of color during the 1980s. For example,

whereas Blacks represented 9.8 percent of the first-time, full-time freshmen en-rolled in the nation's four-year colleges and universities in 1988, they accounted for 11.5 percent of the freshmen planning to pursue physical science majors. Similarly,

Hispanic students represented 1.8 percent of the first-time, full-time freshman population this past fall and 2.1 percent of the aspiring freshman engineering students. (477)

With respect to the preparation of future teachers, Green's analysis of freshman trends indicates that although interest in teaching rose in the eighties, the levels were still far below those of the late sixties and well below those needed to meet future needs. "Even with the recent gains in student interest in teaching careers, the CIRP data indicate that comparatively little of that interest is in secondary school assignments (just 3.2 percent in 1988, as compared to 14.4 percent in 1968). This should be particularly distressing for science educators, because science and mathematics courses in junior high school and high school stimulate student interest in these fields and provide the academic foundation for subsequent undergraduate work" (477–78).

Sue Maple and Frances Stage analyzed data from the "High School and Beyond" national data base to examine factors affecting selection of quantitatively based college majors.[4] A student's attitude about mathematics was a key predictor. These researchers found that the choice of a college major was signaled and predicted by students' expectations as high school sophomores and that the number of mathematics and science courses taken in high school had a strong relationship to subsequent decisions about a college major. Noting that their findings differed by ethnicity and gender, the authors said that they could "only speculate that white females who are not decided on a quantitative major by the sophomore year may disadvantage themselves for further participation in the quantitative pipeline by terminating their studies of math and science early in their high school careers" (53).

In a study of attrition rates among science, mathematics, and engineering undergraduate majors, Nancy Hewitt and Elaine Seymour found that those who dropped out of SME majors did not differ from those who persisted in terms of their background characteristics; the difference derived from how people in the two groups responded to challenges. "Nonswitchers were more likely to make effective use of situational resources, to employ a variety of other strategies, and to find ways to tolerate or surmount the same types of difficulty reported by switchers."[5] The challenges that confronted these two groups read like a litany of the problems reported below by Sheila Tobias: poor teaching, unapproachable faculty, the fast pace and heavy work load, and inadequate help and advice from faculty through periods of academic difficulty.

Problems in College Science Teaching

Sheila Tobias is one of a group of researchers who pinpoint college as the place where many talented students defect from science. Furthermore, she argues that it is in college that many "different" students, including women and minorities, are discouraged from pursuing science further. The undergraduate years are especially important, she argues, because it is easier to intervene at this level than to try to change the curriculum policies of more than ten thousand widely scattered school districts, each with its own school board.

Tobias suggests two reasons why those studying human resources in science have focused excessively on elementary and secondary education and insufficiently on higher education. First, "reformers—and insofar as they become educational reformers scientists are no exception—are most comfortable dealing with problems that have their origins (and, hence, their solutions) elsewhere." Second, studying the science choices and experiences of college students is more complex and messier than studying elementary and secondary students, not as scientifically "clean." "Because they are good researchers, scientists prefer situations in which variables can be isolated and controlled. . . . For many scientists, then, it seems more logical to begin with pure substances (the nation's six-year-olds) and uniform initial conditions, than to flounder in the messy bog of motivation, attributes, and prior training exhibited by post-secondary students in their early years at college."[6]

Citing studies that indicate that many scientists and engineers chose their careers early in their childhood because of intrinsic interest in the subject matter, and not because of inspirational elementary school teachers, Tobias argues that the scientific community attracts and recruits students who are clones of today's scientists.

From this perspective, the low representation of women as well as racial and ethnic minorities in science may not be the result of social discrimination per se (scientists are surely too professional to discount good people because of ethnic origin, skin color, or gender, viz. their welcoming of non-WASPs, to science in the 1940s and of Asians in the 1970s), but of too narrow a vision of what kinds of attributes, behaviors and lifestyles the "true" scientist displays. What we have here is an outsider-insider problem which results in a preference for "in-group" types. (11)

Tobias devised an intriguing ethnographic experiment to discover why great numbers of vary capable college students avoided science. She hired seven postgraduates from a variety of fields in the humanities and social sciences, each of whom was high-achieving and literate. All but one had avoided science totally in college, and none had selected a scientific career. These researchers were asked to audit seriously a semester-long, calculus-based course in physics or introductory chemistry. They were asked to focus on why students like themselves might find introductory science "hard" or even "alienating" (15). Each student was asked to keep extensive notes on his or her experiences and observations about the course, the instructor, and the material and to write a final essay drawing together those observations.

"Eric" was a summa cum laude graduate in literature from Berkeley. One of his note observations relates directly to the notion of cooperative study groups (discussed in chapter 6):

My class is full of intellectual warriors who will someday hold jobs in technologically-based companies where they will be assigned to teams or groups in order to collectively work on projects. [But] these people will have had no training in working collectively. In fact, their experience will have taught them to fear cooperation, and that another person's intellectual achievement will be detrimental to their own.

Tobias notes that Eric thought that one consequence of students' doing their work "in private" was "the absence of any opportunity for them to talk about the physics they were studying. They seemed inhibited, he observed, even about asking questions" (27).

Eric concluded that, while the material covered in a physics course like the one he was observing was inherently difficult, the way it was taught made it much more difficult, and for some students impossible, to master. He noted that the instructor raced through the material, giving students little time to digest one topic before tackling another. Students were quite reluctant to speak out, to ask questions, and to articulate what they did or did not understand. These problems were exacerbated by the competitive nature of the grading process and by the significance this grade held for the students' academic and career development.

Noting that many freshmen who choose science careers abandon that choice during college, while the science disciplines fail to attract many new recruits during those years, Kenneth Green comments,

Science departments themselves are partly to blame for these low retention rates. Many science departments take great pride in the number of students who fail to complete key courses in the lower-division sequence or who ultimately change majors. There seems to be an informal competition on many campuses to see which science classes have the lowest average grades or which programs have the lowest mean grade-point averages. . . . these data should be especially troubling given that the sciences attract a disproportionate number of academically superior freshmen.[7]

Elaine Seymour interviewed 350 students at seven colleges and universities about why they had transferred out of a science, mathematics, or engineering major. One of her findings was that these students, whose grade point averages were only slightly lower than those of students who stayed in these technical fields, more frequently tended to be women and minority students. One of the factors they cited was the perception that the faculty in some of these technical departments were trying to weed out many students. As one White male senior in chemistry put it, "It's the way this gentleman teaches. He believes in grading on a curve and slaughtering people in the first exam. You lose everyone 'cause no one's encouraging you to stay—the professor is very unapproachable. I think you lose a ton a good people because why would they sit here and get slaughtered when they can go to another department and have some interaction with the professor and some encouragement?"[8]

According to Walter Massey, formerly director of the NSF, "The culture of science and engineering may contribute to this failure. The common concept of 'success in science' . . . seems to have created an illusion that only 'the best and the brightest' can do science. Course work is viewed by many faculty as a way to separate the 'men' from the 'boys.' Unfortunately, these courses also tend to separate the men from the women—and the white men from just about everyone else."[9]

Massey points out that in the private undergraduate colleges, such as Oberlin, that produce a high percentage of potential scientists, undergraduates frequently work on research. One study found that during a five-year period the forty-eight colleges designated as "research colleges" had generated about seven thousand journal articles, of which 32 percent had undergraduate student coauthors (1179).

Of course effective teaching involves more than an animated, dramatic presentation. Educators took note of the infamous "Dr. Fox" studies by John Ware and Reed Williams, in which a professional actor was hired to teach the same course to two groups of students under different circumstances.[10] In the first treatment, "Dr. Fox" gave lectures crammed with information in the most boring manner possible. He read from his notes in a monotone, with no emotion or emphasis, and never looked at the students. In the second treatment, he gave exciting, animated presentations filled with jokes and anecdotes but totally devoid of substantive information. The students gave much higher ratings to the animated "Dr. Fox" and claimed they had learned much more from him. It is possible that they actually did learn more. That is, the interesting "Dr. Fox" may have motivated students to read about the subject outside of class, while the boring "Dr. Fox" may have convinced them that it would be useless to waste any time studying for this course.

The problems in college teaching identified by Sheila Tobias partially explain the trends and changes in students' decisions to major in science, but these problems do not occur in a vacuum. They are related to how prestige is awarded in academia, which, in turn, is linked to funding patterns for university research, which powerfully influence how professors spend their time.

Prestige in Academia

After years of studies that purport to rank graduate departments and academic institutions, whose history has been well documented by David Webster,[11] I would suggest that we have solved that problem. That is, we now know how to rank institutions and which institutions rank where; all that remains is detail work. But our understanding of which institutions foster more effective teaching or research is at a primitive level. The important transition from simplistic assessment of structural dimensions to a more penetrating analysis of process dynamics has been delayed in part because of an obsession with unidimensional rankings.

Sociologists carefully differentiate the structure of an organization or social system from the processes that characterize it. Quite frequently, from a theoretical or policy perspective, analysis of the latter is considerably more important than analysis of the former. Our understanding of important organizational dynamics in higher education has been hampered by limited objectives and limited concepts. The first problem is the overuse of such words as *quality* and *excellence*. When virtually every organization in the country announces that its goal is quality, the word loses much of its meaning. Casual observation reveals that, among others, the makers of Ford cars, Midas mufflers, and Budweiser beer all display this word prominently in their mottoes; for example, "The quality goes in before the name goes on."

There is another, more subtle problem with this term. It involves what

philosophers call a *nominalistic fallacy,* an assumption that a word, because it exists, refers to something real, tangible, and identifiable. It might
better be called the Humpty Dumpty syndrome: "When I choose a word, it
means just what I want it to mean, neither more nor less." The connotation
of the word *quality* in both common English parlance and scholarly articles is that either departments have "it" or they don't. Or maybe a department has "it" 80 percent, in which case the department can be ranked
cleanly. Simple connotations and unidimensional rankings are appealing
to funding agencies, gossips, and policymakers, but they mask the complexity of a real organization, in which many people engage in many
functions.

As part of a large evaluation study in 1975, my colleagues and I amassed
a large data set containing multiple indicators of science departments'
structure, function, and productivity over a fifteen-year period.[12] One of
the variables was a national departmental prestige score generated by the
American Council on Education, the so-called "Cartter" ranking. We
conducted multivariate analyses to discover which departmental variables, if any, could predict the Cartter prestige rating.

Surprisingly, only one measure, the departmental rate of publication in
the twenty most highly cited journals in the field, predicts national rankings almost perfectly ($r = .87$).[13] A graph produced by plotting the journal
data (the total of the twenty journals summed over the four years) against
the Cartter ratings indicated that the relationship was an inverse exponen-
tial curve (due, in part, to the ceiling imposed by the Cartter ratings, 5
being the highest possible score). The curve took the form $Y = 5 - 5e^{-bx}$,
where $Y =$ the ACE rating and $x =$ the number of publications. Applying
this transformation to linearize the data yielded one final improvement in
the predictability, a correlation of .91.

Why did this publication index yield much higher correlations with
national ratings than did the publication measures of previous researchers,
such as Warren Hagstrom?[14] Perhaps the explanation has to do with the
fact that scholars tend to assess the quality of faculty in other departments
in their field based on how frequently they have seen those departments
mentioned in a high-quality context. Thus, a mathematician who sees the
University of Michigan given as the institutional affiliation of the author of
an article in the *Bulletin of the American Mathematical Society* is likely to
elevate his assessment of that department a bit, albeit subconsciously. If,
on the other hand, he sees the author and department listed in a rather

obscure journal with a poor reputation, he probably will not raise his subjective judgment of the department.

It should be underscored that although a department's excellence is initially based on whether it has been referenced in a quality arena, once the department has entered that arena, its reputation seems to grow cumulatively, that is, quantitatively, with no further quality assessments being made. This point is supported by the failure to achieve higher predictability by weighting the journals with an impact factor or by factor analysis. The thrust of these finds was that, given a set of journals defined as being of high quality, the way to maximize correlations with the subjective ratings was simple accumulation—across journals and across years—not further refinement on the basis of quality. In short, such ratings are not a pure quality measure but are contaminated by quantity.

As further evidence of this point, when publications per faculty member, as opposed to overall departmental publication rate, was used as a predictor, much lower correlations resulted. That is, a hypothetical department of fifty people who produced two articles each would receive a much higher rating than another hypothetical department of five people who produced ten articles each. Thus, rankings seemed to confound quality with departmental size, so that a larger department was likely to receive a higher rating than a small department of comparable quality.

Empirical findings have revealed both the strength and the weaknesses of such unidimensional rankings. The strength is that an objective correlate of the subjective rankings has been found. The weaknesses are, first, that too great an emphasis in such peer evaluations, and in the academic world, has been given to research as compared with teaching; and, second, that quantity is confused with quality, large departments being favored over small departments of the same quality.

So, step one is acknowledging that it is insufficient, and probably deleterious, to rank the departments in, say, physics from Berkeley or Harvard on down to Podunk. Rather, a matrix should be presented, as in studies by the National Research Council (NRC) in which each department is evaluated on each of a number of structural dimensions, perhaps fifty. This information is useful to a decision maker, whether that person is a government funding official, a college senior choosing a graduate school, or a new Ph.D. considering job offers.

But the really important information still is missing from the matrix. What is the process for conducting research at the university? How are research projects structured? What kinds of resources are available, and under what circumstances? Is the environment one of collegiality or cut-throat competition? What is the quality of the teaching? How are graduate students mentored? What processes are used to facilitate the career growth of young professionals?

Of course, a complete evaluation system should allow for different kinds of quality processes. Some departments will emphasize traditional research criteria, while others may downplay research in favor of teaching and the preparation of skilled professionals. Moreover, even among departments with similar goals there can be differing, equally legitimate processes for achieving the goals.

How Professors Spend Their Time

Some have argued that a professor can be an excellent teacher or an excellent researcher but not both: each role is demanding, and there simply is not enough time in the day to do both well. Others, including myself, believe that it is possible to excel at both tasks. Examples abound of world-class researchers whose teaching is superior. Unfortunately, examples illustrate but do not prove the point. For that, we need data. There are two sources of data: information about how professors spend their time and studies that attempt to correlate research productivity with teaching evaluations.

A number of faculty surveys have asked how professors divided and prioritized their work time. Unfortunately, few have presented respondents with the same list of choices. (This is a classic example of the comparability problem plaguing national studies, discussed below.) Nevertheless, it is instructive to review what recent surveys reported about the distribution of faculty time.

In 1993 the National Center for Education Statistics of the U.S. Department of Education conducted a national study of postsecondary faculty. In this study, 31,354 faculty members in 974 public and private nonproprietary higher education institutions were surveyed (86.6 percent responded). A key conclusion was that "among full-time faculty and instructional staff, approximately two-thirds indicated that their principal activity at their institution was teaching. Of the remaining one-third, approximately 12 percent indicated that their principal activity was research, 12 percent indicated administration, and 11 percent indicated that they were principally involved in something else."[15]

Table 4.2

Allocation of Professors' Time Per Week, Fall 1987
(%)

Type of institution	Teaching	Research	Other[a]
All institutions	56	16	29
Public			
Research	43	29	28
Doctoral	47	22	31
Comprehensive	62	11	26
Two-year	71	3	25
Independent			
Research	40	30	31
Doctoral	39	27	33
Comprehensive	62	9	29
Liberal arts	65	8	27
Other	59	9	33

SOURCE: H. R. Allen, "Workload and Productivity in an Accountability Era," in *The NEA 1994 Almanac of Higher Education* (Washington, D.C.: NEA, 1994), 29.

NOTE: Percentages may not add up to 100 because of rounding.

[a]Administration, community service, professional development, and other work.

Henry Allen has analyzed work-load data from the 1988 National Survey of Postsecondary Faculty.[16] Allen notes that the mean hours regular faculty worked per week was fifty-three, of which forty-six were spent at the institution. This statistic ranged from fifty-seven hours per week in public research universities to forty-seven hours in public two-year colleges. Table 4.2 shows how that time was allocated among the professors' areas of responsibility.

Consider next studies of the association between research productivity and teaching evaluations. (Critics have asserted that measures of the former confuse quality and quantity and measures of the latter confuse pedagogy and popularity.) Jill Tronvig studied whether these multiple job-related roles, especially teaching and research, created role conflict or stress. She surveyed chemistry, economics, and English professors and department chairs at forty-five national and thirty California university departments. Among her findings were the following:

Lower departmental prestige, increasing institutional emphasis on research, and poor faculty morale or working conditions were found to be institutional environment factors which were related to role conflict, dissatisfaction, and lower research productivity. Age, rank, tenure, years of experience, and years at present institution were negatively related to role conflict and positively related to job satisfaction and research productivity. English professors tended to have more role conflict than chemists and economists. . . . A large majority of the professors indicated they believed that faculty research enhanced undergraduate education, but there was no correlation between professors' self-reported teaching evaluations and research productivity.[17]

One economics professor in Tronvig's survey said that "in economics, if you only know the material at the textbook level—which is the case for most non-researchers—you are probably a very poor economist and, on that account, a poor teacher" (154). Another economist observed, "There is an added pressure to bring outside grants for research and for the support of the Ph.D. program . . . one cannot be a fiddler and a ticket seller at the same time" (153).

Kenneth Feldman conducted a meta-analysis (i.e., a rigorous, quantitative review and integration) of such studies.[18] He estimated the mean correlation reported in these studies between research and teaching excellence to be .13. His analysis compensated for such factors as different sample sizes. Squaring the correlation coefficient, .13, yields the coefficient of determination, .0169, which indicates the percentage of one variable associated with the other is less than 2 percent. In short, there is almost no relationship between research and teaching excellence. Good researchers are neither necessarily good teachers nor necessarily bad teachers. Thus, universities should be hiring outstanding researchers who are also outstanding teachers.

The faculty members at a university can easily discover what their administration really values. Confusing rhetoric can always be clarified by examining who gets promoted or by comparing teaching loads across institutions. They vary incredibly. It is revealing that administrators recruiting bright young Ph.D's refer to "research opportunities" and "teaching responsibilities." The latter are often measured in terms of "contact hours," as though one were being exposed to an infectious disease.

According to one professor, "There were—and are—only two kinds of professors on this and hundreds of other campuses: teaching professors and entrepreneurial professors. That's the polite way to say it. In their most unbuttoned moments, usually after the third martini, professors from the 'hard' disciplines bluntly divide the faculty into the 'winners' and 'losers.' Winners are funded. Losers are not. Losers spend most of their time teaching, especially undergraduates. Winners have better things to do."[19]

Peer Group Effects

Both sociological theory and empirical studies have clarified the impact of a student's peers on his or her self-esteem and educational and career aspirations. One of the earliest studies of the powerful effects of peer group pressures on students was a fascinating social psychological experiment conducted by Solomon Asch.[20] Asch asked groups of five undergraduates to study two squares, A and B, projected on a screen; square A was much smaller than square B. He then asked each of the undergraduates to state which square was larger. The first four undergraduates, who were actually stooges, would announce that A was larger than B. The question was whether student five, the only real subject in the experiment, would state the obvious (that square B was larger than square A) or conform to the peer pressure to announce the ridiculous (that square A was larger than square B). It is astounding and depressing to read how many students made sure that their "perceptions" matched those of the other students in the room.

A series of studies conducted over the past thirty years have identified, isolated, and articulated the importance of the sociological concept of relative deprivation, a phenomenon first identified in studies of World War II soldiers. James Davis began a theoretical exchange in his now classic "frog pond" article, in which he applied the theory of relative deprivation, first elaborated by Samuel Stouffer in his studies of the American soldier, in a special analysis of the aspirations of college seniors based on data from the National Opinion Research Center (NORC).[21] Essentially, relative deprivation theory asserts that being "a big frog in a little pond" leads to increased self-esteem. Davis argued that undergraduate career choice is a function of "academic self-concept," which, in turn, is based in part on the student's assessment of his performance relative to that of other students in his own school, not the national pool of undergraduates. To support this hypothesis, he reported data showing that the graduating senior's career choice is more highly related to his college grade point average (a local measure of performance) than to his school's quality or reputation (a measure that reflects the national distribution) when initial freshman career choice and aptitude are controlled. Unfortunately, Davis was forced to work with rather limited measures of both school quality and scholastic aptitude.

A different school of thought is represented by the environmental press theorists, who argue that students' achievement and aspirations are a function of the social context. The basic difference between this theory and relative deprivation theory is the role that it assigns to college quality or selectivity. According to the relative deprivation theory, selectivity should have a negative effect on aspirations because it has a negative effect on academic achievement (that is, a given student will have a harder time getting good grades at a highly selective college). Environmental press theory maintains that selectivity should positively affect aspirations, since an undergraduate will perform best and aim highest at a school where most of his fellow students have high aspirations and are superior academically. Charles Werts and Donivan Watley used a multiple regression model with a national sample of undergraduates to test the relative predictive power of the two theories and reported findings that tended to support relative deprivation theory. But they too lamented their crucial missing link: a measure of academic self-concept.[22]

Alexander Astin and I tested these theories using the CIRP longitudinal data base.[23] A basic assumption underlying our work was that these middle-range theories belong in a conceptual framework within the context of reference group theory. Reference group theory, of course, has been invoked to explain undergraduate phenomena other than career aspirations.[24] In addition, it has been shown that what appear to be college effects can vanish when the characteristics of the students entering that college are controlled.[25] A complete analysis of student body reference group impact requires that all possible control variables be considered. Astin and I controlled simultaneously a rather large number of variables. In addition, we had available, through the CIRP data base, several critical variables that had been missing in previous analyses. Our results showed that the relative deprivation theory and the environmental press theory were both valid, since each had an effect on specific kinds of educational aspirations, and that previous investigators who had forced a choice between the two theories had been creating a straw man.

Michelle Patterson and I repeated the tests of these theories with the CIRP data base, carrying out separate analyses for men and women.[26] Our results indicated that relative deprivation was more pronounced for the men than for the women; that is, women needed a stronger absolute indicator of their ability, for example, faculty praise for an outstanding project, to motivate them to increase their aspirations (particularly in the 1960s, when the data were collected). These results were consistent with other research on the development of career goals and educational aspirations among women.[27]

Subsequently, several studies were published that tested and refined these formulations. In each case, the research represented a successful attempt to uncover effects by making more subtle differentiations than the previous researchers had, for example, by exploring different kinds of status.

Jeffrey Reitz argued that the previous researchers had cavalierly equated educational aspirations and career choice and that this equation was inappropriate, since college selectivity affects the two differently. He found that "selective colleges reinforce preferences for educationally high-level careers within each field, thereby increasing the desirability of career fields with lower overall educational levels."[28] He substantiated this reasoning with a reexamination of the NORC data (the data set for the original Davis analysis). Reitz also developed the notion of relative versus absolute self-assessment. While his definition of those concepts is not precisely parallel to the notions advanced by Patterson and myself, the Reitz distinction may be quite meaningful in comparing the aspirations of men and women.

Karl Alexander and Bruce Eckland differentiated two dimensions of the student body, ability and social status, and found that they affected the students' educational attainments differently.[29] The "college environment" is not a single entity; its components and effects must be analyzed carefully. Michael Bassis argued that reference group effects can be isolated more effectively using multiple linear path analysis.[30] Peers and other reference groups, for example, faculty and friends, are powerful influences on the college student, affecting the student's satisfaction with, and achievement in, science courses.

Student Experiences with Science Courses

In a study that I conducted as part of the Astin-Astin project discussed above, I examined the attitudes and feelings of college students about science and the scientific research process, paying particular attention to those who majored in science, mathematics, or engineering. In addition, I studied the science-related experiences of these students, for example, working on an independent research project. The focus of these analyses was students' satisfaction with their experiences, the faculty, the curriculum, and the resources supporting the curriculum. Study of these affective and behavioral components of the undergraduate experience complements analyses about the flow of students into and out of SME. The attitudes of college students about science faculty and the science curriculum reflect the quality of the undergraduate experience.

This study utilized new data available from HERI's CIRP to examine the impact of psychological and sociological factors during the undergraduate years. The sources of data for the analyses included a freshman Student Information Form (SIF), administered to a huge sample of students (279,985) in the fall of 1985 as part of CIRP, as well as a follow-up questionnaire in 1989. Furthermore, faculty at each of 169 institutions in the sample completed a survey instrument in 1989. Additional institutional data were provided by a survey of registrars, and test scores, for example, from GREs, SATs, and GMATs, were obtained from the appropriate agencies.

The freshman SIF is a four-page questionnaire that contains a variety of items about the student's demographic background characteristics, high school experiences, political attitudes, career and educational aspirations, expectations about college, and self-concepts. The follow-up instrument repeated many of the same items and also retrieved information about many aspects of the college experience. The faculty survey gathered data about the respondent's background characteristics, professional experience and training, productivity, attitudes about academic issues, and political opinions.

For most of the analyses reported below I used a subsample of respondents who were still in college at the time of the 1989 follow-up survey. This group consisted of 12,197 students, of whom 2,697 were science majors, defined as those who were in either the biological sciences, the physical sciences, or engineering (1,513 men and 1,184 women). Responses to each of the key variables were analyzed separately for science and nonscience majors, men and women, and ethnic groups, and attitudinal factors that might affect the career development of women and minority students were examined.

Frequency distributions for each of nine variables measuring satisfaction with the college experience were analyzed separately for each of the sixteen subgroups presented in table 4.3. These variables were the following:

—Science and mathematics courses
—Courses in the student's major field
—Overall quality of instruction
—Lab facilities and equipment

Table 4.3
Mathematical Ability Self-Concept, 1989 Follow-Up
(%)

Subgroup	N	Lowest 10%	Below average	Average	Above average	Highest 10%
Anglo						
Male						
Science	1,269	0.1	2.0	12.2	41.6	44.1
Nonscience	3,018	2.0	13.9	35.2	36.1	12.8
Female						
Science	881	.2	3.3	20.2	46.9	29.4
Nonscience	5,647	3.0	18.9	41.1	31.1	5.9
African American						
Male						
Science	36	0	2.8	5.6	63.9	27.8
Nonscience	118	2.5	14.4	41.5	28.8	12.7
Female						
Science	79	0	1.3	26.6	50.6	21.5
Nonscience	326	4.3	19.9	44.2	26.4	5.2
Latino						
Male						
Science	17	0	0	5.9	23.5	70.6
Nonscience	50	4.0	18.0	26.0	32.0	20.0
Female						
Science	16	0	25.0	31.3	18.8	25.0
Nonscience	88	3.4	28.4	36.4	28.4	3.4
Asian American						
Male						
Science	106	0	0.9	7.5	49.1	42.5
Nonscience	82	1.2	14.6	30.5	37.8	15.9
Female						
Science	71	0	2.8	25.4	42.3	29.6
Nonscience	167	1.8	9.0	37.7	45.5	6.0

SOURCE: D. Drew, "How Undergraduates Experience Science Education," in Astin and Astin, *Undergraduate Science Education: The Impact of Different College Environments on the Educational Pipeline in the Sciences,* 8–22.

—Library facilities
—Computer facilities
—Opportunity to talk to professors
—Contact with faculty or administration
—Relations with faculty or administration

The subgroups were defined by gender, ethnicity (Anglo, African American, Latino, and Asian American), and whether the student was a science major or not.[31]

A few trends in the data should be highlighted. The general level of satisfaction reported for some of the variables, for example, science and mathematics courses, courses in the student's major field, and contact with faculty or administration, was higher than that reported for the other variables. Except on the two variables that are directly related to science, that is, science and mathematics courses and laboratory facilities, the responses of science majors and nonscience majors were approximately the same.

For the first three variables, which deal with courses and instruction, men and women reported roughly equivalent levels of satisfaction. With some exceptions, men reported higher levels of satisfaction than women with the next three variables, which deal with facilities and resources. Except among Asians, men reported higher levels of satisfaction with laboratory facilities and library facilities. Except among African Americans, male science majors reported higher levels of satisfaction with computer facilities than did women science majors. With some exceptions, women consistently reported higher levels of satisfaction than men on the variables having to do with student-faculty interaction. Specifically, women reported more satisfaction with the opportunity to talk to professors, contact with faculty or administration (although this was true among science majors only), and relations with faculty or administration (except among Latino nonscientists, where males reported higher satisfaction).

Few trends were related to ethnicity. Both Anglos and African Americans tend to report higher levels of satisfaction with science and mathematics courses, and Anglos tend report more satisfaction with library resources, opportunities for contact with faculty or administration, and relations with faculty or administration. Asians report less satisfaction with the opportunity to talk to professors and with coursework in their majors.

Next I analyzed the data about three career activity goals ("making a theoretical contribution to science," "becoming an authority in my field," and "obtaining recognition from my colleagues for contributions to my special field"), three research and teaching experiences ("worked on professor's research project," "assisted faculty in teaching a course," and "worked on an independent research project"), and self-concept about mathematical ability. For the most part, male students had higher scores on science-related activities or aspirations than did female students, and science majors certainly scored higher than nonscience majors. But there were some surprises. For example, scores for minority students tended to be comparable to those for majority, or Anglo, students. Also, within each ethnic group the proportion of female science majors who report working on a professor's research project was higher than the proportion of male science majors. Although the sample sizes are quite small, it should be noted that Latino women scored higher than Latino men on each of the measures of career activity goal.

Given the central importance of self-concept in the development of educational aspirations and career choice, table 4.3 is particularly instructive. The most dramatic differences are between male and female follow-up self-concepts. The percentage of Anglo male science majors who see themselves as being in the highest 10 percent is 44.1, while only 29.4 percent of Anglo female science majors see themselves in that category.

These statistics about self-concept are both revealing and disturbing. But a critic might note that they fail to take into account the actual mathematical ability of the students reporting their self-concepts. Consequently, I performed an additional analysis, using the student's score on the quantitative portion of the SAT as a measure of mathematical ability. For the full sample, the ninetieth percentile, that is, the SAT score that defined those students who actually were in the top 10 percent, was 670. The 10 percent of the longitudinal sample that achieved scores greater than or equal to 670 on the SAT quantitative subtest included 1,723 people, of whom 1,152 were male and 571 were female. Among the males in this elite group, 53.5 percent considered themselves in the top 10 percent, and an additional 35.1 percent considered themselves "above average." Among the women in this group, only 32.6 percent considered themselves in the top 10 percent, and an additional 51.3 percent considered themselves "above average." One-sixth of the women whose scores placed them in the highest 10 percent defined themselves as either average, below average, or in the lowest 10 percent!

The cutoff for this sample was a score of 670, which actually is higher than the threshold that marked the top 10 percent of those who took the test during that year (high school seniors in 1984), which was 580. Thus, this is a conservative definition; these students may actually have been in the top 5 percent. Furthermore, each of them would have received a report from the Educational Testing Service indicating not only their score but also their percentile.

Relating follow-up mathematical ability self-concept to the self-concept reported by the student as an entering freshman sheds further light on this important construct. As can be seen in table 4.4, of those men who indeed were in the top 10 percent, 734, or 63.7 percent, defined themselves that

Table 4.4

Math Ability Self-Concepts of Top Math Students, 1985 and 1989

1989 Self-concept	1985 Self-concept		
	Below top 10%	Top 10%	Total
Males			
Below top 10%	315	221	536 (46.5%)
Top 10%	103	513	616 (53.5%)
Total	418 (36.3%)	734 (63.7%)	1,152
Females			
Below top 10%	248	137	385 (67.4%)
Top 10%	50	136	186 (32.6%)
Total	298 (52.2%)	273 (47.8%)	551

SOURCE: See table 4.3.

way when they entered as freshmen. Four years later that percentage had declined to 53.5 percent. Two hundred and twenty-one of the 734 who initially had accurately placed themselves in the top 10 percent reduced their own self-assessment, while another 103 students who initially had erroneously placed themselves lower now considered themselves in the highest 10 percent.

Among women, of the 571 women who actually were in the top 10 percent, 273, or 47.8 percent, defined themselves that way when they entered college. Four years later 137 (half of the group) of the 273 no longer defined themselves as being in the top category; 50 women who had erroneously placed themselves in the lower category as freshmen correctly placed themselves in the highest category four years later. Nevertheless, the proportion of high-ability women who correctly placed themselves in the top 10 percent dropped from 47.8 percent to 32.6 percent during the college years.

It is important that researchers explore the dimensions of the impact of college upon these students so that we can understand how the self-concepts of both men and women are affected by those experiences. Are these relative deprivation effects? Are declines in self-concept more frequently experienced in certain kinds of college environments?

The effects of the educational system, as well as other forces in the culture, on the self-concepts of women, including high-ability women, is deplorable and tragic. *Only 23 percent of the women who actually were in the top 10 percent (probably all in the top 5 percent) believed themselves to be in that group in both their freshman and and their senior year.* We need to understand better why many college students, especially women, underestimate their own ability, particularly in the area of mathematics. Why is it that only one-third of college senior women who actually are in the top 10 percent in mathematical ability define themselves that way?

SME includes a wide variety of fields and activities. Many policymakers will consider the variable that assesses whether the student plans to make a theoretical contribution to science central in discussions of human resources in the national research enterprise. Regression analyses confirmed that college environment variables significantly impacted each of the criterion variables that was examined. Further evidence of the impact of reference groups was found by examining the significant predictors that emerged in the multiple regression analyses. I conducted hierarchical multiple regression analyses to identify individual and institutional factors related to the key dependent variables for the science majors. The criterion variables were the three satisfaction composite variables and "making a theoretical contribution to science." I employed a wide array of predictor variables in a stepwise algorithm.[32] The potential input variables were assessed sequentially in eight blocks:

1. A pretest estimate of the criterion variable
2. Demographic and other background characteristics
3. Major and career aspirations
4. Freshman living arrangements and aid
5. Curriculum, peer, and faculty measures
6. Institutional characteristics, for example, selectivity
7. The magnitude of the exposure to the environment, that is, years enrolled
8. Intermediate outcomes

The first three variable sets could be classified as freshman input variables, and the next three as environment variables. The last two sets involve intermediate outcomes. Thus, while the analysis was a free-entry regression within a variable set, the order of the variable sets was predetermined in a hierarchical fashion. In the case of each criterion variable, separate regressions were run for men and for women. The sample for these regressions included only science majors and, of course, only students who were still in school at the time of the follow-up survey.

Considerable information was contained in these regression results. The predictive power (as reflected in the multiple R) was somewhat lower for factor 2 (courses and instruction) than for the other variables. Also, the predictive power for the males was higher than that for the females in the case of each of the three satisfaction composite variables. Perhaps the most interesting finding revealed by the regression coefficients is that, for these satisfaction factors, the variables indicating that faculty reported a high orientation toward students (in the separate survey of faculty) consistently has a powerful impact. This variable typically yields a beta (a statistical indicator of its importance) that is substantially higher than the betas for all the other background and environment measures. This finding confirms results from a considerable body of previous research about student-faculty interaction. There is no question that the degree to which faculty are oriented toward working with students is very strongly related to students' satisfaction with their college science experience.

In a subsequent study of mathematical self-concept, Linda Sax found relative deprivation effects. "Among students who display initially high levels of math self-confidence, those who enroll in more selective colleges experience greater declines in the perception of their own math abilities," said Sax. "Additionally, the decline in math self-confidence in selective colleges appears to be more pronounced for women than for men. This finding suggests that women might be more strongly affected than men by a sense of 'relative deprivation' with respect to math ability."[33] As a result of a series of multiple regression analyses with mathematical self-concept as the dependent variable, Sax concluded that environments associated with selectivity, or "aspects of selective environments (competitiveness, high enrollment of men, public universities), rather than selectivity itself . . . contribute more powerfully to the decline in math self-concept" (17). Although she was analyzing longitudinal data from the college years, Sax found that variables reflecting the high school experience strongly influenced college attitudes toward, and aspirations involving, mathematics.

Further research is needed about the differential impacts of the college experience upon men and women and upon students from each ethnic background. These studies using CIRP data and prior research repeatedly have emphasized the powerful effects of reference groups, especially peers and faculty, upon the self-concepts, aspirations, and experiences of undergraduates. Understanding these factors better will enable us to improve the quality of the college experience and of career decision making for students choosing majors in science and other fields. Ultimately, these psychological and sociological forces affect not only the quality of the student science courses but also the number of undergraduates who choose careers in science, mathematics, or engineering.

The Supply of Scientists and Engineers

America's technology base will be weakened further if we experience a shortfall in the supply of scientists and engineers, as many leading policy analysts have predicted. The high-tech, information economy described in chapter 1 requires highly skilled human resources, from technical workers, such as CAD/CAM machinists, to Ph.D.-level scientists, engineers, and mathematicians. Will there be a shortfall? If so, in which fields? and when? The data about this issue are confusing.

One of those who expressed alarm about a likely shortfall of scientists and engineers, a former director of the NSF, observed that "the models used to project supply and demand for scientists and engineers have been subject to criticism. But most of the dispute turns on quantitative details rather than the fundamental conclusion; namely, that unless corrective actions are taken immediately, universities, industry, and government will begin to experience shortages of scientists and engineers in the next four to six years, with shortages becoming significant during the early years of the next century."[34]

In a 1988 article entitled "Meeting the Scientific and Technical Staffing Requirements of the American Economy," Eileen Collins summarized the results of simulations she and her associates at the NSF had conducted. "If present trends continue," she said, "there will be a shortage of engineers under high-growth scenarios that cannot be readily filled by plausible increases in the rate at which American women and minority students obtain engineering degrees."[35] Describing the NSF simulation, she reported:

- The demand side simulations are comprised of four inter-related modules:
- an aggregate projection model of the American economy,
- a projected input-output matrix for each industrial sector of the economy,
- a projected occupational requirements matrix for employment in each sector, and
- a new entrants module to derive requirements for new additions to the ranks of science and engineering job holders. (338)

In the simulation, the NSF analysts first projected the size of the 22-year-old cohort for each future year. Next they determined the fraction of contemporary 22-year-olds obtaining a baccalaureate degree in each science field. This was computed separately for each ethnic/gender group. Finally, these contemporary fractions were applied to cohort projections for future years. These calculations yielded "the number of science and engineering baccalaureates by field and year if current propensities persist" (338).

In the April 1990 issue of *Science,* Robert Pool wrote that in 1988

foreign students with temporary visas earned eighteen percent of all life science Ph.D.'s awarded by U.S. colleges and universities, thirty percent of all physical science Ph.D.'s, and a staggering forty-five percent of all engineering doctorates. . . . The effect has been particularly noticeable among engineers. In 1985, two-thirds of all postdoctoral positions went to noncitizens, and about half the assistant professors under thirty-five were temporary residents.[36]

With respect to the ability of foreign graduate students to fill the jobs in industry for scientists and engineers, Collins commented that "the number obtaining permanent resident status is sufficiently small to suggest that foreign personnel flows can fill only a limited portion of the gap between employers' and entrants' opening bids."[37]

Similar conclusions were reached in a 1990 NRC report entitled *A Challenge of Numbers.*[38] The report projected that mathematics-based jobs would grow at twice the rate of other jobs in the U.S. economy during the nineties but that the pool of students who traditionally study mathematics in college—White male students—will shrink. It emphasized the necessity of attracting more women and underrepresented minorities into mathematics-based fields.

The NSF simulation study described by Collins was directed by Peter House, whose findings that the United States faced a crippling shortfall of scientists and engineers were widely cited. A number of researchers, myself included, discussed the implications of a "scientist shortfall" for the economy and the educational system based upon the results of this study. The simulation and report have come under increasing criticism, particularly given the reality of increasing unemployment among scientists and engineers in some disciplines.

On Labor Day of 1992, a front-page story in the *San Francisco Chronicle* carried the headline "Tough Times for Scientists: Ph.D.s Find Once-Plentiful Jobs Are Scarce." According to the article, "Engineers and scientists, some lured into those fields by once-bright employment prospects, no longer have their pick of jobs. They must hound company recruiters and national laboratories that have been hit hard by a sagging economy and budget crises. They also face tough competition from foreign students and academics from the former Soviet bloc nations." The article quoted Sally Asmundson, director of the California Institute of Technology career development center, as saying that there was 30–50 percent less hiring than two years before in private industry.

Noting that there had been a dramatic increase in the number of Ph.D.'s awarded in science and engineering between 1985 and 1991, the article went on to say that Susan Hill, who tracked the job market for the NSF, attributed most of the growth to the increase in the number of foreign students, particularly from the Far East, receiving doctorates. And it quoted Scott Hotes, a graduate student at the University of California at Berkeley who had applied for fifty positions but had not yet received a positive response, as saying that now veteran scientists and academics from Eastern Europe and the former Soviet Union presented strong competition for positions in academic and technical research, especially in physics. Some disciplines will experience a shortage of scientists at the same time that specialists in other disciplines are in the unemployment lines. The *San Francisco Chronicle* article noted that "chemical engineers are thriving, as well as chemists, geologists and mathematicians. In contrast, doctoral students in physics, civil and electrical engineering, operations research and management science are scrambling for employment."[39]

The analyses forecasting a shortfall of scientists were based on a number of assumptions, at least two of which have proved questionable. It was assumed that in the mid-1990s a substantial number of faculty who had reached retirement age would leave academia. But the lifting of the retirement age cap and hard economic times have altered that trend. The second assumption was that the needs of industry for scientists and engineers would continue to increase. But many of those industrial personnel needs have been met by the large numbers of scientists and engineers who lost jobs in the defense and aerospace industries with the end of the Cold War.

Some researchers and analysts have concluded that projecting the supply and demand for scientists and engineers involves so many variables that are difficult to measure and so much random fluctuation that the effort is futile. As one researcher put it, "It's not the fault of the modelers . . . it's the nature of the beast." And another said, "There are at least twenty crucial factors that I would put between a demographic analysis of support and likely outcomes that would be equally valid . . . a strong case can be made that the demographics of eighteen-year-olds have little impact on supply and demand in the scientific marketplace."[40]

Some have argued that a projection of the future supply of scientists and engineers, particularly Ph.D.'s, must more fully take into account fluctuations in the demand. For example, some projections fail to take into account the well-trained scientists who moved into industry in the 1980s and could be lured out by universities, if needed.

A fundamental problem in building models of human resources is the scarcity of information. It is striking how little aware experts in this field, let alone beginners, are of sources of data besides their own. Beyond this, however, the problems that may arise in examining an existing data bank for use in model building essentially parallel the steps taken in a study. Thus, for example, sampling is a preliminary concern in conducting research; sampling problems, for example, survey data based on very low response rates, characterize many existing data banks.

Obviously, a researcher who is going to use a secondary source must live with how the original researcher asked questions and defined theoretical constructs. A related issue is item comparability. Robert Schoenberg, among others, has argued that all researchers should use the same form for certain basic demographic items, such as ethnicity.[41] While this level of coordination among U.S. researchers is virtually impossible in any event, there are convincing arguments against this proposal. The diversity reflected in these items is often based on sound substantive and theoretical reasons, and data bank users must learn to live with a little diversity. However, at present we are forced to live with too much variation, which reduces the utility of the data for policy making.

There are a number of ways to raise survey response rates to a high level, or at least an acceptable level. Yet, some data banks contain information based on very low response rates. This point should be underscored, since researchers approaching such information may note naively that there are thousands of respondents but fail to pursue this further to the point of discovering, say, that those respondents represent only 10 or 20 percent of the initial target sample. Data based on minuscule response rates may be worse than no data at all for certain research objectives.

Perhaps the most pronounced need for improvement is in the area of documentation. Often information on tape or disk has been coded from interview schedules or open-ended questions. The potential users should have available detailed information on how this coding was done. Similarly, the strategies for dealing with missing observations should be documented. This is particularly vital when the data are going to be used in multivariate statistical analyses. Researchers have been known to leave such observations blank, fill them with zeros, replace the observations with the variable mean, replace them with a value based on an extrapolation, arbitrarily assign a value based on a particular theoretical prediction, and so on. The users should know which strategy was employed; ideally they should have the option of replacing missing observations using their own techniques.

Similarly, one would hope that the idiosyncrasies in the data that are a function of the particular computer system—hardware or software—for which the data were developed are well-documented. This is particularly important if the secondary data analysis is to be performed at a different computer installation. For example, data files originally prepared to run on systems that accept large physical records may require reformatting and reduction of the record length before they are used on a smaller system. There are techniques for structuring data files to make them amenable to a maximum number of computer configurations and software packages. One step forward would be the establishment of these techniques as standard operating procedure throughout the profession.

Finally, social researchers have an obligation to their respondents to guarantee confidentiality of the results. In addition, the promise of confidentiality has the practical effect of reducing prospective respondents' anxieties and making them more likely to participate in the research.

Lack of comparability from survey to survey is the lethal flaw that can destroy attempts at longitudinal policy analyses by decision makers. Paradoxically, if retrieval activities that presently are diverse were better coordinated, federal agencies (and related national organizations) could make fewer information requests and the data they received would be more useful. Redundant requests for data about graduate science—about enrollment, Ph.D.'s produced, expenditures, and so on—constitute an unjustified burden for academic institutions.

More to the point, it is difficult, if not impossible, to relate data from different agencies. In several studies, such as an evaluation of the NSF's Science Development Program[42] and research commissioned by a White House Biomedical Research Panel,[43] I and others attempted to create such a merged data file. This was necessary because different agencies or groups retrieve the best (or the only) data about different characteristics of science departments. For example, the NSF has the best data on federal expenditures by discipline, while the NRC has virtually complete information about Ph.D.'s and their job placement. The following are some of the problems we encountered.

— Academic fields are defined and classified differently. For example, in the NRC Doctorate Record File, Ph.D.'s indicate their own fields (which may not match their departments), while the key file about NIH funding references actual departments and the NSF's funding file aggregates departments into "disciplines."
— During the past decades many state universities have developed strong branch campuses with graduate programs. Agencies may report activities at the main campus only or at the main campus and branch campuses separately, or they may lump them together. In addition, the point at which a branch campus is considered sufficiently active to be recognized by an agency (or, in fact, by the university itself) varies.
— Some files fail to separate data about the medical or agriculture schools from data about the main unit. Thus, all federal expenditures for biochemistry are reported as one datum for a particular university.

Policy analysts frequently discover that indicators of the same phenomenon provided by two agencies do not agree. One reason is that different organizations use different sources. For example, the NRC polls doctorate recipients. The NSF obtains information about enrollments from department chairpersons. The Center for Educational Statistics of the U.S. Department of Education retrieves both enrollment and Ph.D. statistics from university-level administrators such as registrars. Agencies develop their own definitions and retrieval techniques consistent with their organizational objectives. And agency officials may fear that the loss of control over these activities that standardization might require will undermine the realization of those objectives. Although this is a problem, it need not be an insurmountable obstacle.

Confessions of a Nonscientist

In his article "Confessions of a Nonscientist," Bill Long, a Presbyterian minister, notes that it was assumed that he would become a scientist.[44] He won science awards in high school. His father was a pioneering computer designer, and his older brother was studying science at Rensselaer Polytechnic Institute. He had received top scores in the SAT achievement tests in mathematics and science. However, once in college, he quickly transferred out of the sciences. As you read his reasons, think about Sheila Tobias's research.

Of the many things that I recall about my college math and science professors, three things stand out. First, all of the professors seemed terribly indifferent or even hostile to me, the student. I suppose they thought that they were trying to motivate me when they told me to look at my neighbor on either side and then realize that one or two of us would not be there in a few months. I suppose they were trying to humble me when they emphasized that if I had not made my major contribution by age twenty-three I would forever be an insignificant force in math and science.

I suppose they were trying to teach me something about responsibility when they said that they didn't care whether I showed up for class or lab. But that is not how I heard it. Instead, through this experience, I heard them saying, "You students are really worth very little. Most of you will not be around very long, so I'm not going to be too concerned about you. If you sink, that is fine with me. If you swim, I will perhaps notice you, but even in that case, I will probably not get around to you for a few more years. I have so many more important things to do than to be with you." . . .

. . . They somehow acted as if they had a presumptive right to science itself. Science was less a field in which they were a humble fellow-student than a private preserve in which they wanted to control the poachers. . . .

. . . It was another factor, however, which gradually convinced me that science and math were not for me. The more I applied myself to the study of physics, calculus or abstract algebra, the more I got the impression that the goal of the field was the mastery of minutiae. Perhaps I was mistaken in my perception, but I never heard any of my professors speak of the wonder of science or the reasons why they were captivated by the field. Chesterton once said that what was lacking in the modern world was not wonders but a sense of wonder. I never felt that my professors were awed or overwhelmed or even impressed by anything in nature or math.

PART II

The Solutions

FIVE

Hidden Talent
Underrepresented Groups as a Resource

> How many Ramanujans, his life begs us to ask, dwell in India today, unknown and unrecognized? And how many in America and Britain, locked away in racial or economic ghettos, scarcely aware of worlds outside their own?
>
> Robert Kanigel, *The Man Who Knew Infinity*

I state in the Introduction that science education has become a vehicle through which the inequalities of our society are perpetrated and exacerbated. Women, people of color, and poor people are underrepresented. In this chapter I present data about these inequalities and argue that scientific research and industrial innovation in the United States are less creative and rigorous then they should be, precisely because of these inequalities.

Poor People, Science, and Social Mobility

As background, consider the connection between social mobility and education in the United States. Does schooling matter? This seemingly innocuous question has generated much controversy, debate, and social progress in the United States. These three words can be interpreted in at least two ways: as asking, Do children learn something worthwhile in school, and if so, what? or Can schools help poor or disadvantaged groups improve their position in society? American history is filled with tales of wealthy, successful, educated men and women who arrived on these shores illiterate and hungry. President John Kennedy referred to "a nation of immigrants." We traditionally have looked to education as a key factor in advancement. But is education still crucial?

Wealth, Status, and Power

Sociologists specialize in the study of social class, asking such questions as, How are different societies structured? Who has power, or authority, or wealth? What are the opportunities for social mobility or advancement? After decades of research, innumerable studies, and painstaking theory development, sociologists have a rich understanding of social class to bring to the schooling controversy.

In nineteenth-century America, quite frequently the railroad tracks literally divided towns into two classes, the wealthy and the poor. People were ashamed of being from the "wrong side of the tracks." In the twentieth century, sociologists have differentiated additional classes. During the 1940s, in a sleepy Massachusetts coastal community, Lloyd Warner, a pioneering researcher, identified six, each with definite characteristics:

1. upper upper class: the "old families," inherited wealth;
2. lower upper class: the nouveau riche;
3. upper middle class: professionals and substantial businessmen;
4. lower middle class: small businessmen, white-collar workers;
5. upper lower class: semiskilled workers; and
6. lower lower class: unskilled workers, welfare recipients.

During the past quarter-century, our understanding of social stratification has become more sophisticated and our urbanized, transient society has become more complex. Modern sociologists reject the notion of two, six, or twelve "classes." They recognize that social status is the result of several factors: occupation, education, and income. These factors usually coincide or are correlated; typically, those with the most education have the best jobs and earn more income than those with little education. But there are many exceptions. Sociologist Gerhard Lenski coined the term *status inconsistency* to identify those who might be high on one scale but low on another, for example, the wealthy but uneducated gambler or the very well educated but underpaid college professor.

The Pernicious Effects of Poverty

I believe that the largest barrier to educational achievement is poverty. It is no exaggeration to argue that if poverty in this country had been eliminated during the past decade, even if no attempts had been made to improve the schools, American education would have improved more than it has as a result of all the educational task forces and reform movements. The level of poverty in a rich, developed country like ours is shocking, and the percentage of children in poverty is even higher than that for adults.

Consider a 10-year-old Latino girl from Miami or a 10-year-old African American boy from Harlem who aspires to become a scientist. They will face a series of barriers, the girl because she is female and because she is Latino, the boy because he is African American. Now, add to this equation growing up in an environment where there is inadequate health care for the entire family, including the wage earners; parents work one or two jobs each to earn enough to get by; violence is rampant and random killings are a part of life; and the levels of alcohol and drug abuse in the neighborhood, and perhaps in the family, are high. These children live with an incredible amount of stress. Under such circumstances, survival becomes the goal for most children, and thinking about any career, let alone a career as a scientist, is a luxury.

At the end of the 1990–91 school year, Jeffrey Lantos, a teacher at Hancock Park Elementary School in Los Angeles, published an article on the *Los Angeles Times* op-ed page called "Farewell to a Classroom of Young Heroes." Noting that he would watch his sixth grade class graduate that day with sadness, he said,

I will watch Sharona, from Tehran, who was shot at by soldiers as she escaped with her family over the Makran Mountains into Pakistan. I will watch Mayra, who endured the sullen stares of border guards and three days of hunger and thirst as she and her mother rode rickety buses up the twisted spine of Central America.

I will watch Vinod, who wrote that what he missed most about his native India was his baby cow, born the day he left. . . .

I will watch these children, so many of whom have known few of the joys and little of the security of childhood, children forced by the demands of their new country to become parents to their own parents (translating, explaining the customs, the laws, the school system), children who, in the afternoons, walked (or ran?) through grimy, gang-governed neighborhoods and who, upon arriving home, unlocked and relocked the deadbolts and plopped into frayed armchairs in darkened corners of empty apartments where they were kept company by Oprah and Phil and Geraldo. . . .

I will miss my young heroes and heroines, because that is what they are. In a country crazed with violence, in a country whose elected leaders have all but abandoned them, these children have risen above their circumstances and performed heroically. They have noble qualities, all of them. Their accomplishments made me feel exalted.[1]

In a classic article called "Keeping the Poor Poor," Paul Jacobs presented compelling evidence that it is more expensive to live in a poor neighborhood than in an affluent area.[2] The rent is higher per square foot in poverty-stricken East Los Angeles than in affluent West Los Angeles. Across this country, banks have withdrawn from violence-ridden inner cities. Consequently, residents of these areas have to pay inordinately high fees to cash checks at special establishments. It is virtually impossible for the people who need financial resources the most to get a loan. Those people and institutions who will loan them money charge unbelievably high interest rates. Since major supermarkets also have withdrawn from these areas, most residents must obtain food and other necessities from convenience stores and other small markets, where the prices are considerably higher than in the more affluent areas of town. It is much more difficult for someone who has been trapped in poverty to climb out than it is for the rest of us to stay out.

Citing studies that repeatedly demonstrate that the amount and quality of schooling experiences can change students' IQ test scores, David Berliner states,

It has become clear that the more schooling you acquire, the smarter you will appear on the test. The corollary is one that our democracy is having difficulty facing, namely, that higher social class standing will make a child intelligent, at least as measured by tests of intelligence. Higher social class standing allows parents to buy high quality day care, preschool, and K-12 schooling; permits the purchase of instructional toys, encyclopedias and computers; and ensures first-rate health care.[3]

Discussions of poverty usually conjure up images of inner-city persons of color, but in fact the devastating effects of poverty know no ethnic boundaries. A 1992 article in the *Los Angeles Times* noted that poor Whites, who lived largely in rural areas and small communities, "defy the public image of poverty as primarily a problem of Blacks and Latinos in the inner cities."[4] According to the 1990 census, those living in poverty in California included about 1.8 million Anglos, 1.6 million Latinos, and 400,000 African Americans. Of course, the percentage for Latinos and African Americans (approximately 21 percent) is considerably higher than that for Anglos (approximately 9 percent), and the forces of poverty and racism combine in pernicious ways.

Harold Hodgkinson has published numerous articles and reports about the rapidly changing demography of the United States and its effect on the educational system and the work force. He cites some startling statistics. For example, "California . . . already represents in human terms what New York did at the turn of the century—the point of entry for millions who immigrate to the U.S. Two-thirds of the world's immigration is to the U.S., which means that California is now accepting almost one-third of the world's immigration, and immigration rates are on the increase."[5] According to Hodgkinson, the Southern California Gas Company, the nation's largest gas company, "can tell you how to hook up a gas stove in Chinese, (either Mandarin or Cantonese) Spanish, Korean, Vietnamese and English, all in their thirteen million person service area! Only fifteen percent of Los Angeles school children are Caucasian" (2).

Hodgkinson comments that California seems to be committed to "a Brooks Brothers system of higher education for students prepared in Robert Hall Schools" (5). He adds that the higher education system in California cannot operate independently of the public schools. "With great ethnic and economic diversity, the largest classes in the nation, in a decade of declining achievement scores, the schools represent the well from which higher education must drink. This is as true in Iowa as in California" (9). Hodgkinson has reported many disturbing statistics. For example, an African-American male born in California is more likely to be murdered than to enroll in the University of California! And every day in America forty teenage girls give birth to their third child!

The Quality Education for Minorities Project reported that

slow productivity growth has translated into stagnant real incomes. The real wages of full-time working males were lower in 1987 than in 1973, and wages are higher in Germany, Sweden, and Japan than in our own land. As wages have fallen, poverty has grown: thirty-two million people, about thirteen percent of all Americans, now live in poverty. Twice as large a percentage of American children are in poverty as in Japan or any major Western European country. A growing number of citizens are threatened with permanent second-class status, and society's unwillingness to equip all Americans to participate in the national economy may well consign the nation to like status in the global economy.[6]

Owing to their heritage and social system, Americans have advantages over the citizens of most other countries with respect to social mobility. In Japan, England, and many other countries a student's career path is largely determined by testing and choices made at a very young age. One of America's great competitive strengths is that it gives people second and third chances. This is entirely consistent with human nature and with what we know about how people develop during childhood, adolescence, and adulthood. The class and social structures in many nations, including Western industrialized nations, greatly restrict educational opportunities for many people. In a recent article about comparative educational achievement, Joel Kotkin commented that

exacerbating Europe's youth problems are rising numbers of new immigrants, mostly from the Islamic countries of the Near East and North Africa. A recent U.N. International Labor Organization report referred to the estimated seven million children—roughly one-tenth of the youth population of Western Europe—as a "demographic time bomb." These youngsters have virtually no hope of rising to even the middle rungs of the highly structured European education system. In the western part of Berlin, for example, Turks account for roughly one in five young people; yet only seven percent ever attend gymnasium, the secondary-education level required for university admission. Barely three percent ever enter university. In France, admission to university-level education for the large Algerian Muslim population is rare indeed; the rector of the Ecole Polytechnique in Paris, one of France's elite technical institutions, could not recall one Algerian-French student attending his institution in recent years.[7]

Classic Policy Studies

Sociological research has contributed directly to national decisions about social progress and racial equality during the past quarter-century. The central questions in the schooling debate are

—How can we equalize the opportunities available to children of all classes from all ethnic backgrounds?
—How is schooling linked to adult achievement?
—What aspects of the school experience most relate to student learning?

A major Supreme Court decision in 1954 mandated integration of the nation's elementary and secondary schools with "all deliberate speed." In a footnote to that decision, the justices cited the research of Kenneth Clark, who focused on a crucial variable: self-esteem. In cleverly constructed studies, Black and White children were asked to describe Black and White dolls. The answers indicated that the self-esteem of Black children was suffering under the "separate but equal" schooling policy that many southern states had pursued.

The study about the equality of educational opportunity that had the greatest policy impact was directed by James Coleman at the Johns Hopkins University and Earnest Campbell of Vanderbilt University. The results were published in what became known to many as the Coleman Report.[8] A major piece of progressive legislation, the Civil Rights Act of 1964, had mandated that the government commission a study of the degree to which equal educational opportunities were being presented to White and minority children. The researchers could have satisfied the letter of the law simply by reporting on the facilities, for example, books, buildings, and budgets, available to both groups of students; however, they believed that a full response to the legislation required assessing how well the schools were educating each group.

Their study was massive; the sample included all the teachers and administrators from many school districts as well as children in the first, third, sixth, ninth, and twelfth grades. Over six hundred thousand children were included; each took an achievement test as part of the research. Advanced statistical techniques and computers were used. The results were startling and provoked debates that still simmer. Among the conclusions were the following:

— Minority students performed below White students throughout the school years, with the gap widening in the later years.
— Facilities, such as books and buildings, were not a major predictor of student achievement.
— Important determinants of student achievement were the social characteristics of the other students.
— Self-concept also played an important role in student achievement.

Policy studies like the Coleman Report require many difficult methodological decisions. For example, ideally studies of student development are longitudinal, not cross-sectional. In longitudinal studies, researchers measure the growth of students between the first and twelfth grades by following a group of first graders for twelve years. In cross-sectional studies, researchers study a group of first graders and a group of twelfth graders at the same time, the assumption being that the differences between them reflect the impact of twelve years of schooling. Cross-sectional studies are a weaker basis from which to draw policy inferences, but they are more practical and less expensive.

In the Coleman project, the researchers were constrained to a cross-sectional design because Congress mandated that the study be completed in two years. Nonetheless, it was one of the largest policy research studies ever conducted, drawing upon the most sophisticated computer-based techniques available. Its conclusion that it was not school facilities but the nature of a student's classmates that most affected his or her achievement, that is, that poor children learn best in schools with-middle class classmates and that minority children learn best in school with Whites, spurred movement toward the integration of American schools. And the findings about self-concept were noted by educators.

Pygmalion in the Classroom

As outlined in the Introduction, a fascinating study by Robert Rosenthal of Harvard University suggested that the expectations teachers have about a student's potential exert a strong impact on the student's learning.[9] In his prior research Rosenthal had been interested in whether researchers unconsciously biased seemingly scientific observations in support of hypotheses they expected. For example, he studied experimental psychologists who were conducting research about how white rats learn mazes. He randomly sorted rats into two groups and told some research psychologists that one group contained "maze-bright" rats, while the other contained "maze-dull" rats. At the end of numerous trials, the experimenters reported that the "maze-bright" rats learned significantly faster than the others. Actually, of course, the groups were indistinguishable. Findings such as these about how researchers, even experimental psychologists in a laboratory situation, can unknowingly bias results have helped social scientists detect and avoid such bias.

If researchers can unknowingly bend objective phenomena to match their expectations, couldn't teachers do the same thing? Rosenthal and his colleagues next selected some elementary school students totally at random. The researchers then informed the teachers that these students had tremendous intellectual potential of a kind that had not been revealed on standard intelligence tests. In other words, these particular students were alleged to be potential geniuses in disguise. Once the teachers held these expectations about these otherwise typical children, the students' grades improved dramatically. It turned out that the teachers were spending more time with them and were predisposed in subconscious ways to perceive the students as doing well; student performance responded to this extra treatment.

This study by Rosenthal has been the subject of some methodological controversy. Critics have suggested facetiously that Rosenthal's own theory about experimenters' bias explains why he found the results he expected in the classroom. But the idea is intriguing and powerful. Think of the implications: perhaps some children fail in school because their teachers expect them to.

And what if students incorporate low teacher expectations as part of their own self-concept? Research in the social sciences—clinical psychology, sociology, anthropology—substantiates the great importance that a person's self-concept plays in his or her achievement in school and at work. Perhaps, then, the most destructive impact of low teacher expectation is the damage to the student's self-concept. What is more cruel than the destruction of a child's self-concept, particularly on false grounds? Some people never recover. On the positive side, teachers with high expectations for their students may bolster their self-concept, a potentially liberating impact.

Increasing a student's self-esteem, by itself, without accompanying resources such as effective instruction and hard work by the student, will not be enough. My argument is that low self-esteem causes many students to opt out of the mathematics and science education system. Furthermore, if they can get past that barrier, they will discover that they are capable of mastering these subjects. But it is not enough merely to increase someone's self-esteem. In fact, it can be a cruel joke simply to raise the self-esteem of youngsters without also helping them to learn and requiring them to achieve.

Thomas Sowell has criticized some steps that have been taken in the name of increasing self-esteem:

The practical consequences of the self-esteem dogma are many. Failing grades are to be avoided, to keep from damaging fragile egos, according to this doctrine. Thus, the Los Angeles school system simply abolished failing grades in the early years of elementary school and many leading colleges and universities simply do not record failing grades on a student's transcript. Another way of forestalling a loss of self-esteem is to water down the courses to the point where failing grades are highly unlikely. A more positive approach to self-esteem is simply to give higher grades. The wide-spread grade inflation of recent decades owes much to this philosophy.[10]

While self-esteem is a central concept in the case I present in this book, it should be clear by now that I am not advocating grade inflation or watering down of courses. To the contrary, I believe we must expect students to excel and to realize that this will require hard work. One thing is sure, though: students with a depressed self-concept are unlikely even to attempt advanced mathematics and science courses.

Many teachers erroneously assume that only a very small percentage of students can master science and mathematics. Their expectations exclude the great majority of middle-class White males. Only a very small group of students will "meet their standards," they believe. The chances that a poor person, or a minority person, or a young woman will fall into that select group are even lower. Calvin Sims, an African American journalist, grew up in inner-city Los Angeles and received a degree in engineering from Yale. He describes his experiences in a science fair he entered while a high school student:

With all this fuss about science, it's no surprise that I entered the L.A. County science fair. I worked for months on my project on thin-layer chromatography, running samples and testing substances, and I was picked as a finalist. I fully understood that project and I think I explained it well to the judges—but they clearly did not believe I had done it on my own. One asked if I'd gotten my idea from another student's project. They weren't trying to find out how well I understood the material, they were trying to find out how an inner-city kid could do such work. I got an honorable mention instead of a prize.[11]

People of Color and Science

Pioneers always have the toughest challenge. Consider the impressive achievements of African Americans who attended major colleges and universities in the United States while slavery still existed. John Chavis attended Princeton, John B. Russwurm graduated from Bowdoin in 1826, Edward Jones graduated from Amherst in 1825, and an African American graduated from Ohio State in 1828.[12]

According to a report prepared by the Congressional Research Service,

By the year 2000, approximately eighty-five percent of the new entrants to the U.S. labor force are expected to be minorities, women, handicapped, and immigrants, groups which for the most part have been historically underrepresented in science, mathematics, and engineering. Presently, Blacks and Hispanics are twenty-five percent of the precollege level, and, by the year 2000, they will comprise forty-seven percent. Approximately twenty-three of the twenty-five largest school systems in the United States are majority minority school systems—systems in which students from minority groups predominate. . . . The role of minorities is no longer viewed just as an equity issue; the demands of a scientific and technical workforce must also be met. . . . Blacks are approximately twelve percent of the U.S. population and constitute 2.6 percent of all employed scientists and engineers.

Table 5.1
U.S. Citizen Ph.D.'s in Natural Science and Engineering, 1985–1991

Year	Total[a]	White		Asian		Latino		African American		American Indian	
		Men	Women	Men	Women	Men	Women	Men	Women	Men	Women
1985	8,161	5,797	1,587	224	80	83	34	69	29	13	09
1986	8,090	5,675	1,654	240	83	96	41	53	33	20	11
1987	8,216	5,652	1,709	279	83	109	43	60	33	23	07
1988	8,685	5,960	1,862	290	72	141	46	63	33	21	06
1989	8,811	5,824	2,060	324	93	127	48	72	38	25	09
1990	9,249	6,205	2,134	310	86	143	67	68	35	15	02
1991	9,281	6,150	2,110	352	128	152	61	87	46	25	09

SOURCE: Commission on Professionals in Science and Technology, "Professional Women and Minorities," *Science* 256 (June 1992): 1765.
[a]The total includes minority groups not listed.

Hispanics comprise nine percent of the U.S. population, and represent less than two percent of all employed scientists and engineers.[13]

Statistics compiled by the Commission on Professionals in Science and Technology demonstrate that during the 1980s the number of African Americans earning Ph.D.'s in SME declined by 20 percent. There actually are fewer African American males earning Ph.D.'s in SME than there were twenty years ago. "In 1988 . . . only one Black U.S. citizen earned a Ph.D. in mathematics and only one in computer sciences."[14] Table 5.1 presents data about ethnicity and Ph.D. attainment in SME.

Betty Vetter, the executive director of the Commission on Professionals in Science and Technology, lamented, "We're losing a whole generation of children, and probably their children too."[15] According to a report by the Quality Education for Minorities Project,

Forty-four years after Mendez v. Westminster School District, and thirty-five years after Delgado v. Bastrop Independent School District, and thirty-five years after Brown v. The Board of Education of Topeka—all cases that declared segregated schools unconstitutional—most minority children remain in schools that are separate and decidedly unequal. Educational opportunities for most minority youth lag behind those available to white students, and that lack of opportunity is reflected in the lower educational achievement of minority children.[16]

Here is a summary of research findings about the loss of women and minorities from the scientific pipeline:

Using national data, Sue Berryman found that losses of women from the pipeline occur primarily at the end of the precollege years and during college. The lower adult participation rates of women were traced to two factors: (1) they obtain advanced degrees at lower rates generally, and (2) they select quantitative college majors at lower rates than men do. In contrast, most Blacks and Hispanics are lost to science much earlier in the schooling process, and other minority losses occur throughout the years of schooling. *The underparticipation of minorities thus can be largely attributed to their lower levels of achievement in mathematics during the precollege years.* However, even those Blacks and Hispanics who remain in the precollege pipeline are less likely than whites to choose quantitative fields of study.[17]

SAT Performance

Table 5.2 presents data on SAT verbal and mathematics scores of students of differing ethnic groups for selected years between 1979 and 1989. While Whites continue to score higher than persons of color on the SATs, minority students' scores increased considerably during the eighties, probably reflecting improvement in their elementary and secondary education.[18]

One study found that among students who scored 550 or above on the SAT quantitative exam, minority students persisted in science, mathematics, and engineering majors at rates equaling or exceeding those of Anglos.[19] The researchers cited the central importance of role models who also were persons of color.

In this context, consider an extraordinary study by Nancy Gray.[20] Gray assessed the impact of an academically rigorous urban high school magnet program on disadvantaged students of color. Despite weak preparation in elementary school, these students achieved at a high level. Furthermore, their SAT scores improved dramatically. Gray stated that her

results generally support the premise that what students study in high school, how well they master the concepts presented, and the advanced academic skill levels they achieve during those last years of pre-college schooling are indeed major factors in later SAT performance. Findings do suggest, however, that although rigorous academic preparation in high school is associated with significant gains in SAT scores, many aspects of students' basic achievement patterns are set earlier, at least by the end of middle school. . . .

For the publishers of the SAT, the findings support what they have long been saying: those who want to improve their SAT-scores should take demanding high school programs. For schools under the gun to improve the SAT performance of those they serve—privileged or disadvantaged, majority or minority, native-speakers of English or the limited English proficient—the experience of this project points the way to at least modest score improvement for students who receive suitable academic treatment and goes a long way toward defining what that treatment might be.

Table 5.2
*Mean Scholastic Aptitude Test Scores, by Ethnic Group,
in Selected Years, 1979–1989*

Ethnic group	1979	1982	1985	1987	1989	Change 1979–89
Verbal						
American Indian	386	388	392	393	384	−2
African American	330	341	346	351	351	+21
Mexican American	370	377	382	379	381	+11
Puerto Rican	345	360	368	360	360	+15
White	444	444	449	447	446	+2
Math						
American Indian	421	424	428	432	428	+7
African American	358	366	376	377	386	+28
Mexican American	410	416	426	424	430	+20
Puerto Rican	388	403	409	400	406	+18
White	483	483	490	489	491	+8

SOURCE: Quality Education for Minorities Project, *Education That Works: An Action Plan for the Education of Minorities* (Cambridge: MIT, Jan. 1990), 19.

By implication the findings exonerate the SAT as a possible major contributor to postsecondary-admissions inequity and cast its role perhaps more realistically as a mirror of widespread inequity in academic preparation in the nation's schools— inequity which has obviously already occurred by the time students fill out their college admissions applications. (181–82)

Tracking, Achievement, and Aspirations

In a rigorous study of the connection between ethnicity and "cognitive ability," Herbert Ginsburg and Robert Russell studied preschool and kindergarten children, focusing on cognitive abilities that are thought to be associated with later mathematics abilities and achievements, for example, counting, conservation, and enumeration.[21] At no point did Whites significantly outperform African Americans. There were some differences related to socioeconomic status, but most of those differences had disappeared by the time the children reached kindergarten.

A 1990 study published by the Rand Corporation assessed the delivery of educational programs to poor people and persons of color.[22] A particular focus was the efficacy of tracking and how it relates to issues of racial equality. The Rand findings were based upon both an exhaustive review of the literature and analysis of data from a survey administered to principals and teachers in a national probability sample of twelve hundred public and private elementary and secondary schools.

The researchers found that small differences exist between the science and mathematics experiences of most White students and those of poor, or minority, or "low-ability" students in elementary school. They also found that these differences had increased significantly by the time the students entered secondary school. Being placed in a low track greatly reduces students' opportunities to learn science and mathematics; furthermore, persons of color are much more likely to be placed in lower tracks. The authors note that

the inequitable practices related to ability-grouping that we have identified in this study are commonly viewed as natural responses to differences in student aptitudes and achievements. But even if supposedly objective ability groupings appear logical, they are easily confounded with race and social class.

Moreover, the differences in opportunities they provide actually limit instruction, rather than fine-tune it. . . . *High-ability students at low-socioeconomic-status (SES), high-minority schools may actually have fewer opportunities than low-ability students who attend more advantaged schools.* (vii, emphasis added)

They conclude, "although schools may think that they ration good teaching to those students who can most profit from it, we find no empirical evidence to justify unequal access to valued science and mathematics curriculum, instruction, and teachers" (xi).

The study also reports findings that indicate not only that tracking works poorly for middle- and lower-ability groups but that it does not necessarily improve learning and achievement among high-ability students. "Many studies show that highly capable students do as well in mixed-ability classes" (6).

Sociologist Daniel Solorzano has conducted extensive studies of science aspirations and achievements among Latinos. In one study he examined Chicano mobility aspirations, attempting to disentangle the complex interactive affects of race/ethnicity and social class. Table 5.3 summarizes the key results. Solorzano noted that "when social class was controlled, Chicano eighth graders had higher educational aspirations than white students at the lowest SES quartiles. . . . At the highest SES quartile, Chicana females have slightly higher aspirations than white females, but the opposite is true for Chicano males."[23] Among students with high aspirations, Chicanos do not attain as much education as their White counterparts. Solorzano concluded that for Chicanos "high aspirations have become a necessary but not sufficient condition for later attainment" (54).

Table 5.3

Percentage of Eighth Graders Planning to Attend College, 1988

Students	Overall	Socioeconomic quartile			
		Low	Low/middle	Middle/high	High
Chicanos					
Female	70.4	67.7	74.9	83.3	98.5
Male	66.7	56.5	75.3	80.9	89.7
Whites					
Female	87.5	58.5	77.8	88.0	96.8
Male	78.6	48.9	68.7	87.6	94.9

SOURCE: D. Solorzano, "Chicano Mobility Aspirations: A Theoretical and Empirical Note," *Latino Studies Journal*, Jan. 1992, 53.

NOTE: Students responded to the question, "As things stand now, how far in school do you think you will get?" The response was coded "College Aspiration" if the student expected to attend college and more. Socioeconomic status was constructed from father's occupation, father's education, mother's education, family income, and material items in the household and then broken down into four quartiles.

Higher Education

In the book *Blacks, Science, and American Education,* Willie Pearson, Jr., and H. Kenneth Bechtel have brought together a number of papers that present detailed data about the experiences of African American students on each rung of the educational ladder.[24] Table 5.4 presents enrollment data on African Americans and Whites in four science disciplines in undergraduate and graduate institutions.

Table 5.5 lists the institutions that awarded the most bachelor's degrees to African Americans in each of the four discipline areas from table 5.4. This table says a lot about the importance of the traditionally Black institutions (TBIs) in the preparation of Black scientists and engineers. According to Gail Thomas, the data clearly illustrate that the TBIs continue to play an important role in educating Black students. "It is predicted," Thomas points out, "that TBIs will be required to assume an even greater responsibility in educating Black students as tuition and academic standards for admissions continue to escalate at the PWIs [predominantly White institutions]."[25]

Table 5.6 presents current data on educational attainment, by ethnic group, and table 5.7 presents current data on recipients of doctorates, disaggregated by discipline, gender, and ethnic group.

Jerry Gaston argues that, in addition to the legal, moral, and equity reasons for increasing participation in science by African Americans and other persons of color, it can improve the range and quality of theorizing

Table 5.4

Science Enrollments in Undergraduate and Graduate Institutions, Fall 1982

(%)

Group	Biological Sciences	Engineering	Mathematics	Physical Sciences
		Undergraduate		
African Americans	8.3	5.9	9.8	4.6
Males	3.1	3.6	4.9	2.5
Females	5.2	1.4	4.9	2.1
Whites	80.4	79.6	80.7	85.9
Males	42.0	68.0	45.2	63.7
Females	38.4	11.6	35.5	22.2
		Graduate		
African Americans	2.5	1.2	1.4	1.2
Males	1.2	1.0	.8	.9
Females	1.3	.2	.6	.3
Whites	80.5	49.7	55.8	70.9
Males	48.5	42.5	38.8	55.8
Females	32.0	7.2	17.0	15.1

SOURCE: W. Pearson, Jr., and H. K. Bechtel, eds., *Blacks, Science, and American Education* (New Brunswick, N.J.: Rutgers University Press, 1989), 65. Copyright © 1989 by Rutgers. The State University. Reprinted by permission of Rutgers University Press.

Table 5.5

Institutions Awarding the Most Bachelor's Degrees to African Americans, 1980–1981

Biological Sciences		Mathematics	
Howard University	Washington, D.C.	South Carolina State*	South Carolina
Tennessee State*	Tennessee	Fayetteville State*	North Carolina
CUNY-City	New York	Morgan State*	Maryland
South Carolina State*	South Carolina	University of the District of Columbia	Washington, D.C.
Morehouse*	Georgia		
		Bowie State*	Maryland
Engineering		Physical Sciences	
Prairie View*	Texas	Embry-Riddle University	Florida
Southern University*	Louisiana		
North Carolina Agricultural and Technology*	North Carolina	Howard University*	Washington, D.C.
		Xavier University*	Louisiana
CUNY-City	New York	University of the District of Columbia	Washington, D.C.
University of the District of Columbia*	Washington, D.C.		
		Alcorn State*	Mississippi
		Hampton University*	Virginia
		Fisk University*	Tennessee

SOURCE: Pearson and Bechtel, *Blacks, Science, and American Education*, 72.

NOTE: Asterisks indicate predominantly Black colleges and universities.

Table 5.6

Educational Attainment of the U.S. Population, by Ethnic Group, 1990

Highest education level	Total	American Indian	Asian	African American	Latino	White
Eighth grade or less	10.4	14.0	12.9	13.8	30.7	8.9
Some high school, no diploma	14.4	20.4	9.5	23.2	19.5	13.1
High school diploma	30.0	29.1	18.5	27.9	21.6	31.0
Some college, no degree	18.7	20.8	14.7	18.5	14.3	19.1
Associate degree	6.2	6.4	7.7	5.3	4.8	6.3
Bachelor's degree	13.1	6.1	22.7	7.5	5.9	13.9
Graduate or professional degree	7.2	3.2	13.9	3.8	3.3	7.7

SOURCE: Census Bureau, as reported in *Chronicle of Higher Education Almanac*, 1 Sept. 1994.

NOTE: The figures are based on the 1990 census and cover adults age 25 and older. The total includes those whose racial or ethnic group is not known. Latinos may be of any race. The figures may not add to 100 percent because of rounding.

and research. "The support for this thesis involves evidence suggesting that social processes affect who becomes a scientist, what kind of scientist they become, and what specialties they choose. It will be argued that problem choice is influenced by the same kind of social processes. If that is correct, than it is desirable to recruit scientists from all social categories in order to maximize the probability that particular research problems are not neglected."[26] Undergraduate courses, to say nothing of precollege education, are structured so as to encourage certain kinds of White male students to persist in studying science, mathematics, and engineering. In addition to being inequitable, this makes for poorer science.

Icons from the 1960s

Two African American men who rose to national prominence and visibility during the 1960s by entirely different paths have reemerged in the nineties as mathematics and science educators.[27] The first, Robert Moses, was a doctoral student at Harvard when he became immersed in the civil rights struggles in Mississippi in the early 1960s. According to Alexis Jetter, in a 1993 article in the *New York Times Magazine,*

Moses set out on a solitary tour of rural Mississippi, written off by most civil rights leaders as too dangerous to organize. . . . Exhibiting almost mystical calm in the face of terrible violence, the soft-spoken young man quickly became a legend. When a sheriff's cousin gashed his head open with a knife handle, a badly bleeding Moses still managed to stagger up the courthouse steps to register two black

Table 5.7
Characteristics of Ph.D. Recipients, 1992
(%)

Characteristic	All fields[a]	Arts and humanities	Business and management	Education	Engineering	Life sciences	Physical sciences	Social sciences	Professional sciences[b]
Sex									
Male	63.0	53.7	76.0	40.5	90.7	60.7	80.3	52.6	57.0
Female	37.0	46.3	24.0	59.5	9.3	39.3	19.7	47.4	43.0
Citizenship									
U.S.	66.4	77.7	56.7	86.8	38.7	65.7	54.2	74.3	75.8
Non-U.S., permanent visa	5.0	5.5	7.7	2.4	7.5	4.9	5.5	4.5	5.0
Non-U.S., temporary visa	25.5	13.7	31.9	8.3	50.3	26.9	37.7	16.7	16.1
Unknown	3.1	3.2	3.7	2.4	3.5	2.5	2.7	4.4	3.1
Ethnic group[c]									
American Indian	0.5	0.5	0.2	0.8	0.4	0.4	0.4	0.5	0.5
Asian	6.2	3.0	9.6	2.4	17.8	7.0	10.0	3.5	4.5
African American	3.9	2.7	3.2	8.3	1.9	2.2	1.0	4.4	5.9
Latino	3.2	3.8	2.0	3.5	2.9	2.7	2.8	3.7	2.3
White	84.5	88.6	83.5	84.0	74.7	86.1	83.7	86.3	84.5
Other or unknown	1.6	1.4	1.5	1.0	2.3	1.6	2.0	1.6	2.2

SOURCE: National Research Council, as reported in *Chronicle of Higher Education Almanac*, 1 Sept. 1994.
NOTE: Figures may not add up to 100 percent because of rounding.
[a] Includes degree categories not listed separately.
[b] Excludes business, which is listed separately.
[c] Figures cover only U.S. citizens and those with permanent visas.

farmers. Seemingly oblivious to danger, he fell asleep in a SNCC office where only hours before workers had leaped out a window to escape an armed mob of local whites. And in Greenwood, when three Klansmen opened fire on his car, Moses grabbed the steering wheel with one hand, cradled the bleeding driver with the other and somehow managed to bring the careening car to a halt.

Jetter quotes Taylor Branch, author of *Parting the Waters*, a Pulitzer Prize–winning account of the early civil rights movement, as saying, "Bob Moses was the equivalent of Martin Luther King" (32).

In 1964 Robert Moses was risking his life to register poor Blacks as voters because voting was the key to a fuller participation in society. By 1994 Moses believed that mathematical literacy was the key to fuller participation in the economy. Since 1964 Moses has been on a personal odyssey that has included marriage, divorce, remarriage, children, protesting the Vietnam War, and living for ten years in Tanzania. Today, according to Jetter,

he's seeking to open another closed society: the world of educational opportunity denied to poor children, black and white alike. His trademark overalls and baby face are gone, but the curiously unblinking gaze and hushed voice haven't changed at all. And now, in the same Delta towns where he was beaten and jailed three decades ago, Moses has reappeared—retooled for the 90's as director of the Algebra Project, a crusade that experts say could revolutionize math education. (32)

In the early eighties, while re-enrolled at Harvard Graduate School, Moses became dissatisfied with the mathematics instruction his daughter was receiving. Out of that dissatisfaction was born the Algebra Project, an innovative, experienced-based approach that now has been disseminated widely across the country, including in rural Mississippi. As a result of these efforts, Robert Moses was awarded one of the rare, coveted MacArthur "genius" grants. Moses took his young students on the Cambridge and Boston subways, specifically the Red Line. They were able to master the concept of positive and negative numbers by assigning positive numbers to stations that were inbound toward Boston from Central Square and negative numbers to stations that were outbound.

A second African-American male who became nationally recognized in the 1960s is Richie Havens. Havens was a popular folk singer with a modest following before the Woodstock celebration in 1969. He opened Woodstock with a stirring performance of "Here Comes the Sun" and emerged as one of the performers who symbolized the 1960s. Havens still performs today, and in the summer of 1994 he appeared at one of the Woodstock twenty-fifth-anniversary celebrations. But for several years his energies also have been directed toward his organization the Natural Guard, an environmental education organization.

The Natural Guard, of which Havens is chairman of the board, began with fifteen students in New Haven in 1990. Presently, the organization is working with a thousand young people, including all but two of the original fifteen. Natural Guard activities continue in New Haven but also have been initiated in Brooklyn, several cities in New Jersey, on the island of Hawaii, and in Central America. According to Diana Edmunds, executive director of the organization, their goal is to engage and empower young people who often have no food at home and sometimes must dodge bullets on their way to school. Weekly meetings are held for the students, who range from kindergarten through high school, the largest contingent being middle school students. Recently, a bilingual group of kindergarten and first-grade students helped prepare a lead-awareness booklet that has been distributed to health and day-care centers. Other students have transformed vacant lots into organic vegetable gardens, in the process learning about science, mathematics, nutrition, economics, and health. Some of these students, who have subsisted on fast foods, had never used a knife and fork.

Social Support: The Role of the Family

Nathan Caplan and his associates studied the academic achievement of students from Indochinese refugee families. These children, many of whom had suffered from many years without schooling, "quickly adapted to their new schools and began to excel. Some of these children had lived for years in relocation camps." The authors concluded that although some of their findings were culturally specific, others pointed overwhelmingly to the pivotal role the family played in the children's academic success.[28]

The authors surveyed 6,750 recent immigrants in five urban areas in the United States. They found that these immigrants were "more ordinary" than those who had fled Saigon and other parts of Vietnam in 1975. "These newer displaced persons had had limited exposure to Western culture and knew virtually no English when they arrived. Often they came with nothing more than the clothes they wore" (36).

An in-depth qualitative study was made of 536 children from 200 families. The students consistently achieved high grades, especially in mathematics. In sharp contrast to findings from previous research, student achievement was positively correlated with the number of siblings. The researchers reasoned that sisters and brothers helped to transmit cultural values. The Indochinese high school students averaged three hours and ten minutes per day on homework compared with about one and one-half hours per day for American students. Many of the parents reported routinely reading aloud to young children.

Interestingly, one of the strongest predictors of high grades was parental belief in egalitarianism between the sexes, especially with respect to the roles of the parents. Consistent with prior research, children of parents who had a strong sense of personal efficacy, that is, who believed they had the ability to control external events, achieved higher grades. However, for these Indochinese families this sense of efficacy may turn out to be more one of familial efficacy than one of personal efficacy. The authors' findings ran contrary to expectations.

Rather than adopting American ways and assimilating into the melting pot, the most successful Indochinese families appear to retain their own traditions and values. . . . *Although different in origins, both traditional Indochinese and middle-class American values emphasize education, achievement, hard work, autonomy, perseverance and pride. The difference between the two value systems is one of orientation to achievement. American mores encourage independence and individual achievement, whereas Indochinese values foster interdependence and a family-based orientation to achievement.* (41, emphasis added)

Journalists have labeled Asian Americans the "model minority." There is no question that Asian Americans generally achieve well in mathematics and science and, in fact, cannot be appropriately labeled an underrepresented minority. Bob Suzuki, president of the California State Polytechnic University, Pomona, notes that this image first was projected in the mid-1960s. He and other scholars analyzed empirical data, such as the 1970 census, to determine how accurate the image was. They concluded that

the model minority characterization of Asian Americans was inaccurate, misleading, and a gross overgeneralization. They noted that while many Asian Americans had, indeed, achieved middle-class status, there was still a far larger proportion of people with incomes below the poverty level among Asian Americans than among Whites. In fact, many of these poorer Asian Americans lived, and still live, in inner-city ghettos, such as the Chinatowns and Manilatowns, which have been among the most impoverished areas of the cities in which they are located. . . . On the basis of such analyses, it was concluded that Asian Americans were typically underemployed in lower level positions that were not commensurate with their levels of education, age, and experience. Although Asian Americans had invested heavily in education, it did not appear to gain nearly as much earning power for Asian Americans as it did for Whites. This disparity was largely attributed to the persistence of racial discrimination.[29]

In this highly technical report, Suzuki does not mention his own direct experience with discrimination (as a child during World War II he was imprisoned in a U.S. government internment camp).

Audrey Yamagata-Noji analyzed physiological, sociological, and cultural factors associated with the educational achievement of Japanese American college students.[30] Several of the results from her survey of 180 students supported previous research: students who achieved high grades had parents who exerted control over them, praised them, and included them in adult conversations. However, the parents of these students did not teach their children academic skills at home; nor did they monitor school progress. "The Japanese cultural variable 'haji' (not shaming the family) correlated positively with high school grades. 'Haji,' 'sunao' (obedience to parents), and interdependency correlated highly with students' achievement self-concepts" (ii). Finally, most students in the sample reported that their parents expected or encouraged them to attend college and that they felt guilty when they did not do well in school.

Equity 2000, an intervention project of the College Board, is attempting to bring the success rates of minority students to the same level as that for nonminority students. According to Donald Stewart, president of the College Board, "If we are to make the fundamental changes in our educational system that will allow all students to enter and succeed in college, attitudes and beliefs about the ability of students to learn must change." He reported that at the end of Equity 2000's first year, which focused in great part upon educating teachers, the percentage of students that mathematics teachers and guidance counselors believed were capable of passing algebra and geometry increased dramatically. In the project's pilot site, Fort Worth, Texas, there was a concomitant 36 percent increase in the number of students who enrolled in algebra classes in one year.[31]

In a powerful study, Marian Maddox presents case studies about poverty-stricken, disadvantaged single African American mothers who attempted to break the poverty cycle by going to college.[32] The courage and determination that shine through in these narratives is striking. These women had to constantly fight against many barriers—family responsibilities, financial hardships, racism, eighteenth-century attitudes about the role of women—to achieve their goal of a college education.

Historically, dominant cultures have attempted to justify their subjugation of minority groups by asserting that the minorities were mentally inferior. This was nowhere more dramatic than when White, European colonial powers conquered countries where the population consisted of people of color. The emergence of brilliant thinkers from those populations has shocked the so-called experts and forced a reevaluation of the thesis.

Ramanujan: An Astonishing Example of Hidden Talent

For many decades, British intellectuals deprecated the intellectual capabilities of people from India. Against this background, the contributions of East Indians to mathematical and statistics are impressive. For example, Mahalanobis made fundamental contributions to the development of multiple group discriminant function analysis, including defining a complex multivariate generalized distance measure, Mahalanobis's D^2. But for sheer drama few stories in the history of science and mathematics can match that of the short, troubled life and extraordinary accomplishments of Srinivasa Ramanujan. Top graduate students in mathematics today will carefully study Ramanujan's theorems. Although he died young and had a brief professional career, Ramanujan is recognized as one of the towering figures in the history of mathematics.

One would not have guessed this based on his first twenty-five years. A sickly youth, Ramanujan grew up in an ordinary village in South India, stumbled through school, flunked out of college, could not keep a job, and had a troubled marriage. But he discovered mathematics as an adolescent, devouring a British volume he acquired, Loney's 1893 textbook *Trigonometry*. He became obsessed with mathematical games, puzzles, and theorems and recorded these in notebooks that he carried around South India as he lurched from failure to failure.

In 1913 he wrote to three of the world's leading mathematicians, at Cambridge University in England. One, G. H. Hardy, immediately recognized the genius that had produced these questions. A correspondence and then a friendship ensued. Hardy eventually arranged for Ramanujan to travel to Cambridge, where he proceeded to light up the mathematical world. However, his poor health continued, compounded by isolation from his family in India and his inability to adjust to British life. He died at the age of 32. In his powerful biography of Ramanujan, *The Man Who Knew Infinity*, Robert Kanigel writes:

"Srinivasa Ramanujan," an Englishman would later say of him, "was a mathematician so great that his name transcends jealousies, the one superlatively great mathematician whom India has produced in the last thousand years." His leaps of intuition confound mathematicians even today, seven decades after his death. His papers are still plumbed for their secrets. His theorems are being applied in areas— polymer chemistry, computers, even (it has recently been suggested) cancer— scarcely imaginable during his lifetime. And always the nagging question: What might have been, had he been discovered a few years earlier, or lived a few years longer?[33]

Kanigel notes how tenuous and fragile the events that led to Ramanujan's recognition were and speculates that things might have turned out differently.

It is a story of one man and his stubborn faith in his own abilities. But it is not a story that concludes, Genius will out—though Ramanujan's, in the main, did.

Because so nearly did events turn out otherwise that we need no imagination to see how the least bit less persistence, or the least bit less luck, might have consigned him to obscurity. In a way, then, this is also a story about social and educational systems, and about how they matter, and how they can sometimes nurture talent and sometimes crush it.

An incident from Ramanujan's teenage years underscores both his genius and his insecurities. When he was in high school, Ramanujan discovered how trigonometric functions could be expressed in a form that was unrelated to the right triangles, in which they were, superficially, rooted. But when Ramanujan found out that the great Swiss mathematician Leonhard Euler had made this very discovery 150 years earlier, he was so mortified that he hid the papers on which he had recorded the results in the roof of his house (50).

Why did the British-controlled educational system not recognize and nurture Ramanujan's genius? Consider this quotation from a report about India written by William Thackeray: "In India that haughty spirit, independence and deep thought which the possession of great wealth sometimes gives ought to be suppressed. They are directly averse to our power and interest. The nature of things, the past experience of all governments, renders it unnecessary to enlarge on this subject. We do not want generals, statesmen and legislators; we want industrious husbandmen."[34]

Twenty years after Ramanujan's death, E. H. Neville made the following observation:

Ramanujan's career, just because he was a mathematician, is of unique importance in the development of relations between India and England. India has produced great scientists, but Bose and Raman were educated outside India, and no one can say how much of their inspiration was derived from the great laboratories in which their formative years were spent and from the famous men who taught them. India has produced great poets and philosophers, but there is a subtle tinge of patronage in all commendation of alien literature. Only in mathematics are the standards unassailable, and therefore of all Indians, Ramanujan was the first whom the English knew to be innately the equal of their greatest men. The mortal blow to the assumption, so prevalent in the western world, that white is intrinsically superior to Black, the offensive assumption that has survived countless humanitarian arguments and political appeals and poisoned countless approaches to collaboration between England and India, was struck by the hand of Srinivasa Ramanujan.[35]

The same idea was expressed in 1946 by the statesman Jawaharlal Nehru:

Ramanujan's brief life and death are symbolic of conditions in India. Of our millions how few get any education at all; how many live on the verge of starvation. . . . If life opened its gates to them and offered them food and healthy conditions of living and education and opportunities of growth, how many among these millions would be eminent scientists, educationists, technicians, industrialists, writers, and artists, helping to build a new India and a new world?[36]

Mathematics and Culture

An excellent discussion of the links between mathematics, culture, philosophy, and reality, that is, the sociology of knowledge, can be found in David Bloor's book *Knowledge and Social Imagery.*[37] Bloor argues that mathematics is not immutable, that a sociology of mathematics (as opposed to a sociology of mathematicians) is possible. Questioning whether there can be an alternative mathematics, Bloor notes, "The idea that there can be variation in mathematics just as there is variation in social organisations appears to some sociologists to be a monstrous absurdity."[38] He quotes the sociologist William Stark, who stated, "Surely, there can only be one science of numbers, forever self identical in its content."[39] He contrasts Stark's statement with Oswald Spengler's claim that "there is not and cannot be number as such. There are several number worlds because there are several cultures."[40] Bloor adds that "Wittgenstein is reported to have read and been impressed by Spengler's book. He, too, embraces this 'monstrous absurdity' in his sociologically oriented 'Remarks on the Foundations of Mathematics.' Perhaps this explains the relative neglect of that work. Philosophers who feel at home with Wittgenstein's other writings often discern little coherence or sense in his account of mathematics."[41]

In a fascinating chapter, Bloor illustrates this debate by tracing the history of the concept of number, discussing historical differences about such questions as, Is one a number? the metaphysics of root two, and the assumption underlying the calculus and other procedures that a curve is really made up of many little straight lines, or infinitesimals.

Bloor concludes, "A number of cases . . . can be read as examples of alternative forms of mathematical thought to our own. The examples . . . have shown mathematics to be grounded in experience but experience which is selected according to varying principles and endowed with varying meaning, connections and uses."[42] In other words, another argument for *welcoming* people from diverse cultures to the mathematics and science enterprises is that their work may stretch, enliven, and reframe these fields.

Women in Science

Jadwiga Sebrechts began an article in the *Journal of NIH Research* with the following question:

What do the inventors of the following have in common?
- The cotton gin
- The microelectrode
- Nerve growth factor
- Nuclear fission
- COBOL computer language
- Apgar score
- Smallpox inoculation
- Tetracycline

A clue: It's the same thing that is common to the scientists who identified and catalogued more than 300,000 stars, who cofounded the Marine Biological Laboratory at Woods Hole, Mass., who founded ecology, who made the calculations necessary to split the atom, and who invented the branch of mathematics known today as functional analysis.[43]

The answer is that all these scientists were women.

Women and Science Careers

Bernadine Healy, former director of the National Institutes of Health, called it "astonishing . . . that young women pursue careers in science at all!" Healy sees one exception to the discouragingly subtle, and not so subtle, biases against women in American schools and colleges: "All women's colleges lose fewer of their science majors to other fields. Based on my own personal experience, I believe that women's colleges can engender an environment and a mindset in which there are no barriers based on gender, an environment that encourages women to pursue 'nontraditional' fields—like science and medicine."[44]

Bryn Mawr, a small woman's college, graduates more women physics majors than all but two institutions in the United States.[45] At Douglas College, of Rutgers University, a special residence hall has been created for women science students. It has computer and library resources, and ten women graduate students in science live in the dorm as mentors and tutors.

Sebrechts discusses a study by the American Association of University Women in which the authors observed that the perception by others that girls are less able in mathematics and science correlates, unfortunately, with a general loss of self-esteem among adolescent girls. "Even objective positive evaluations of competence in math and science, such as respectable grades, tend to be dismissed by the girls as irrelevant."[46] This research finding corresponds dramatically to the mathematics self-esteem results reported in chapter 4. Etta Falconer, director of science programs at Spelman College, said about Spelman students, "We expect them to succeed and they do."[47] This is what should be happening to both men and women, majority students and students of color, across the United States.

Table 5.8 compares the success of coeducational schools and women's colleges in recruiting and retaining women in science disciplines. A bulletin from the Women's College Coalition notes that "the percentage of majors in economics, math and the life sciences is higher in women's colleges today than it is even for men in coeducational colleges." And it notes that according to the Great Lakes College Association, "between 1970 and 1982, only 4.3 percent of women received their baccalaureate degrees from women's colleges, but these graduates went on to comprise 7.2 percent of all women with doctorates in math and physical sciences and 6.6 percent with doctorates in the life sciences."[48]

Those who persist in their studies and become researchers and professors often encounter a glass ceiling in academia. Jonathan Cole commented that even after taking into account factors "such as career interruptions and the quantity and assessed quality of research performance of men and women," he finds that "women are still less likely to be promoted to high academic rank. And when they are promoted, it is not apt to happen as quickly . . . the pattern of promotion to high rank has persisted for the past fifty years at much the same level."[49]

Table 5.8

Graduates of Coeducational and Women's Colleges Earning Degrees in Science Disciplines, 1986

Discipline	Coed colleges	Women's colleges
Economics	1.4	4.0
Life Sciences	3.6	5.4
Mathematics	1.5	2.3
Physical Sciences	1.2	1.7

SOURCE: J. S. Sebrechts, "The Cultivation of Scientists at Women's Colleges," *Journal of NIH Research* 4 (June 1992), 24.

NOTE: The figures represent data collected from the National Center for Educational Statistics, 1986.

Given that observation, data in a recent report by the American Mathematical Society and the Mathematical Association of America should not be surprising. The report notes that women make up 24 percent of U.S. citizens receiving doctorates in mathematics, which represents a 3–4 percent increase over previous levels. However, in the mid- to late 1980s only 16 percent of new professors hired in mathematics by American universities were women. Participants in a recent conference about the glass ceiling in mathematics concluded that the barriers to progress were subtle but important. For example, female students see few female professor role models and thus are less encouraged to pursue careers in mathematics.

According to figures from the Association for Women in Mathematics, the mathematics departments at the University of Chicago, Harvard, MIT, and Princeton are among those who have no tenured women on their faculty, and the mathematics department at Berkeley has only one.[50] Rhonda Hughes, chair of the mathematics department at Bryn Mawr College, says, "Mathematicians are decent types, but sadly, mathematics is still very much a man's world."[51]

In a recent article in *Science,* Marcia Barinaga discusses what she says is a very real issue for virtually all the women scientists she contacted for her article, namely, "the feeling that women, on average, run their labs, interact with colleagues, and pursue their careers in characteristically female ways, probably as a result of their cultural conditioning." Barinaga says that

If such a "female style" exists, it is certainly not absolute, and many researchers can tick off exceptions: women who operate more like the average male scientist, and men who seem to fit the putative female mold. Furthermore, there is no way to evaluate the science that a "female style" creates—whether it's better or worse than the science produced by the dominant male model. Nonetheless, many female scientists do feel that their style is not as readily accepted in the inner circles of research, and they argue that barriers to their approach must be broken down if they are to achieve fully equal status in the world of science.[52]

Beyond anecdotal evidence, this thesis has not been studied systematically and empirically. Several studies have indicated that women scientists publish fewer papers than their male counterparts, even when variables such as the quality of graduate training are controlled. Among the explanations proposed for this finding are that women wait until a paper is perfect before submitting it to a journal, while men more rapidly move to publication; and that eminent scientists, who are more likely to be male, choose different kinds of problems, with different publication possibilities, than do less established scientists, who tend to choose safer topics.

Among the skeptics that such a "female style" exists is a leading sociologist of science, Harriet Zuckerman. Zuckerman and Jonathan Cole examined the publications and citations of matched pairs of men and women scientists over the first twelve years of their career, following the receipt of doctorates in 1969 and 1970. They found that

women published slightly more than half (fifty-seven percent) as many papers as men, with that proportion decreasing somewhat as time passed. However, women now account for twenty-six percent of the most prolific scientists in the cohort (those who published at least 1.6 papers annually) as against just eight percent in the cohort of 1957–1958 in comparable years. Since highly productive scientists contribute disproportionately to the literature and presumably to the development of scientific knowledge, the increased representation of women in this group is significant.[53]

In another study, Cole and Zuckerman reported analyses indicating that gender differences in publication rates cannot be explained by marriage and family obligations of women. "Married women with children publish as much as their single female colleagues do." Further, "the divorce rate for both women and men is unrelated to published productivity." Cole and Zuckerman found that "married women scientists with children do pay a price to remain scientifically productive. They report having had to eliminate almost everything but work and family, particularly when their children were young. As an eminent psychologist observed, what goes first is 'discretionary time. I think I can only work effectively . . . fifty hours a week. . . . If I didn't have children, I'd probably read more novels . . . or go to more movies.'"[54]

Helen Astin studied the research experiences of men and women whose work is frequently cited. After comparing essays written by both male and female authors of highly cited works, Astin concluded:

When we examine their perceptions about what led them to undertake the highly cited research in the first place, women appear to be responding to others rather than being driven by their own quest. That is, they are less likely to undertake the work because they are interested in solving a problem, but rather that the work was the outcome of the dissertation or they were invited to prepare the piece. Furthermore, when it comes to explaining why their work is so frequently cited, the women appear to be more interested in how their work can be useful to others (their research can help and the findings can be applied by others). They also make more positive attributions about the importance of their work than do the men. They see their research as integrating knowledge and providing direction for further work: "a useful procedure for calculating the affinity of the drugs for the receptor"; "the hope that this approach might lead to a new type of cancer immunotherapy."

There were strong differences between the publishing experiences of social scientists and those of natural scientists. In fact, Astin says that "the results reported thus far suggest that overall, field may be more of a factor than gender in the experiences reported by scientists who produce highly cited research."[55]

Discrimination or bias against women can occur at all stages of the growth, education, and professional life cycle. Michele Paludi and Lisa Strayer found that college students judged a given article more favorably if they believed the author was male than they did if they believed the author was female. "This pro-male bias was present even for articles in feminine and sex-neutral fields. Furthermore, this bias was more evidenced when subjects perceived the sexually ambiguous author's name to be female instead of male."[56]

Obstacles and Barriers

Like the early African American scientists and inventors, the earliest women mathematicians had to overcome both prejudice and insufficient recognition of their work. For example, both Sophia Germaine, who received the grand prize of the French Academy of Sciences in 1816 for her paper "Memoir on the Vibrations of Elastic Plates," and Mary Fairfax Somerville, who presented a paper entitled "The Magnetic Properties of Violet Rays of the Solar Spectrum" to the Royal Society of London in 1826 and who subsequently was elected an honorary member of the Royal

Astronomical Society, were self-taught.[57] Both had to hide their studies of mathematics from their families, who did not approve of their daughters studying such material. Both received little or no formal training in mathematics. Somerville's personal study of mathematics was delayed for three years when she was married to a man who opposed the education of women. Many years later the Women's College at Oxford was named Somerville College in recognition of her achievements.

Because intelligent women were suspect, Sophia Germaine signed the name LeBlanc to her writings and letters. Similarly, Augusta Ada Byron Lovelace, arguably the world's first computer programmer, published under the initials A.A.L. Most students of statistics are not aware that one of the pioneers in this field was Florence Nightingale. In fact, Karl Pearson, in a letter to Sir Francis Galton, called her "the prophetess." Marti Rice and William Stallings have documented her accomplishments in the field of statistics, including calculating mortality rates, developing statistical records for hospitals, and conducting impact and evaluation studies.[58]

In the latest edition of her classic book *Overcoming Math Anxiety,* Sheila Tobias reports on one of the earliest studies of the links between gender and mathematics:

In 1974, John Ernest, a professor of mathematics at the University of California at Santa Barbara, put mathematics and sex on the public's agenda for the first time. Assigned to teach a freshman seminar about elementary statistics, Ernest decided to turn his seminar into an investigation of the relationships, real and imagined, between gender and performance in mathematics. His students fanned out into neighboring junior and senior high schools to interview teachers and students about girls' and boys' performance in mathematics. The results of their inquiry were nearly always the same. Both boys and girls, they were told, have a fair amount of trouble doing math, and most of them do not like the subject very much. The difference between them was that boys stuck with math, because they felt their careers depended on it and because they had more confidence than girls in their ability to learn it. The problem, concluded Ernest, was not math inability in females; it was their math avoidance at crucial stages of their schooling. Society expects males to be better than females at mathematics. This affects attitudes; attitudes affect performance; performance affects willingness to study more mathematics; and, eventually, males do better than females. His findings, modest though they were, were considered so important that the Ford Foundation published and distributed forty thousand copies of his little book.[59]

Tobias has led the way in articulating, developing, and describing the concepts "math anxiety" and "math avoidance." She suggests that there are several internal, though not innate, variables that cause girls to do more poorly than boys in many mathematics courses and tests. One of these is "female isolation." "Unless they are blessed with a math-oriented family, or collected in a special dormitory for math/science majors, girls find themselves isolated both in class and outside of class when it comes to math. Not having anyone to talk to about what they're learning, they fail to learn to *speak mathematics;* worse yet, they do not get the opportunity to extend their knowledge, their skills, and their imagination through discussion" (78).

Tobias found that boys attribute their success to ability and their failure to not having worked hard enough. Girls, conversely, attribute their success to effort or sometimes luck and their failure to lack of ability. Tobias adds that Gary Horne, who teaches mathematics to young adults in the juvenile system, observes that "disempowered groups in general—and not just women and girls—attribute failure to lack of ability" (81).

In their book *Failing at Fairness*[60] and related journal articles, Myra and David Sadker report on the persistent pattern of discrimination against girls and young women in American education. Their research focuses on verbal interaction patterns in classrooms. Among their findings:

- From grade school to graduate school, girls receive less teacher attention and less useful teacher feedback.
- Girls talk significantly less than boys do in class. In elementary and secondary school, they are eight times less likely to call out comments. When they do, they are often reminded to raise their hands while similar behavior by boys is accepted.
- Girls rarely see mention of the contributions of women in the curricula; most textbooks continue to report male worlds.
- Too frequently female students become targets of unwanted sexual attention from male peers and sometimes even from administrators and teachers.[61]

The authors note that when biology teachers are asked to assist students with microscopes, they tend to explain to the boys how to adjust the microscope but to make the adjustment directly for the girls. "Boys learn the skill; girls learn to ask for assistance" (18). In light of the work of the Sadkers and the consistent findings about the positive impacts of women's colleges, some high schools are experimenting with single-gender math and science classes. Preliminary results are that girls respond enthusiastically to such classes. They conclude, "Twenty years after the passage of Title IX, the law prohibiting gender discrimination in U.S. schools, it is clear that most girls continue to receive a second-class education" (14).

Grieb and Easley have studied patterns of communication in elementary school classrooms.[62] They began with the thesis that "persons with successful mathematics-based careers have, at an early time, achieved personal trust in their own intuitions and thus avoided becoming afraid of the social consequences of error." Through participant observation research, these researchers observed that some children are passive and compliant in solving problems exactly as the teacher has described. Others, who have more potential to become successful and creative in mathematics, challenge the limitations of the problem as designed by the teacher. What is crucial, according to Grieb and Easley, is how the teacher responds to this latter group of students.

We attempted to identify a social mechanism in primary schools which allows white, middle class male students who are creative in their study of mathematics to preserve an independent attitude while keeping females and minorities in an attitude of dependence on knowing the algorithm before proceeding with the problem.
   . . . while there may be other roles that are available to minorities and females, the "pale male math mavericks" very often have a distinct advantage over minorities and girls with similar mathematical creativity: they can develop habits of independent thinking in mathematics from early primary grades because they are not being expected by most teachers to conform to the social norms of arithmetic." (317)

Because of the practically assured success of white middle- or upper-class males, they are perceived as holding potential with less regard as to how hard they work or how dutiful they are in school. This implicit potential is one reason why teachers can allow white males who show some interest and capability in mathematics to pursue math in their own way. If the white male child also performs well and appears particularly bright, there is even less reason for forcing him to conform to standard procedures. (344)

In a thorough article entitled "Women in Science and Engineering," physicist-historian Stephen Brush asks, "What is preventing more women from going into science and engineering?" "There is no simple answer to this question," he says. "In the past two decades overt discrimination may have become covert, but it is still effective. And some new factors have emerged to reinforce the old obstacles."[63] Among the obstacles Brush cites are the negative popular culture stereotype of the scientists as a nerd, textbook portrayals of scientists and engineers that disproportionately discuss and picture males, wide-ranging publicity about the so-called mental inferiority of females, inadequate precollege preparation, biases in the SAT, cutbacks in financial aid, inappropriate teaching methods, sexist attitudes of professors and students, and the tradition of combative inter-actions among scientists. Among the remedies Brush proposes are deem-phasizing the SAT, giving publicity to recent research on cognitive sex differences, removing the "glass ceiling" in academia and other disincen-tives to women in industry, and funding intervention programs for the long haul.

With respect to the textbook portrayals of scientists and engineers, Brush observes,

The scientists and engineers mentioned or pictured in textbooks are almost always male. When a discovery made by a women is discussed, she is often not given credit. At the high school level, Marie Curie may be the only woman mentioned, perpetu-ating the belief that science has been created almost entirely by men. A striking example of the clumsiness of attempts to include women scientists is provided by a widely used high school physics text. C. S. Wu is pictured in the front of the book; the caption says she is well known for an experiment that disproved a basic princi-ple of physics, but does not say what the experiment was. The experiment, which demonstrates that parity is not conserved in certain interactions of elementary particles is discussed later in the same text, but Wu is not mentioned there! (406)

With respect to the continuing controversy over whether there are ge-netically based differences in brain functioning and capabilities between men and women, Brush notes that a 1974 book by Eleanor Maccoby and Carol Jacklin and a 1980 article in *Science* by Camilla Benbow and Julian Stanley both argue that there is evidence for some differences.[64] He quotes Patricia Campbell and Susan Geller, who assert that the Benbow-Stanley article "has been used to support and encourage the continuation of ineq-uity. The social implications of its publication may prove to be catastroph-ic."[65]

Brush summarizes findings from more recent research on cognitive sex differences:

—The "well-established" sex differences reported by Maccoby and Jacklin are actually very small.
—Many of the studies purporting to prove male superiority on spatial tests did not yield statistical significance.
—Cognitive sex differences have declined precipitously over the past three decades.
—There is strong evidence that the differences that do exist are not genetically based, but are environmentally based. For example, cross cultural studies have shown that females in some cultures do better than males on exactly the same tests and skills.

Brush concludes that "the more general thesis, that cognitive sex differences are innate, is therefore currently without any proof. . . . Reports of cognitive differences between the sexes received widespread publicity, perhaps in part because of hostility toward the women's movement. The studies that called cognitive sex differences into question, on the other hand, have received comparatively little attention. Thus misconceptions linger. Scientists and journalists have an obligation to correct them " (413–14).

One of Brush's final observations should be underscored: "When more women become successful scientists, the culture of science may change; it is very unlikely to change if women stay out of science" (415). I shall return to this point again in this book. I will argue that science progresses, as Thomas Kuhn has observed, when creative people shed the constraints of current theory to propose innovative shifts in our frame of reference, that is, our paradigms. One liability of a system that recruits only Anglo males with a particular personality profile is that the range of potential creative solutions to scientific problems is truncated.

Research has consistently revealed that the SATs overestimate the college performance of males and underestimate that of females. A muchdebated issue is males' consistently better performance than females' on the SAT. Phyllis Rosser has examined this SAT gender gap. Among her more interesting findings is that certain SAT items favor one sex over another by 10 percent or more. Table 5.9 lists the seven SAT verbal items and the ten mathematics items for which this is true. (In the latter items, all differences were in favor of males.) Rosser observes:

When estimating their math and English abilities, both men and women perceived their abilities to be more in line with their test scores than with their grades. Unfortunately, this meant that girls believed themselves to be less able than their grades would indicate, and less able than boys. And girls were less likely to aspire to "super-elite" colleges. Further, sex differences in these two areas also persisted when SAT scores were controlled for, with men ranking their abilities moderately higher than women and aspiring to "super-elite" colleges at a moderately higher rate, suggesting the complexity of the operation of sex bias in education.[66]

Cognitive Style and Self-Confidence

Commenting on U.S. Department of Education findings that high school girls score about five points lower than high school boys nationally on mathematics tests, Patricia Clark Kenscaft, a mathematics professor at Montclair State College in New Jersey, noted that centuries ago Europeans

Table 5.9

SAT Verbal and Math Items Favoring One Sex by at Least 10 Percent

Section	Item No.	Description	Female % minus male %
Verbal			
1	No. 1	"setback," opposite "improvement"	−10.7
1	No. 5	"sheen," opposite "dull finish"	+18.3
1	No. 23	author's tone, science passage	−11.8
1	No. 44	"mercenary" is to "soldier"	−15.7
4	No. 21	"pendant" is to "jewelry"	+ 9.6
4	No. 24	"love" is to "requite"	+14.5
4	No. 31	"betrayal" (in human relations item)	+10.2
Math			
2	No. 8	"liters per hour"	−10.3
2	No. 15	"chore 994th boy will have at boys' camp"	−12.3
2	No. 16	"number of boy with chore at boys' camp"	−15.6
2	No. 19	"parallelogram ratios"	−12.2
2	No. 20	"$\frac{1}{6}$ as decimal, sum of digits"	−10.7
2	No. 21	"basketball team win/loss record	−27.0
2	No. 22	"$<(a - b)<$"	−11.0
2	No. 25	"n as odd integer"	−10.8
5	No. 17	"length of right triangle"	−10.7
5	No. 25	"inequalities with x^2, $-x$"	−10.6

SOURCE: Adapted from P. Rosser, *The SAT Gender Gap: Identifying the Causes* (Washington, D.C.: Center for Women Policy Studies, Apr. 1993), 31–32.

believed that if a girl learned geometry her internal organs would be so upset that she would not be able to bear children. "Centuries from now people will laugh, like we laugh at those Europeans, about reasons why girls score lower on standardized math tests than boys."[67]

Jacquelynne Eccles has developed a model that predicts academic choices on the basis of expectancies for success, cultural norms, experience, aptitude, and personal beliefs and attitudes. The model helps explain why few women pursue careers in science and engineering despite their own track record of success in early studies in those areas. "If anything," Eccles observes, "the elementary school females reported slightly more confidence than the males in their English ability. Sex differences, however, began to emerge in junior high school, at which point the females had lower estimates of their math ability than did the males. The size of this sex difference grew as the students moved into high school."[68]

Eccles concludes,

It appears that there are certain kinds of learning environments that are not particularly conducive to most females' motivation to study math and science. These characteristics include competition, social comparison, high use of public drill, and domination of student-teacher interaction by a few students. In contrast, there are certain kinds of learning environments that appear to be more beneficial to females. These include controlled hands-on experience, use of nonsexist and nonracist materials, cooperative or individualized learning formats that ensure full participation by all children in the class, and active career counseling. [One researcher] has labeled this latter type of classroom a "girl-friendly" classroom. What is interesting about this set of characteristics is that they facilitate the motivation and performance of minority students and low achieving males as well.[69]

Hazel Markus and Daphna Oyserman have reviewed the literature on gender differences in cognitive style. In a chapter called "Gender and Thought: The Role of the Self-Concept," they begin by saying that it is important to acknowledge at the outset that "this body of research is unsystematic, largely atheoretical, and the gender-related differences obtained are usually small." Discussing the literature on differences between men and women in field dependence and spatial abilities, they say that "most recent explanations center on brain-based differences such as sex-related differences in brain lateralization. Building on the early suggestion that these differences are probably best interpreted as a reflection of individual differences in cognitive style, we suggest that differences in how men and women represent themselves is another causal factor worthy of serious consideration."[70] Furthermore, they suggest that the differences in how men and women represent themselves relate to the fact that boys are encouraged to separate from their mother at an earlier age than girls.

With respect to gender differences in cognitive ability, Oakes observes,

A recent reanalysis and synthesis of studies of gender differences performed over the past twenty years makes most of these debates moot: Linn and Hyde (in press) report that gender differences in mathematics and science abilities have dwindled to almost nothing over the past twenty years. While one sex difference remains (males mentally rotate figures more rapidly), girls' poorer performance can be remedied with training. Most important, growing numbers of solid theoretical and empirical studies are demonstrating that cognitive skills can be learned . . . and that both girls and minorities can acquire them. . . . Thus, even if important group differences in cognitive abilities do exist, they may not necessarily be unalterable. That is, interventions can be constructed to overcome these differences and, potentially, the achievement disparities they cause.[71]

Concerning the role of self-confidence, Oakes observes that children's belief in their ability is linked to their mathematics performance and to selecting college courses and majors in mathematics and science. Beginning in junior high school boys will have a higher self-concept than girls who actually are equally able. In other words, the self-confidence differences precede the differences in performance and course selection.

In light of the findings I reported above about the self-esteem of college freshmen, the following statement by Oakes is instructive: "One recent study found that male college students tended to attribute their difficulties to external factors, e.g., the inherently difficult nature of the course material or poor instructors, whereas women tended to place the blame on their own perceived inadequacy."[72] And Sheila Tobias reports that in a 1991 survey of students at Barnard (an all-women's college) who scored well above average on precollege quantitative tests, students whose ability in mathematics ought to have inclined them toward science, "twenty-five percent indicated that their previous achievements in mathematics did not translate either into a desire to continue or into increased confidence." In fact, it was their "desire to avoid mathematics" that had a significant effect on their career choice.[73]

According to Oakes, it is well known that teacher expectations can influence student performance.

The phenomenon is documented, for example, in the series of studies following Rosenthal and Jacobson [*Pygmalion in the Classroom*] and the more recent literature on "effective schools". . . . When teachers differentiate expectations on the basis of race, gender, or handicapping conditions, these expectations are likely to erect barriers for minorities, girls, and physically disabled students. Additionally, because of their less-powerful positions in society, lower-class and minority children are more influenced by teacher expectations. . . . The same hypothesis may apply to girls and physically handicapped students.[74]

In 1989 Lynn Friedman conducted a meta-analysis of recent studies on sex differences in mathematics.[75] Systematic and rigorous analysis and comparison of many studies, combined with the results from an earlier meta-analysis by Maccoby and Jacklin[76] and analyses of SAT gender differences, suggest that the gender difference in mathematical performance, if it exists, is very small. Furthermore, reported gender differences have been decreasing over time.

Carol Klein conducted an extensive review of both the literature and data from assessment tests to determine what factors influence the interest and achievement of girls and young women in science.[77] Among her findings were that

—Girls have less direct, hands-on experience with materials than they would like (28).
—On assessment tests boys scored better on items that related, directly or indirectly, to activities that boys participated in more often, for example, using flashlights and batteries. Conversely, girls scored

higher on items that related to activities that girls participated in more often, for example, opening a jar and using heat. "Boys did better on test items that had to do with mechanics, forces, and model construction. Girls did better on those about plants or health-related topics" (29).

—Both boys and girls perceive science, particularly physical science, as "masculine." This image is conveyed by textbooks, textbook illustrations, by so-called sex-appropriate toys, and the like.

—While girls do as well as, or better than, boys with respect to tests of spatial abilities in the early elementary grades, the pattern is reversed after that. Some researchers consider these differences favoring boys to be genetic; most, however, believe "that the disparity comes from differences in the in-school and out-of-school activities of boys and girls" (29).

—There are far too few role models for young girls or women actively engaged in science. This is because of the perpetration of the image of science as masculine, an image that is culturally defined. Klein notes that in Poland "societal views differ, and sixty percent of the women go into science" (30). Connected to this societal expectation is a scheduling phenomenon that mitigates against girls choosing science. Science courses are often scheduled at the same time as language, writing, music, or art courses, the assumption being that the former are largely for boys and the latter are largely for girls.

—Girls generally achieve more in science and show greater interest in science in single-sex schools than in coeducational schools.

—Girls tend to be more comfortable with the traditional lecture approach and more intimidated by an open-ended, hands-on, experimental approach. However, they have no such hesitations in elementary school.

Power and the Concept of Intelligence

Historically, elites often have justified their positions of power by asserting that the less powerful lack the intelligence to succeed in society. The early Roman conquerors believed that the inhabitants of what is now Great Britain were much less intelligent than Romans. Nineteenth-century European imperialists mocked the alleged intellectual inferiority of colonial populations. As I discuss in the conclusion, a prominent British scientist argued that empirical evidence from tests of aptitude revealed that Jewish people were not intelligent enough to benefit from schooling. At one time, it was popular in scientific circles to try to measure the brain size of people from various ethnic groups.

Even today, assumptions about intelligence and who possesses it often are implicit in discussions of education and its problems. Such assumptions include the notion that highly intelligent men marry highly intelligent women and are likely to succeed economically; and that the children of the poor are not as intelligent and therefore it is no surprise that they fail in school. The question may be asked, Why invest so heavily in educational resources for African American children, when they are not as intelligent as majority children? Or, Since SAT results show us that there is a gender gap in mathematics, why not just accept the fact that girls can't do as well as boys in mathematics and science?[78]

Such unjustified assertions are at the core of the negative expectations about mathematics and science education that permeate our society. They go a long way toward explaining why "under-represented groups" are underrepresented in the study of mathematics and science (and other fields). I would like to isolate and analyze the assumptions implicit in such assertions. In brief, I will argue that

— *Even if these assumptions were true,* they would not change the fundamental arguments and recommendations in this book.
— Fewer and fewer social scientists are clinging to the notion of a single, unitary "intelligence." Attempts to measure head and brain sizes were rejected by most scientists years ago.
— Discussion of differences in the intelligence levels of population subgroups usually involves the notion of inherited aptitude. Arguments based on this notion display considerable confusion about the manner in which genetics and environment interact.

What if science had indeed demonstrated that one gender or ethnic group was superior to another in native intelligence? This would not alter the demand expressed throughout this book that mathematics and science education be provided for all students. If such differences had been shown to exist, the variation between groups would be small relative to the variation within groups. Consequently, if such assertions were true, say, in the case of males and females, there would be two overlapping normal curves, one for young men and one for young women. A tiny percentage of those in the male normal curve would have a higher I.Q. score than that of the highest woman, and a tiny percentage of those from the female normal curve would have an I.Q. score below that of the lowest scoring male. The vast majority of both young men and young women would fall in the same I.Q. range.

Aptitude is but one of many factors that affect whether a student masters a subject and can successfully apply that knowledge in subsequent studies and in the workplace. Learning is affected by the health of the student, the quality of the teaching, the nature of the curriculum, and other factors discussed at length in this book. As we have seen, expectations and self-concept play a vital role. So does hard work. Perhaps the most interesting finding from the cross-cultural studies comparing Japanese and American students, studies in which the Japanese students excel, is that Japanese teachers attribute student success or failure to hard work, while American teachers attribute student success or failure to innate ability. In conclusion, while there is no convincing evidence that one group is more intelligent than another, *even if there were,* my conclusions and recommendations about mathematics and science education would remain unchanged.

In fact, there is little or no evidence to justify such assertions. Consider the central concept that intelligence is a unitary, underlying, innate trait. This "research finding" really was an artifact of the statistical techniques used in the early studies of intelligence. In his book *The Mismeasure of Man,* which every educator should be required to read, Stephen Jay Gould questions a definition of intelligence based upon tests developed through the use of orthogonal factor analysis.[79] The error being made here, one that is repeated frequently in research, is epistemological rather than statistical. Researchers employ a mathematical technique to simplify and summarize data, but they mistakenly claim that the statistical results, determined in part by arbitrary analysis assumptions, actually represent an underlying social or psychological reality.

Consider the mathematics and interpretation of factor analysis, a set of procedures developed to summarize, condense, and reframe matrices of multivariate data. The essential goal of factor analysis is to replace a large set of variables, say, fifty variables, with a few new variables, or "factors," say, four factors, that contain most of the statistical variation from the original variables. The technique relies upon a mathematical procedure that yields *eigenvalues* and *eigenvectors*. These procedures are applied to a matrix of Pearson product-moment correlation coefficients.

The idea of a single, underlying, general intelligence factor received its greatest legitimation from the work of Charles Spearman. Gould has shown that Spearman's *g*, which purports to measure general intelligence, is largely an artifact of Spearman's use of a specific form of factor analysis: principal components. In this method, the data are analyzed so as to produce the largest possible single factor. Other forms of factor analysis, based on different assumptions, would have yielded two or three "medium-sized factors." According to Gould,

This error of reification has plagued the technique since its inception. It was "present at the creation" since Spearman invented factor analysis to study the correlation matrix of mental tests and then reified his principal component as *g* or innate, general intelligence. Factor analysis may help us to understand causes by directing us to information beyond the mathematics of correlation. But factors, by themselves, are neither things nor causes; they are mathematical abstractions. Since the same set of vectors . . . can be partitioned into *g* and a small residual axis, or into two axes of equal strength that identify verbal and arithmetical clusters and dispense with *g* entirely, we cannot claim that Spearman's "general intelligence" is an ineluctable entity necessarily underlying and causing the correlations among mental tests. (254–55)

The notion that there are multiple intelligences is precisely what current psychological and educational researchers, like Howard Gardner, whose work is considered to be on the cutting edge, have concluded.[80]

Arguments about the epistemological implications of analytical assumptions constitute a special case of arguments about the links between mathematics and reality. Some would argue that mathematical elegance and beauty underlie the seemingly chaotic physical reality we observe and even would attribute theological characteristics to mathematics. Galileo once remarked that mathematics is the language with which God wrote the universe. I know a statistics professor who asks each of his students to gather a thousand maple leaves and measure precisely the distance between the first and third points of the leaf. He then plots and graphs the combined data points from all students in the class and demonstrates that the result is a perfectly defined statistical normal curve. Some students are awe-struck when they first discover the precise mathematical relationships underlying physical phenomena. But the key philosophical question is whether these mathematical properties represent underlying realities or simply complex assumptions that help us explain and predict the empirical reality. That question obviously is beyond the scope of this book. But researchers and statisticians need to be sensitized to these issues.

The perpendicular coordinates utilized in these analyses are referred to as *Cartesian coordinates*, after the French mathematician René Descartes. The French, incidentally, reify mathematics. Several years ago I attended an international conference convened in a suburb of Paris by a French technical institute. The purpose of the meeting was to assess the relative merits of objective, multiple-choice tests and the traditional French baccalaureate examination in college admissions. At one point I engaged in a debate with the dean of one of France's leading medical schools. He stated flatly that since his school wanted to admit only the most promising students, rigorously selected, there was only one criterion for admission, namely, the student's score on a demanding mathematics test! Much as I like mathematics, I replied that if I were undergoing surgery, I would hope that the surgeon had demonstrated skills and knowledge in other areas besides mathematics when he or she entered medical school.

Incidentally, Gould reports the repeated failures of earlier researchers who tried to compare head and brain sizes of various groups. First, he demonstrates why it is virtually impossible to measure brain size accurately. More to the point, such researchers kept generating study "results" that demonstrated that prison inmates in Britain clearly had larger brains than the leading scholars at Oxford or Cambridge.[81]

Even if one accepts the increasingly dubious notion of a generalized intelligence or the notion that I.Q. is inherited (or partially inherited), one must be circumspect in considering the erroneous and confusing logic that some invoke. Christopher Jencks articulates some of these errors well:

In order to illustrate both the basic logic of genetic explanations and their potential pitfalls, it is helpful to begin with an example in which the causal links are relatively clear, such as hair length. In our society variation in hair length is largely attributable to the fact that some people have their hair cut shorter than others. In most cases, moreover, men cut their hair shorter than women. This means that if you are born with two X chromosomes, your hair usually ends up longer than if you were born with an X and a Y chromosome. In a statistical sense, therefore, the presence or absence of a Y chromosome predicts much of the variation in hair length—let us say sixty percent. But the fact that genes currently predict hair length fairly accurately tells us nothing about society's ability to alter hair length. If men and women became convinced that equal hair length was important, achieving this result would be no harder than making hair length equal among males alone. Likewise, if some zealot decided that shorter (or longer) hair would contribute to human happiness, he would be a fool to abandon his campaign simply because someone pointed out that people's genes currently "explained" sixty percent of the variation in hair length. And if some social scientist read a study showing that genes explained sixty percent of the variation in hair length, he would be an even greater fool to conclude, as many now do, that environmental influences explained only forty percent. Environmental variation (in the way people have their hair cut) would explain virtually all the variation in hair length, despite the fact that genetic variation explained sixty percent.[82]

Jencks continues,

This means that heritability estimates set a lower bound on the explanatory power of the environment, not an upper bound. If genetic variation explains sixty percent of the variation in IQ scores, environmental variation *must* explain the remaining forty percent, but it *may* explain as much as 100 percent. If, for example, genes affected IQ scores solely by affecting children's appearance or behavior, and if their appearance or behavior then affected the way they were treated at home and at school, everything genes explained would also be explicable by environmental factors. In such a world, environmental differences would explain 100 percent of the variation in IQ scores. But if genetic variation explained sixty percent of the variation in children's environments, there would be no contradiction between the claim that genes explained sixty percent of the variation in IQ scores and the claim that the environment explained 100 percent. (107)

A Concluding Comment

The arguments in this book, both problems and solutions, apply to middle-class White males as well as to the groups discussed in this chapter. But poor people, women, and people of color each face additional barriers. Furthermore, the obstacles accumulate rapidly for a person who falls into two or three of these categories, for example, a poor, African American, young woman. Ultimately, all of the students who are "underrepresented" in the study of mathematics and science represent an enormous resource for the U.S. economy. When the meaningless but powerful barriers to their studying and achieving in mathematics and science are destroyed, the technical skills and knowledge available in the American workplace will increase dramatically. At the level of the individual, the removal of these barriers can transform lives.

SIX

Workshop Groups and Calculus Instruction

> The carver . . . rarely sets out, at least consciously, to carve, say, a seal, but picks up the ivory, examines it to find its hidden form and, if that's not immediately apparent, carves aimlessly until he sees it, humming and chanting as he works. Then he brings it out: seal, hidden, emerges. It was always there: he didn't create it; he releases it; he helped it step forth. Edmund Carpenter, Frederick Varley, and Robert Flaherty, *Eskimo*

The need for a higher level of scientific literacy among American students and workers has already been examined. Projected changes in the demographic composition of the American work force during the next twenty-five years were contrasted with the underrepresentation of women, minorities, and poor people in technical fields. Trail-breaking research by Uri Treisman, along with follow-up research by Martin Bonsangue and others, suggests one dramatic solution to these problems.

Treisman developed calculus workshop study groups in which minority students have not only achieved, they have excelled beyond anyone's expectations.[1] It is very important to understand why the Treisman model has worked and what this means for the development of a talented technocracy in America. As we shall see, there are two crucial components to this success story:

—Students study in groups in addition to their individual study.
—Students are expected to excel and to do extra, more difficult homework problems. This is *not* a remedial approach.

Perhaps this model is most noteworthy for the theories it rejects. The students who succeeded in Treisman's workshops and in subsequent workshops across the country were underrepresented minority students, often from poor or disadvantaged backgrounds. Their success in the workshop environment sometimes surpassed that of Anglos and Asians studying the same subject at the same institution. Thus, these data provide yet another basis for rejecting the notion that some students, because of gender or ethnic background, are less capable of mastering calculus—and, by implication, other mathematical and scientific disciplines. These findings also refute the notion that growing up in poverty or in an environment with a high incidence of neighborhood violence, dysfunctional families, health problems, and the like rules out a technical career or that attending a less respected elementary or secondary school with limited resources rules out success. Certainly, growing up in poverty, with the associated social and family problems, makes it much more difficult for a young person to succeed in technical fields. But it can be done, and the benefits to the individual, his or her family, and society are almost incalculable. Furthermore, Uri Treisman has come up with an approach that facilitates such success.[2]

The Berkeley Calculus Workshop

Treisman's original research is vitally important and should be examined in depth. It is presented in its most detailed form in his 1985 dissertation, *A Study of the Mathematics Performance of Black Students at the University of California, Berkeley.* Treisman observes at the outset that "I had come to question the efficacy of individualized tutoring, self-paced instruction, and short courses aimed at the development of studies skills—the traditional pedagogical arsenal of special programs for minorities. . . . These programs were remedial underpinnings: they focused on minority students' weaknesses rather than on their strengths" (2). He continues:

In the Fall of 1975, while developing a training program for Mathematics Department teaching assistants, I became aware of the high rate at which Black students were failing freshman calculus at Berkeley. I had made it my practice to speak with the T.A.s about the weak and strong students in their teaching sections, and the regularity with which Black students appeared within the former group and Chinese students within the latter struck me as an issue that should be addressed in the training sessions. With this in mind, I began to seek the reasons for this apparent difference in performance. (4)

Treisman then interviewed twenty African American and twenty Chinese students, asking them about their use of instructors' office hours, whom they studied with, how much they studied, and so on. In addition, he asked the students to prepare a report, from memory, of how they had spent their time during the three days preceding the interviews. So far, these are standard research techniques. But Treisman added a wrinkle that produced startling results: he asked permission to accompany the students while they studied. "Many agreed, and over a period of eighteen months I accompanied these students to the library, their dormitory rooms, and their homes in the hope that I might see first-hand how they went about learning and doing mathematics" (5).

Obviously, the students' behavior was not unaffected by the presence of a mathematics instructor looking over their shoulder while they studied. "The students typically responded to their discomfort by asking me questions," notes Treisman, "and I to mine by rolling up my sleeves and helping them with their homework" (5). While this interaction would conflict with the demands of a rigorous experimental design, it facilitated the communication that was so important for Treisman's work in this heuristic, or hypothesis-generating, stage. Under these circumstances, the students really opened up.

Treisman presents some case study narratives about the experiences of several students to illustrate the challenge. Here are some excerpts from his narrative about a student named Joe.

Joe graduated from a predominantly Black high school in East Oakland. . . . few students from this high school went on to college, and most of those who had come to Berkeley had been academically unsuccessful. . . . Joe was president of his Junior class and was interested in school affairs, but he felt that preparing for college required that he hold himself apart from his classmates. . . . Joe was actively recruited by Berkeley (his high school GPA was above 3.8), and was admitted directly into the College of Engineering. . . . Joe's first few weeks at Cal were difficult. He had trouble understanding his professors' lectures and was often unable to complete his homework. When he received a D on both his calculus and computer science mid terms, he was stunned. He believed he was well prepared for the University, and he knew he was trying hard to excel. . . . upon learning at the end of the term that he had failed both Chemistry and Computer Science—the final examinations contained few questions on material that Joe had reviewed—he decided to refrain from all social activity and to devote even more time to study. This new regimen, however, had little effect on his performance. After his winter quarter mid terms, Joe stopped going to class; by then he was depressed and believed no matter what he did, no matter how hard he tried, he would fail his courses. (6–7)

Joe withdrew from Berkeley at the end of the academic year.

Treisman also gives a case study example of an African American student from a predominantly White high school who experienced difficulty adjusting to the university. Treisman observes that "among Black students in the Berkeley 1975 freshman class, only two of the twenty-one students who had enrolled in first-term calculus (Math 1A) went on to complete the final course in sequence (Math 1C) with a higher grade than C."

What did Treisman find when he compared the study habits of Chinese and African American students? First, African American students almost invariably studied alone. In contrast, most of the Chinese students studied with other Chinese students. This allowed them to have support and intellectual exchanges; they tried to work out homework problems and the like, and they shared grapevine information about the course and the university. For example, they discovered that the professors' expectation of two hours of study for one hour of class was a serious underestimate. The Chinese students averaged fourteen hours of study per week for a four-unit class, while the African American students had been devoting the eight hours per week that the professors recommended. The Chinese students critiqued one another's work, correcting errors and suggesting innovative solutions. Compounding the performance discrepancy was the tendency for African American students to avoid remedial tutoring programs. These were students who had excelled in high school, many of them valedictorians, and they identified such programs with low-achieving students. They rarely approached their teaching assistants. "But, even when they did, their inability to define their needs clearly coupled with the low expectations that many T.A.'s held for the academic achievement of Black students usually precluded a fruitful exchange" (19).

Treisman designed a workshop to confront the problems his observational research had identified. Following a short pilot, the workshop program began in the fall of 1978. Participation was voluntary, and the students typically met for two hours a day, three or four days each week. "Only one of the forty-two participants in the 1978–79 workshop failed the calculus class, and more than half of the students received grades of B– or better" (29). Following this initial success, the program was expanded, and external funding was received in the form of a three-year grant from the Funds for the Improvement of Post-Secondary Education. The program grew rapidly—within four years over three hundred students were participating—but Treisman notes that the guiding philosophical principles remained the same:

(1) the focus on helping minority students to excel at the University, rather than merely to avoid failure;

(2) the emphasis on collaborative learning and the use of small-group teaching methods; and

(3) the faculty sponsorship, which has both nourished the program and enabled it to survive. (30–31)

The program would begin with an orientation session. "Throughout the orientation, students are warned of the dangers of studying in isolation from their peers. They are encouraged to seek out classmates who share their high standards and goals, and to form study groups—even if they do not wish to participate in (the program)" (38). Since students' success seems to be so closely tied to workshop participation, Treisman's description of those sessions assumes particular importance.

A visitor entering a workshop session might mistake it at first for a noisy study hall or a lively math club meeting. Many of the students are engaged in discussion, some huddled in groups of three or four, some in pairs. Several students appear to be joking; others are working on a problem by themselves, ignoring the buzz about them.

But after observing for a while, the visitor perceives the organization of the workshop more clearly. The grouping of students is transient; the small clusters form and reform to compare notes on the various problems that appear on a worksheet that has been distributed at the beginning of the session. Occasionally, a student will address the entire group, asking in a loud voice if anyone has solved a particular problem.

Meanwhile, the workshop leader circulates unobtrusively, observing the students at work on the problems he has chosen for them. From time to time he sits down a short distance behind one of the groups and listens in for a few minutes. He might move on without addressing the group at all, or he might join in the discussion. Quite often, after working with a group, the leader takes one of its members aside for a brief period of private instruction.

On occasion, the leader stops the proceedings and addresses the group as a whole. He might comment on a group's work, discuss one of the more perplexing worksheet problems, or ask one of the students to present his work to all in attendance. Such interruptions typically account for about twenty minutes of the two-hour session. During the remaining time, it is the students who seem to be in control; each is free to choose the problems on which he works and the students with whom he discusses his results. (41–42)

The workshop leaders spend considerable time preparing for the sessions; most of that time is devoted to creating problems. These include problems like those on tests, problems designed to reveal individual student deficiencies, problems that illustrate major course concepts, problems to provide experience with mathematical symbolism and language, and "street mathematics," that is, computational shortcuts.

Treisman notes that the leader's role is not to duplicate the instruction provided by the teaching assistants.

The leader's role is more like a manager or moderator than an instructor. *The basic premise of this workshop instruction is that through the regular practice of testing their ideas on others, students will develop the skills of self criticism essential not only for the development of mathematical sophistication, but for all intellectual growth.* Moreover, by continually explaining their ideas to others, students acquire the same benefits of increased understanding that teachers themselves regularly experience. (45–46, emphasis added)

Students do not participate in the workshop during their sophomore year and are discouraged from studying there. However, they are not simply dumped, unprepared, into deep water after their freshman year, a year in which virtually all of them have been successful at calculus. Rather, considerable attention is given to providing them with the skills and resources that will carry over into their subsequent undergraduate studies. For example, they are encouraged to maintain the network of friends developed during the workshop sessions and to become actively involved in other campus organizations.

When the calculus grades achieved by African American workshop students were contrasted with those of African American nonworkshop students for the years 1973–84, "the principal finding" was that "the average grade earned by Black workshop participants has been approximately one full grade higher than that earned by Black students not participating in the program" (62) (see table 6.1). More than half of the workshop students received a B- or better in Math 1A, compared with fewer than one-fourth of the nonworkshop students (64). Additional analysis revealed that the workshop students consistently outperformed nonworkshop students in the courses following Math 1A, for example, in the second- and third-term calculus courses.

African American workshop students are considerably less likely than African American nonworkshop students to drop out of school in the two years following this calculus course, that is, at the end of two and a half years of college. Furthermore, workshop students were far more likely to graduate from college than were nonworkshop students. The rates for workshop students, for example, the graduation rates, were roughly comparable to those of nonminority students at Berkeley, while the rates for nonworkshop participants were substantially lower. Finally, African

Table 6.1

*Mean Grade Earned in Math 1A by African
American Students, 1973–1984*

Year	Nonworkshop students	Workshop students
1973	1.8	
1974	1.5	
1975	2.0	
1976	1.4	
1977	1.9	
1978	1.1	2.4
1979	1.9	2.7
1980	1.5	2.8
1981	1.5	2.6
1982	1.5	2.7
1983	1.8	2.7
1984	1.4	2.5

SOURCE: P. U. Treisman, "A Study of the Mathematics Performance
of Black Students at the University of California, Berkeley" (Ph.D.
diss., University of California, Berkeley, 1985).

American workshop students were more likely to persist in a mathematics-based major until graduation than were African American nonworkshop students. When SAT level was controlled—that is, when students who entered Berkeley with the same SAT level were compared—the African American workshop students outperformed all other groups in Math 1A, including the White and Asian students!

Despite these impressive achievements, a reader of this report might ask whether these workshops would be effective at other institutions. After all, the University of California at Berkeley is one of the top universities in the country, and students who are accepted there, including minority students, have already demonstrated that they are outstanding. Also, would these same effects be observed among students from other underrepresented minority groups, for example, Latinos?

The Calculus Workshop Programs at California State Polytechnic Institute, Pomona

The most extensive application of the calculus workshop model has been at the California State Polytechnic Institute in Pomona. Martin Bonsangue conducted a thorough, systematic evaluation of this program, in which the majority of participants have been Latinos. The evaluation focused upon a sample of 133 workshop and 187 nonworkshop Latino American, African

Table 6.2
*Best Calculus Grade Means for Workshop and
Nonworkshop Minority Students, 1986–1991*

Course	Workshop group	Nonworkshop group
M114	2.67	2.07
M115	2.65	1.91
M116	2.48	1.80
M214	2.66*	2.26
M215	2.56*	1.97
M216	2.61*	2.18

SOURCE: Adapted from M. V. Bonsangue and D. E. Drew,
"Long-Term Effectiveness of the Calculus Workshop" (report to
the National Science Foundation, Apr. 1992), 4.
*Former workshop student.

American, and Native American students who were followed for a five-year period.[3] Both the treatment and comparison groups consisted largely of Latino students (87 percent of the workshop students and 85 percent of the nonworkshop students were Latino). Both groups also contained mostly men (74 percent of the workshop students and 80 percent of the nonworkshop students). The workshop program was patterned after the Berkeley experience. Students met in groups to work on calculus problems twice a week for two hours each session. Statistical comparisons revealed no significant differences between the workshop and nonworkshop students in terms of their background and other pre-intervention variables such as SAT scores, high school grade point average, and their score on a precalculus diagnostic test. A comparison of workshop and nonworkshop students' grades in first-quarter calculus is presented in table 6.2. Further analysis revealed that each of several workshop subgroups—Latinos, African Americans, and women—outperformed the corresponding nonworkshop group.

One of the hidden factors in patterns of calculus achievement is that a substantial number of students who fail introductory calculus take it again, in some cases again and again. Consequently, Bonsangue developed the Course Attempt Ratio (CAR), in which the numerator is the number of times a student attempted a course and the denominator is the number of courses he or she completed successfully (5). Table 6.3 reports CARs for both workshop and nonworkshop minority students in first-year calculus.

Additional analyses show that the workshop effects persisted in subsequent second-year calculus courses. Although the CARS of groups in the second-year courses did not differ, the workshop group successfully completed one and a half times the number of second-year mathematics

Table 6.3

*Course Attempt Ratios for Workshop and Nonworkshop Minority Students
in First-Year Calculus, 1986–1991*

Course	Workshop students	Nonworkshop students
Math 114	1.19	1.43
Math 115	1.19	1.56
Math 116	1.34	1.87
3-quarter calculus sequence	3.63	4.64

SOURCE: Bonsangue and Drew, "Long-Term Effectiveness of the Calculus Workshop," 6.

Table 6.4

*Persistence and Mathematics Completion Rates for Workshop
and Nonworkshop Minority Students, 1986–1991*

Students	Group	N	Enrolled or graduated N	Enrolled or graduated %	In MSE major N	In MSE major %	Math requirement completed N	Math requirement completed %
All	Workshop	78	75	96	66	85	60	77
	Nonworkshop	131	76	58	63	48	36	27
African Americans	Workshop	7	7	100	6	86	6	86
	Nonworkshop	20	9	45	9	45	4	20
Women	Workshop	22	22	100	19	86	19	86
	Nonworkshop	23	12	52	7	30	4	17
Transfers	Workshop	11	11	100	10	91	4	36
	Nonworkshop	48	23	48	20	42	9	19

SOURCE: Bonsangue and Drew, "Long-Term Effectiveness of the Calculus Workshop," 10.

courses that the nonworkshop group did, even though there were initially 40 percent fewer students in the workshop group than in the non-workshop group (8).

Workshop students were significantly less likely to drop out of the institution, "with forty-two percent (55/131) of the non-workshop minority students in the 1986–89 sample leaving the institution by spring 1991, compared to fewer than four percent (3/78) of the workshop students" (9). Table 6.4 reports these attrition rates as well as the degree to which those students who remained enrolled completed their mathematics requirements and stayed in MSE majors. "Of those students still enrolled in Mathematics, Science, and Engineering, more than ninety percent of the workshop students had completed their mathematics requirements for their individual majors, compared to less than sixty percent of the nonworkshop students" (10). And workshop students who persisted in their MSE field achieved higher grade point averages overall than did the nonworkshop students. However, they held only a slight advantage in terms of grades within the major, and there were no differences between the two groups with respect to number of units completed overall or within their majors.

In a further assessment of the relative importance of precollege academic measures and workshop participation, two multiple regressions were run predicting, first, MSE persistence and, second, mathematics completion. "None of the precollege measures entered the regression equation for either dependent variable. Thus, the traditional pre-college cognitive measures held minimal power in predicting persistence in an MSE major and mathematics completion. Workshop participation was the only statistically significant predictor of mathematics completion, accounting for twenty-three percent of the variation in mathematics completion among men, while nearly twice that amount, forty-four percent, among women" (15).

Table 6.5 presents information on the precollege measures and some academic and social involvement variables for different ethnic groups. The academic and social involvement variables were assessed using the Student Involvement Questionnaire, an instrument developed by Ernest Pascarella that was administered to 186 workshop and nonworkshop students enrolled in calculus during the 1990–91 academic year.

An additional aspect of this analysis was to examine the calculus achievement of minority workshop and non-workshop minority and majority students, with workshop students achieving a grade mean nearly one full grade point higher than that achieved for non-workshop minority students. *In fact, workshop students earned a calculus grade mean of at least .75 grade points higher than any non-workshop ethnic group, including Asian and white students, even though some precollege cognitive factors for the workshop group were significantly lower than those for white and Asian groups.* (16–17, emphasis added)

Additional regression analyses showed that the only significant predictor of calculus course grade for workshop students was the number of hours spent in individual and group study, which accounted for 26 percent of the variation in course grade. Interviews with the students from the 1987–88 cohorts revealed that about half formed study groups in their upper-division courses after completing the workshop program, a finding that parallels the goals and experiences of the Berkeley program. The following interview finding is relevant to the discussion in chapter 5 of women's experiences in college science and mathematics courses: "Most of the women interviewees reported feelings of isolation or self-doubt to

Table 6.5
*Group Means of Involvement Variables, Cognitive Measures,
and Course Grades for Calculus Students, 1990–1991*

| | Ethnic Group | | | | | |
| | African American and Latino | | | Other | | Total |
Variable	Workshop (N = 36)	Nonworkshop (N = 24)	Filipino (N = 18)	Asian (N = 59)	White (N = 37)	Nonworkshop (N = 150)
Student hours	8.23	6.88	4.00[a]	5.77[a]	6.76	6.20[a]
Group hours	4.09	1.83[a]	0.56[a]	1.15[a]	0.62[a]	1.13[a]
Involvement	8.51	7.54	5.67[a]	6.07[a]	7.08	6.58[a]
High school GPA	3.35	3.29	3.34	3.38	3.37	3.35
SAT-Verbal	408	383	461[b]	373	469[b]	411
SAT-Math	517	491	555[b]	569[b]	589[b]	557[b]
Parent education	2.12	2.08	3.00[b]	2.57[b]	3.19[b]	2.27[b]
Course grade	2.43	1.47[a]	1.18[a]	1.60[a]	1.68[a]	1.58[a]

SOURCE: Adapted from Bonsangue and Drew "Long-Term Effectiveness of the Calculus Workshop," 17.
[a]Group mean score significantly lower than workshop, $p < .01$.
[b]Group mean score signficiantly higher than workshop, $p < .01$.

varying degrees, despite earning grades as high or higher than those of their male colleagues. Several women openly discussed barriers of sexism that they had experienced within their majors. Overall, women described a college experience that was qualitatively different from that described by men" (19).

Bonsangue conducted an additional analysis to assess the financial implications of these research findings. He found that the per-student cost-effectiveness for an intervention program is equal to the reduction in CAR times the cost to the university when a student takes a course minus the cost to the university of conducting a workshop. This relationship can be summarized as

$$\text{C.E.} = (\triangle\text{CAR} \times \text{UNIVCOST}) - \text{WKCOST}.$$

Bonsangue reports financial data indicating that the cost to the university for a four-unit, one-quarter calculus course was $517. Figures from the Academic Excellence Workshop Budget Report indicate that the total direct and indirect costs of that effort were $335 per student.

Thus, the Cost Effectiveness per workshop student in 1990–91 was $1.01 \times \$517 - \$335$ or $187 per student. Thus, using the difference in Course Attempt Ratios from the 1986–89 cohorts (the mean CAR for non-workshop students was 4.64 while the mean CAR for workshop students was 3.63), students who participated in the workshop each cost the institution $187 less than students who were not in the workshop. (22)

Moreover, the savings to the institution may be even greater when subsequent calculus courses are considered and when the persistence and retention rates are considered.

In summarizing the implications of the data yielded by this important workshop program, the evaluators state: "The data strongly suggest that achievement among under-represented minority students in mathematics, science and engineering disciplines may be less associated with pre-college ability than with in-college academic experiences and expectations" (23).

High School Workshops

John Marlowe and Katharyn Culler have reported on their attempt to implement the Berkeley workshop model at the high school level, specifically at Albany High School in California. "During the interviews, we explain that the workshop program isn't out to rescue people and that success will come only from the kids' own hard work. We also emphasize that parents are expected to be involved in the program. When students are accepted, they—and their parents—receive congratulatory letters." Marlowe and Culler report that since they initiated the mathematics workshop program in 1983, "the failure rate of Black students in introductory algebra has been cut in half."[4] Encouraged by this success, they have also launched a workshop program in chemistry. The University of California at Berkeley now admits more minority students from this high school than it did in previous years.

The Harvard Assessment Seminars

The work of Treisman and Bonsangue demonstrates that minority students who traditionally have been underrepresented in science, mathematics, and engineering can excel in these disciplines. Many of these students enter college with enormous social handicaps, for example, having lived a childhood below the poverty line, yet they can achieve in calculus and subsequent courses. In fact, with the aid of the workshop program, they have achieved at levels exceeding those reached by Anglo and Asian students. The key philosophical components of these workshop programs are an emphasis on academic excellence rather than remediation and the formation of study groups with other students.

Now I would like to report a surprising research finding from the other end of the academic spectrum: how super-achieving students learn best at Harvard College. Richard Light conducted extensive explorations with students and other faculty in the Harvard Assessment Seminars, an effort initiated by President Derek Bok in 1986 and continued with the support of his successor, Neil Rudenstine. Light's main finding was that "students who get the most out of college, who grow the most academically, and who are happiest, organize their time to include interpersonal activities with faculty members, or fellow students, built around substantive academic work."[5] Light adds that this is difficult for some students.

Another principal finding from the Harvard Assessment Seminars related directly to science. Noting that "more than half of Harvard freshmen express a strong interest in doing some work in science and . . . nearly half plan to concentrate in the sciences," Light describes how this group of freshmen divides into two subgroups during the undergraduate years. The members of one subgroup love their science experience and plan to study and work more in science. The other subgroup find their science courses dull and lose interest in a technical career. What accounts for the difference? Light concludes that it results directly from how their professors organize their science courses.

When asked to describe how they approach their work, students from these two groups sound as if they are describing different worlds. Those who stay in science tell of small, student-organized study groups. They meet outside of formal classes. They describe enjoying intense and often personal interaction with a good lab instructor. In contrast, those who switch away from the sciences rarely join a study group. They rarely work together with others. They describe class sections and lab instructors as dry, and above all, impersonal.

Science professors who succeed in structuring their classes and labs to help undergraduates work collegially are honored by students and mentioned repeatedly. The word "inspiring" is used often. These professors attract specialists in both sciences and other disciplines to their courses. Their success is not due to some mysterious charisma. It is due to the way they organize the work in their courses. (10)

The Harvard researchers believed that their conclusions would only be useful if their work was consistently oriented toward potential policy implications and was implemented with the utmost scientific rigor. Interviews were conducted with a random sample of 6 percent of all Harvard College undergraduates (the response, or participation, rate exceeded 90 percent for each round of interviews). These students were interviewed twice as freshmen and once as seniors. In addition, a group of researchers conducted special interview analyses contrasting twenty students who had made an extremely successful transition from high school to college in the freshman year with twenty-one students who had not. Also, a doctoral student invited 173 freshmen to keep a log of how they spent their time in a given week. A special study was done of fourteen seniors in the physical sciences. Two other researchers conducted surveys of alumni soliciting their reflections about their college experiences; the respondents to these surveys had graduated from Harvard and Radcliffe Colleges between 1957 and 1983. Another interview study explored how the experiences of students who stayed in the sciences while in college differed from those of students who switched from science to another area.

These findings about Harvard College students from the late 1980s and early nineties parallel the results of a study completed by me in the late sixties.[6] In that research, I hypothesized that student interaction with reference groups—faculty, other students, family—would have an important impact on several key outcomes in the undergraduate experience, including academic achievement. I analyzed extensive longitudinal data on a sample of undergraduates in the Harvard classes of 1963 and 1964 using multivariate statistical methods, that is, stepwise multiple regression and canonical correlation analyses. The data had been collected as part of an ongoing research project, the Harvard Student Study, and included a variety of psychological and sociological measures. Each student in the sample had given several days to the project every semester in college. The results revealed the powerful effect of reference groups, especially faculty members. Those students who interacted with their faculty members got substantially more out of the undergraduate experience, in terms of such measures as academic achievement and satisfaction, than did their contemporaries who worked as hard but failed to initiate such contacts.

The parallels between the specific observations from Light's Harvard assessment and those from the Treisman and Bonsangue research are striking. Consider this comment about suggestions from Harvard students about how undergraduate learning can be made more effective.

The students' second suggestion for interpersonal engagement is not unanimous. Just over half bring it up. It is the value of forming small study groups, with fellow students, that meet outside of class once or twice a week. The typical size of such groups is four to six students. They meet for an hour and a half to two hours. They nearly always include both men and women. Students stress that these are not intended to be "men's groups" or "women's groups"—they really are designed to be *study* groups. Those who participate in such groups take them very seriously.[7]

While the Harvard Assessment Seminars yielded these very clear recommendations about student participation in study groups, they also yielded observations about student involvement in campus life generally. "One of the earliest findings from our seminars . . . is a strong connection between academic success and becoming an active member of the college community. The evidence is overwhelming that students who are active in extracurricula activities adjust far more quickly to college life. And their grades are at least as high as those for students who concentrate narrowly, and only, on course work" (43). This observation mirrors both the theories and the research findings of such authors as Alexander Astin, Ernest Pascarella, William Spady, and others. Perhaps the most consistent finding in the higher education literature about the impact of the college experience on undergraduates has been that academic and social involvement with the campus community leads to success.

Another of Light's findings parallels an observation from the research at the California State Polytechnic Institute at Pomona: "While the advantages of study groups are widespread, there is one group of students for whom they seem especially important: young women concentrating in the physical sciences." Light cites the 1988 undergraduate honors thesis of Andrea Shlipak, who found that "women who concentrate in physics and engineering consider these small working groups a crucial part of their learning activities. Further, her interviews with women who enter college intending to specialize in the physical sciences reveal a sharp break between those women who join study groups and those who don't. Women who join a small study group are far more likely to persist as science concentrators than those who always or nearly always study alone" (54).

In a section about the value of building substantive work in science around more student-student and student-faculty interactions, Light observes,

This is hard to do. To some it will sound vague. Yet this suggestion is brought up more than any other by students. Many perceive serious work in the physical sciences as impersonal. In contrast, they think of classes in humanities and social sciences as "dealing with people—their dilemmas, their joys, their tragedies, their lives," as one woman who switched from chemistry to anthropology put it.

When I shared this point with faculty colleagues in the sciences, one responded, "But physics and chemistry and biology are beautiful, too—just in a different way." I know. And some students know, too. But unless professors make a conscious effort to share their perceptions of this beauty, they will continue to lose some students. And the most promising way to share such perceptions, according to students who have chosen to work in the sciences, is to build small work teams so students interact more. For example, create a discussion group after each major lab experiment. That way, rather than going home alone into the night, each student can share findings, frustrations, and surprises with others. They become part of an ongoing conversation shared by young fellow scientists. (67–68)

Research in three different institutional environments has demonstrated the power of expecting students to excel and the effectiveness of workshop study groups as a vehicle to help them achieve success.

SEVEN

Curriculum Reform and Talent Development

> There are two essential elements to teaching science. One is to know the subject. The other, more subtle and more difficult, is that you have to be able to remember what it was like not to understand something you now understand. That's very hard, because each thing you understand transforms you for life. Nevertheless, the key to teaching that thing is to remember your untransformed self. If you can do that, I think you can teach just about anything.
> David Goodstein, "Needed: An Isaac Newton of Science Education"

In chapter 1, I discuss the gap between the mathematics and science our students learn in school and what they will need in the workplace. In chapter 3, I discuss the gap between the achievement of American students in these subjects and the achievement of students in other countries. How can we close these gaps? The solutions include changing what we teach, changing how we teach it, and finding new ways to develop talent.

Innovation in Mathematics Instruction

Consider this statement from *Everybody Counts* about how students learn mathematics:

Research in learning shows that students actually construct their own understanding based on new experiences that enlarge the intellectual framework in which ideas can be created. Consequently, each individual's knowledge of mathematics is uniquely personal. Mathematics becomes useful to a student only when it has been developed through a personal intellectual engagement that creates new understanding. Much of the failure in school mathematics is due to a tradition of teaching that is inappropriate to the way most students learn.[1]

One reason why there is an insufficient supply of trained mathematics teachers, according to *Everybody Counts,* is "deficit financing of intellectual capital. When demand for mathematics in universities increased sharply during the last decade, most institutions responded either by increasing class size or by hiring under-qualified temporary teachers" (28).

Noting that many students avoid advanced mathematics courses in high school because they believe they lack the ability, Judy Blum-Anderson has identified ten strategies for teachers to employ when confronting these fears. These include using cooperative learning and group projects on a regular basis, increasing public awareness of individual achievement, and making regular connections between the mathematics course content and applications in personal life or work.[2]

I believe that teachers must approach students with a new philosophy. First, their fundamental goal must be for the students to learn as much as possible. This is the bottom line, and it should not be eroded by other, conflicting motivations, such as demonstrating how smart they are, merely trying to survive from paycheck to paycheck, scaring students away or failing them to demonstrate how tough the discipline is, and so forth. Second, teachers must believe that all students can master the material. The question is not *whether* the students will learn but *how* they will learn.

We must teach to the students' frame of reference and tie new material to their lives. They and we should be engaged in the construction of meaning, not the transmission of knowledge. For example, in every introductory statistics course I must teach about variance and standard deviation, concepts that most students do not find intrinsically exciting. The notion is that while two samples may have the same mean or average, the variation or dispersion around those means may differ. Consider the ages of children at childcare center A (4, 4, 4, 4, 4, 4) and childcare center B (2, 2, 2, 6, 6, 6). They exhibit the same mean, but any teacher or parent can tell you that there is a great difference between working with six 4-year-olds and working with three 2-year-olds and three 6-year-olds.

I illustrate the importance of this construct by citing a powerful personal experience of Stephen Jay Gould.[3] He emerged from exploratory surgery in the mid-1980s to be told by his physician that the surgery had revealed a particularly virulent form of cancer and that the median life expectancy for patients with this cancer was six months. Gould comments that since the median is a measure of central tendency, he needed to learn about the variation and the shape of the distribution. He subsequently discovered that, while half the patients with this form of cancer died within six months (this is the meaning of *median*), many survived for many years. He then pursued the medical literature further and discovered that he had many of the characteristics of patients who survived a long time. Invariably I find that this story stimulates students' interest in, and understanding of, the meaning of variance.

The use of stories to communicate concepts should not be confused with presenting anecdotes instead of teaching or with catering to the present college generation's entertainment needs. Once, after giving a lecture to two hundred UCLA undergraduates, I described to a colleague the range of student behaviors I had observed. Some students had listened attentively; others had slept, snapped their chewing gum, drunk coffee, read a newspaper, joked, or fondled one another. "You don't understand," my colleague replied. "This is the television generation. They don't realize that you can see them!"

One of the most dramatic examples of the impact of expectations upon perceptions emerges from the cognitive psychology research of Jerome Bruner.[4] Bruner used a slide projector, which he referred to in this context as a "disambiguator," to project a picture that was totally out of focus. The subjects in the research were asked to study this blurred picture for a few minutes and write down their hypotheses about what the picture might be. Next he brought the picture slightly more into focus and asked the subjects to write down their new hypotheses about what the picture might be. He continued this process, each time bringing the picture slightly more into focus and asking the subjects for their hypotheses. Some subjects became so wedded to their initial hypotheses that they could not see the picture even when Bruner had brought it completely into focus! Such is the power of expectations over perceptions.

The effective teacher will lead students to master and enjoy skills, techniques, and knowledge that they thought they could never acquire. The challenge is to extract and nurture the talent and interest that the student already possesses. This approach is consistent with the epistemology and pedagogy of Paulo Freire. According to Marilyn Frankenstein,

Freire is adamant that the content of an education for critical consciousness must be developed by searching with the students for the ideas and experiences which give meaning to their lives. . . .

. . . In addition, Freirean problem-posing is intended to involve the students in dialogue and coinvestigation with the teachers. Freire insists that people cannot learn through "banking"—expert teachers depositing knowledge in the presumably blank minds of their students, who memorize the required rules in order to get future dividends. He stresses that this dialogue does not involve teachers' pretending ignorance.[5]

A quotation from a professor of mathematics at the University of Utah illustrates the problem: "Our primary responsibility as mathematicians is not to students but to mathematics; to preserve, create, and enhance good mathematics, and to protect the subject for future generations. . . . Good students—the ones destined to become mathematicians—will survive any educational system, and those are the ones with whom our future lies."[6]

The result of attitudes like these, according to Eugene Garfield, the man who developed the Science Citation Index, a valuable resource in science policy research, is that "with respect to math education, the United States is an underdeveloped nation and its students are impoverished."[7] The teaching of statistics provides a striking example. Statistics is required in many graduate and undergraduate programs and occasionally is offered in high school. Most students dread statistics and put off taking it as long as possible. Furthermore, few students remember the material six months after the final exam, and almost none could effectively employ statistical analysis in research or in personal decision making.

The reasons lie not in the odious nature of the subject (some of us truly enjoy it) but in how it is presented—and by whom. People who master and teach statistics tend not to possess superior interpersonal skills. Statistics, and mathematics and science more generally, should be taught by linking the subject to the student's experience base and illustrating its application in real research. Instead, the following occur:

—Professors stand at the board deriving equations, mumbling into their beards. Derivations teach students little that is useful; what they need to know is when and how to apply each technique.
—Students are expected to memorize equations and spit them back in closed-book exams. Researchers don't need to memorize equations; they can always look them up. All statistics exams should be open-book, a structure that more closely matches the research realities.
—Many courses list mathematical prerequisites, sometimes calculus.

While this serves the useful function of scaring away most potential students and easing the professor's workload, it has no pedagogical or substantive basis. Students can master statistics through multivariate analysis even if they know only a little algebra.

—Students are taught and dutifully master an array of techniques—chi square, t test, correlation, regression—but are not shown why or when to choose one technique over another.

—Too many professors simply show students how to employ statistical programs (the most widely used being the Statistical Package for the Social Sciences, or SPSS) to grind out statistics and skip the important material, namely, what the technique is and how to use it.

Each of these behaviors drives students from statistics for the same reason that many junior high school students are turned off by science: no link is made to either their prior experience or their future work.

Students need to be shown how research is conducted and how the statistical methods are used. From this perspective some of the material in standard texts is useless. For example, many statistics textbooks devote about half a chapter to the index of qualitative variation. Yet, in over thirty years of doing research, observing my colleagues' research, and reading studies, I have yet to encounter an index of qualitative variation. Why burden students with something they will probably never need? Similarly, most texts present more probability theory than is necessary or valuable. There should be less time devoted to the matrix algebra underlying multiple regression and more time to important issues that arise in applying regression analysis to real data, for example, multicollinearity and the treatment of missing observations.

Anecdotes, jokes, and other illustrations can link abstract mathematical techniques to the student's frame of reference. For example, I have found it helpful when introducing the concepts of probability, random fluctuations, and statistical significance to describe some highly improbable experiences from my own life. (Once, in trying to salvage a magic trick that had floundered, I handed the Washington, D.C., phone book to a friend. I instructed her to pick a name at random and said that I would tell her that person's phone number. I was bluffing, of course. But she closed her eyes, pointed, and read me the name of my brother-in-law! The probability that she would pick at random someone whose phone number I knew from that huge phone book was infinitesimal.)

In *The Call of Stories,* Robert Coles talks about the power of stories to instruct, to connect to people's lives, and to communicate. In the following passage he describes how the concept "stories" enabled him to make a breakthrough in communication with a recalcitrant psychiatric patient.

She was still hesitant to begin, so I said it—said what no one had suggested I say . . . : "Why don't you just tell me a story or two?"

. . . She looked at me as if I'd taken leave of my senses. I began to think I had: this was no way to put the request I had in mind. Why *had* I phrased my suggestion that way? I explained that we all had accumulated stories in our lives, that each of us had a history of such stories, that no one's stories are quite like anyone else's, and that we could, after a fashion, become our own appreciative and comprehending critics by learning to pull together the various incidents in our lives in such a way that they do, in fact, become an old-fashioned story.

. . . For the first time in my short career in psychiatry I saw a noticeable and somewhat dramatic change take place in a patient—and not in response to any interpretation or clarification of mine, but merely as a result of a procedural suggestion, as it were: how we might get on, the patient and I.[8]

Ernest Fandreyer comments on what he calls the "template method," in which students follow, more or less by rote, an example presented by the teacher in solving more problems of the same kind:

If a sample of more than thirty schools and over 200 periods of class time observed is any indication, then at least eighty percent of the mathematics instruction in our grades 5–12 have been performed with the template method during the last thirty years or longer. During the same time, other countries—England, Germany, France for instance—have relied far more on other methods, e.g. various forms of what might collectively be called guided discovery and have used the template method sparingly in their grades 5–12. Conceivably, it is this circumstance more than any other that enables their students to score higher, in international comparisons, than American students. More importantly, the experience of these countries suggests that most students are capable of solving new problems on their own.[9]

More and more mathematicians are encouraging students to solve problems by writing and keeping journals in mathematics classes. According to Paul Connolly, director of the Institute for Writing and Thinking at Bard College, "Students take conceptual ownership by articulating mathematical concepts in their own language. Language is the medium through which we construct knowledge for ourselves and others."[10] This observation relates to something every professor learns: that the best way to learn something thoroughly is to have to teach it.

Every weekday, 25 million children study mathematics in our nation's schools. Those at the younger end, some 15 million of them, will enter the adult world in the period 1995–2000. The forty classroom minutes they spend on mathematics each day are largely devoted to mastery of the computational skills which would have been needed by a shopkeeper in the year 1940—skills needed by virtually no one today. Almost no time is spent on estimation, probability, interest, histograms, spreadsheets, or real problem-solving—things which will be commonplace in most of these young people's later lives. While the fifteen million of them sit there drilling away on those arithmetic or algebra exercises, their future options are bit-by-bit eroded.[11]

One indication that teachers fail to make mathematics meaningful is provided by the National Assessment of Educational Progress. "Nine-year-olds rated mathematics as the best liked of five academic subjects; thirteen-year-olds rated it as the second best liked subject; and seventeen-year-olds rated it as the least liked subject."[12]

Thomas Romberg, director of a research center at the University of Wisconsin at Madison, believes that mathematics instruction must be made more relevant to daily life if it is to be effective. "The arithmetic we teach through eighth grade is really the arithmetic of the fifteenth century . . . the algebra is from the seventeenth . . . and the geometry? That's pretty much third century B.C." In his efforts to develop mathematics curriculum units Romberg has drawn heavily on the Dutch educational system, where mathematics instruction is closely related to real-world situations.[13]

Lynn Steen, a past president of the Mathematical Association of America, said in an address at the 1988 annual meeting of that organization that, since teachers tend to teach the way they were taught,

the most effective way to promote discovery learning in the schools is to enhance apprenticeship learning in the colleges, where tomorrow's teachers are today learning how to teach by the examples set by their college professors. The time is ripe for department chairs to insist that universities fund teaching at a sufficient level that all undergraduates can be taught by experienced teachers who will involve students in the excitement of discovering mathematics.

Apprenticeship education will require sufficiently better integration both of research mathematics and of contemporary applications in the experience of students. Current research, new applications, and the emerging goals of mathematics education could resonate in ways that would greatly enhance student involvement in mathematical learning.[14]

The state may prove to be an appropriate level for coordinating effective reform of mathematics education. The Washington (State) Center for Improving the Quality of Undergraduate Education received an NSF grant to facilitate calculus curriculum reform in that state. The grant's principal investigators are building their efforts around calculus curricula developed at Harvard and Duke. Project co-director Robert Cole observes that

most of the reform calculus curricula have the following characteristics: (1) they stress *applications* of calculus to "real world" situations, (2) they use various *"active learning"* strategies, rather than rely on traditional lecture methods, (3) they emphasize *collaborative student efforts* in both in-class group activities, and out-of-class group projects, (4) they ask students to *write* about mathematics in order to deepen conceptual understanding, and (5) they use *technology* such as graphing calculators and computer software as an integral part of the teaching of mathematical concepts.[15]

The Dwight D. Eisenhower State Mathematics and Science Program, sponsored by the U.S. Department of Education, operates at the state level. Grants given under this program have been used for in-service activities for teachers and have supported school-university partnerships in upgrading teacher training activities. The significant improvements, while real, are less visible than those achieved through some national efforts because they occur in many, disparate local environments.

For no immediately apparent reason the State University of New York College at Potsdam, a small public institution in rural New York state with about five thousand students, has achieved phenomenal success in teaching mathematics. Twenty percent of the bachelor's degrees awarded by this institution annually are in mathematics, compared with a national rate of 1 percent. The course is rigorous, and the reputation of the mathematics department reaches into the local high school, so that entering freshmen arrive anxious to study calculus. "What is the basis of their success?" asks John Poland, writing in the *American Mathematical Monthly.*

The students say they feel that the faculty members really care about them, care that each one of them can develop to the maximum possible level. The faculty can be quite explicit about it: for example, the chairman tells his classes that he believes in each of them, and cares about them, that he is there to help them achieve their potential. He stresses that a mind is a terrible thing to waste. The faculty win the students over to enjoy and do mathematics. And it is simply the transforming power of love, love through encouragement, caring, and the fostering of a supportive environment.[16]

One result of the perception in the United States that Japan is a world leader in mathematics and science education, on the one hand, and the increased demand for students to learn basic mathematics skills generated by the "back-to-basics" movement of the eighties, on the other, is the

Kumon Educational Institute, a thriving Japanese company that tutors U.S. students in mathematics. Originally devised by a Japanese mathematics teacher who was tutoring his own son, Kumon centers now are franchised in Japan, the United States, and other countries. The Kumon method also is taught in some U.S. schools. The Kumon centers train their own instructors and do not require teacher certification. Students attend instructional sessions twice a week and do homework, but the pace is individualized. Following a diagnostic test, each student is asked to master a set of math problems totally before moving on to the next set. Edward Effros, a UCLA mathematics professor, says "I suspect Japan is more productive because they're better educated. Kumon is not so much a back-to-basics approach. It's really back-to-homework. Kumon is really just a form of homework."[17] It is ironic that the Kumon method is growing in popularity just as mathematics education leaders are pushing the United States away from the back-to-basics calculations and toward critical reasoning and conceptual problems.

Major science organizations, like the American Association for the Advancement of Science and the National Science Teachers Association, are developing new curricula in science. Major mathematics organizations, like the Mathematics Science Education Board and the National Council of Teachers of Mathematics, are developing new mathematics curricula. To what degree are these mathematics reform and science reform efforts being coordinated? Coordination is particularly important since the larger U.S. educational curriculum is predicated on the assumption that mastering mathematics is a prerequisite for learning science.

Curriculum development projects are expensive. George Tressel notes that "the scale of these projects was such that NSF staff occasionally referred to their cost in terms of a 'zach'—a unit of a half million dollars—named after Gerald Zacharias, the MIT physicist who headed the PSSC project and spearheaded the multimegabuck curriculum development approach to science education reform."[18] Tressel adds that the cumulative historical investment by NSF in curriculum development has been $561 million.

The Science Curriculum

In the wake of *A Nation at Risk* and other reports about the inadequacies of America's educational system, several major science education reform efforts have been launched. The most ambitious is Project 2061, a large-scale, long-term project (critics have questioned whether 2061 is the projected date of completion) sponsored by the AAAS. The project directors believe that reforming American education is a huge challenge that requires a huge effort. Project 2061 has been organized in three stages: defining curriculum goals, developing sample curricula, and implementing curriculum change in schools throughout the country. The first stage has been completed, yielding *Science for All Americans,* a volume that specifies goals and objectives. Luther Williams, head of Education and Human Resources at the NSF, said about this volume, "For the first time we have a total representation of what should constitute science education."[19] Presently the second stage, curriculum development, is being carried out at six sites: Pennsylvania, Wisconsin, Georgia, Texas, and California (two sites).

Another project, titled Scope, Sequence, and Coordination (SSC), is sponsored by the National Science Teachers Association. While this project also is large, curriculum reform is already under way in California, Iowa, and Texas. The SSC's guiding principles are that (1) information is learned in thematic blocks and (2) students learn concrete ideas before moving to abstractions. For example, students conduct density experiments, simultaneously learning some physics, chemistry, and biology, as opposed to taking separate courses in physics, chemistry, and biology. One criticism of this approach is that most teachers are specialists in one discipline and may be surprisingly weak in the other disciplines.

Iowa program director Robert Yager comments, "Traditionally kids were told, 'Learn this and you'll find it useful.' But it wasn't useful. Now we turn that around." Commenting on how the courses can stimulate student interest, Yager cites one course that focused on the ozone hole. "To their teacher's amazement, the students were soon clambering for information: 'What's an atom? What's a molecule? What does pH mean?' The class became the community ozone experts, and college bound students began to complain that their course was too dull."[20]

The SSC project has been implemented rapidly at the California sites. Thomas Sachse, the state science education director, believes in moving fast and handing much responsibility for the innovation to the teachers themselves. The state of California supplemented federal grant funds in order to implement the program in as many schools as possible; 214 schools are participating in the project. According to Bill Aldridge, the chief author of the SSC curriculum, "There's no excuse for making the claim that some people can't learn science; it's elitist nonsense."[21]

These two efforts, as well as a parallel effort in mathematics education spearheaded by the National Council of Teachers of Mathematics, share certain characteristics:

- —Less memorization. "One study estimated that students encounter more new words in a high school biology book than in two years of instruction in a foreign language."
- —Upgrading teachers and building reform around them, rather than throwing reform at them.
- —Integrating traditional disciplines in thematic blocks, rather than teaching each discipline separately.
- —Greater emphasis on hands-on activities.
- —A greater focus on listening to students' questions and the ideas about scientific phenomena they bring to the classroom.
- —Linking science to society's problems.
- —Emphasizing the scientific process and how problems are solved.[22]

In a letter to the editor of *Science* magazine, Rustum Roy commented that "surely we should match Rutherford's well-conceived Project 2061 with a Project 5090. If the National Science Foundation and the Department of Education would mandate that fifty percent of the money go for the ninety percent of the citizens and their technological literacy, I feel sure this would reflect better the hopes of Congress."[23] While the numbers are extreme, Roy's recommendation is consistent with the main arguments in this book.

In addition to these ambitious curriculum development projects by the AAAS, the National Science Teachers Association, and the National Council of Teachers of Mathematics, the prestigious National Academy of Sciences was asked to develop and publish national standards for science literacy—what students should know about science and how they should be taught.

As reported in a September 1994 issue of *Science*, the process of developing these standards has taken longer, and been more expensive, than originally projected. A draft document was originally scheduled for late 1993, but it appears that this document will not be available until 1995. Janice Earle, a senior program officer in the NSF's Systemic Science Initiative program, says that the standards have "taken longer than we thought, proven to be more difficult than we thought, and there's less consensus than we thought."[24]

Meanwhile, a number of states have been attempting to revise their own science curricula, many with the aid of substantial grants from the U.S. Department of Education. The original notion was that these state curriculum development efforts would be linked to existing standards provided by the NAS, but many of the states have been unable to wait for those standards to become available. According to Shirley Malcom, the director of education and human resources at the AAAS and the chair of a national committee that reviewed the standards projects in all disciplines, "The delays put states in a very difficult situation. They can't just hold up on the work they're called upon to do. The standards then become a check against work already done, as opposed to the foundation for that work" (1649).

Robert Yager has argued that personal relevance should be the organizing focus for the science curriculum.[25] Citing a review of the literature on cognitive psychology studies by Champagne and Klopfer, Yager notes that "basically the research indicates that there's a wide gap between what is taught in school science and what students learn. In fact, it is apparent that what students really learn, i.e., how they interpret and understand the real world, is more related to their direct personal experiences in the real world and not like the interpretations and understanding advanced in typical K–12 (and college) science courses" (146).

About programs like Project 2061, which attempted to identify the most important subject areas in a given discipline, Yager comments, "Certainly there is little evidence that attempts at identifying the science knowledge of most value have ever resulted in better programs, more student interest, more learning" (147). Yager concludes: "There is every evidence that involved students learn, that students want to know when they need to know. Instead of arguing with students that they will need to know—that they will appreciate their science experiences later, i.e., knowledge acquisition,—why not guide students into activities, questions, situations where they see and feel the need to know? Such students will be motivated" (154).

The traditional, multiple-choice test format militates against curriculum designs and assessment built around student concerns and experience. New tests being developed as part of the California Assessment Program will stress reasoning ability, writing skill, and problem solving instead of multiple-choice questions. For example, here are two essay questions in mathematics:

The cycle for the traffic light on Main Street is green for fifty-five seconds, yellow for five seconds, and red for thirty seconds. What is the probability of having to stop at the traffic light? Explain your reasoning and include consideration of how drivers react to yellow lights.

A visitor from outer space has just arrived. It is confused about our number system. It asks you: "Is five plus twenty-nine equal to 529?" Answer the visitor's question and explain your answer.

And a science question:

A small tree is planted in a meadow. After twenty years it has grown into a big tree, weighing 250 kg. more than when it was planted. Where do the extra 250 kg. come from? Explain your answer as fully as you can.[26]

Of course, it is more difficult to develop consistent and fair scoring standards for essay questions than for multiple-choice questions, but such obstacles are not insurmountable. In fact, the College Board has added an essay component to the SAT, arguably the most important test any student will ever take.

William Wraga and Peter Hlebowitsh articulate an additional rationale for a personally relevant science curriculum, often referred to as the science, technology, and society (STS) approach: the characteristics that distinguish STS from conventional science education can be shown to reflect the major tenets of traditional curriculum scholars such as John Dewey.[27] They quote Dewey: "When material has to be made interesting, it signifies that as presented, it lacks connection with purposes and present power; or that if the connection be there, it is not perceived."[28] Wraga and Hlebowitsh conclude that "though its principal tenets bear a remarkable resemblance to some of the best that curriculum theory and research has to offer, the new rationale for science education has developed seemingly independently from the body of knowledge that comprises the curriculum field. STS education can draw wide theoretical and practical support from the larger curriculum field. A full century of curriculum scholarship is ready to be mined for the purpose of enriching a promising approach to science education."[29]

Science Literacy Courses

Jon Miller, who has done considerable theoretical and empirical work in the area of science literacy, has made several observations about improving the level of literacy in the population:

— Some level of formal science and mathematics instruction, above and beyond informal learning programs like those of museum and television, is necessary.

—Family attitudes toward science are central in socializing young people.

—Post-Sputnik (and other) attempts to strengthen science education created "a view that chemistry, physics, and advanced mathematics courses were only for the best and the brightest—what students call, the 'brains'—and that ordinary mortals need not apply. In my view, too many high school science and mathematics teachers still hold that attitude and those attitudes are partially responsible for the low enrollment rates in these courses."[30]

—Some students avoid advanced science and mathematics courses because they are tougher and therefore potentially detrimental to their grade point average. "Thus, we have the phenomenon of above average students actively seeking to avoid advanced high school science and mathematics courses to improve their chances for college!" (26).

—The middle school and high school years are a critical period in the development of scientific literacy, and we must focus our short-term attention on the revision of those curricula.

A new science literacy program has been developed by faculty members at thirty-six liberal arts colleges using a $20 million grant from the Albert P. Sloan Foundation. Dramatic examples from real life are used to illustrate scientific principles. For example, during a chemistry class at Williams College a hit-and-run accident is staged outside the building. The students assignment is to identify the vehicle that hit the "victim" through a chemical comparison of glass fragments left at the scene with those from the headlights of the suspect's car and other vehicles. In fact, this instructor, Larry Kaplan, presents most topics by imbedding them in a situation that involves forensics. Students are fascinated by crime and detective work, and "all during this time the students think they are not doing any chemistry. But what I'm really doing is teaching them about the scientific method, the importance of clearly identified samples, the use of controls and standards, and other aspects of doing good science."

Wesleyan University physicist Ralph Baierlein creates a spectacular visual demonstration by placing a neon-filled tube in an electromagnetic field. "That is so striking a demonstration, that a picture of it actually showed up last year on the university calendar," says Baierlein.

Wellesley College physicist Theodore Ducas rode an elevator up and down forty floors of a Boston skyscraper while standing on a scale and videotaping the scale. He then showed his class how these data could be used to identify the position and acceleration of the elevator at any given time. In another exercise Ducas introduces his students to decision theory analysis by considering the alternatives and tradeoffs involved with the decision about whether to perform amniocentesis on a fetus that might have Down's syndrome.

In contrast to this approach, Robert Hazen and George Mason University colleague James Trefil have built their science course for nonscientists around what they have defined as the great ideas in science.[31]

Intervention Programs

Beatriz Clewell, Bernice Anderson, and Margaret Thorpe have compiled a list of intervention programs that show promise toward correcting the underrepresentation of women and minorities in the study of mathematics and science. They present examples of case studies from ten particularly effective intervention programs, including the Detroit Area Pre-College Programs (DAPCEP), Operation SMART (Science, Math, and Relevant Technology) in New York City, Project SEED (Special Elementary Education for the Disadvantaged) in Berkeley, and the Saturday Science Academy in Atlanta, Georgia. In a summary table, they list a variety of intervention strategies that research has shown to be effective, for example, the use of adult mentors as role models, field trips, after-school classes, parental involvement, and the like, and indicate through a matrix structure exactly which of those strategies are practiced by each of the ten case study projects.[32]

Linda Hayden and Mary Gray have reported about a successful intervention program—a Saturday academy—for high-ability minority students that has been implemented at the University of the District of Columbia in Washington D.C. The participants are seventh, eighth, and ninth graders from Washington, D.C. The program is designed to provide enrichment experiences in creative mathematics, electrical engineering, and computer science for academically talented minority youth at no cost to them.[33] In the electrical engineering component students are introduced to the basic theory of electricity and the instruments used in measuring such quantities as current and voltage, and they are given specific instruction in soldering, reading schematic diagrams, and the like.

All students construct a light generator, a sound generator, and/or a transistor radio. Assignments for more advanced students in this component include the construction of robots. In the computer science component students learn to program in BASIC on a mainframe computer, either using a modem or by direct link. Some advanced students learn PASCAL. In the mathematics component the focus is on abstract reasoning and the students study such topics as bases other than base ten, basic set theory, and three-dimensional exploration. Minority engineers and scientists address the group. Subsequent evaluation questionnaires administered to both parents and teachers revealed enthusiasm for the program. More than seventy percent of the participants felt that the Saturday Academy program increased their confidence in their ability to get good grades in more advanced courses and their grasp of mathematics/science concepts they were never able to grasp before. . . . Seventy percent felt they could become electrical engineers, whereas fifty-two percent felt they could become mathematicians, and sixty-six percent felt they could become computer scientists."[34]

Even though only high-ability students were selected for this program, it is impressive that 96 percent plan to attend college and 58 percent plan to select a quantitative major.

Follow-up data were gathered and compared with those for a control group of students with qualifications similar to those of the students who had attended the Saturday academy. There was a significant positive relationship between having attended the Saturday academy and high school graduation, college enrollment, and selection of a quantitative major. This relationship was more pronounced, however, for males than for females. Also, the authors were unable to control for the fact that Saturday academy participants had strong parental support and involvement, while the same could not necessarily be said of the comparison group students. The post-program evaluations revealed enthusiasm for the hands-on aspect of the instruction.

The California Institute of Technology, one of the nation's premier universities, has developed an exciting summer program for high school students from disadvantaged backgrounds. As the *Los Angeles Times* reported,

Take forty teen-age science whizzes from disadvantaged backgrounds. Stick them for six weeks in college laboratories crammed with expensive equipment and personalized instruction. What do you get? For seventeen-year-old Angie Gonzales from Porterville in Central California, the answer is sheer ecstasy. "In my high school chemistry class, we had three labs the entire year," said Gonzales, rolling her eyes. "Here we're constantly in the lab, doing stuff we couldn't even imagine at home."[35]

Eduardo Grado, who directs the program for Cal Tech, observes, "Students will rise to the level of expectation, but sometimes expectations aren't high enough, especially for disadvantaged or minority students" (B8). Some of his students have had teachers who discouraged them from enrolling in tough courses.

The University of Southern California has launched a Pre-College Enrichment Academy. Seventh graders from neighborhood schools are selected for the program, which is a six-year effort to help them acquire the academic skills and self-concepts necessary for success in college. According to the program director, James Fleming, "Our focus is on the average student, because our premise is we can take an average student, and in six years render that student a scholar" (B1). At the end of the six-year program, if the students meet USC's admission requirements the university will give them a four-year scholarship, worth approximately $34,000 a year. During the school day the students receive extra instruction in language arts and college skills, and they have an hour of tutoring after school. They also attend a three-hour session every Saturday at USC. The students' parents also must make a commitment to participate in the program.

A major problem for secondary schools, even those engaged in innovative programs, is how to give students the opportunity to work with high-tech science equipment. Occidental College in Eagle Rock, California, has been cooperating with the Los Angeles Unified School District in a program that will send an especially equipped van with high-tech equipment, for example gas chromatrographs, to Los Angeles high schools. Laura Hoopes, an Occidental professor observed that "students are very intellectually prepared and smart when they start college, but we find they've had essentially no lab experience, and we're very concerned about that. Modern science is very equipment-intensive. We're trying to give the students a flavor of that."[36]

Henry Levin of Stanford University has developed the Accelerated Schools Program for disadvantaged students at the elementary level. This program is based on high expectations for all students and particularly emphasizes parent involvement. According to Levin,

The goal of the program is to accelerate the learning of the disadvantaged so that they are able to perform at grade level by the end of elementary school. Such schools must be characterized by high expectations on the part of teachers, parents, and students; deadlines by which students will be expected to meet particular educational requirements; stimulating instructional programs, planning by the educational staff who will offer the programs, and the use of all available resources in the community including parents, senior citizens, and social agencies.[37]

Levin's program, which is being implemented in a number of schools, attempts to bring the students to a high enough level of achievement by the end of the sixth grade that they can join a conventional seventh-grade program at a competitive level. Levin and his associates are hopeful that the Accelerated Schools experience will increase self-esteem and have the consequent effects of reduced rates of dropping out, drug use, and teenage pregnancy. The program involves a full institution, not just one or two classrooms. Both language and practical applications are emphasized in every part of the elementary school curriculum. Virtually all administrative decision making is school-based, and the principal plays a vital role.

The NSF's Human Resources Programs

There is a story about Henry Kissinger, who often lectures at colleges, flying in a small aircraft to give a lecture at a college in Vermont. There were two other passengers, an elderly clergyman and a college student. During a storm the plane encountered severe turbulence, and eventually the pilot staggered into the passenger compartment. "This is a terrible storm," he said. "And the copilot and I have discussed the options. We won't be able to make it to the next airport, and the terrain here is too mountainous to land safely. While it's risky, the safest option is to parachute out. Unfortunately, we only have two parachutes. The copilot and I feel we have to try to land the plane, dangerous though that may be. I'll leave it to the three of you to decide who gets the two parachutes." He then disappeared back into the cockpit.

Immediately, Henry Kissinger jumped up and announced, "I have made many contributions to world peace. Furthermore, in the future I intend to make many more contributions to world peace. Beside, I'm probably the smartest man in the world." He then seized a parachute from the student's hands, put it on, and jumped out the window.

A long silence ensued while the clergyman and the student stared at each other. Finally the elderly gentleman said to the student, "I'm an old man and have lived a full life. I've always been close to God. Why don't you take the other parachute?" The college student replied, "There's nothing to worry about, pops. The 'smartest man in the world' just jumped out that window wearing my backpack!"

In other words, it's not enough to have an intelligent idea. You also have to be able to implement it.

Several times in its history the NSF departed from its usual programmatic structure to create capacity-building programs for higher education. Three such programs are Science Development, the College Science Improvement Program, and the Experimental Program to Stimulate Competitive Research. The implementation of each has been the subject of an evaluation or policy analysis by me.

The Science Development Program

Science Development, which ultimately comprised three subprograms funding graduate education, embodied three innovative concepts:

—a strong emphasis on geographical dispersion of the funded institutions;
—funding of "second-tier" institutions (those not yet considered excellent), together with deliberate exclusion of those universities in the "top twenty";
—funding via institutional rather than project support.

The Science Development program was formally announced in March 1964, and the first grants under the program were awarded during fiscal year 1965. Although the structure of the funding program changed several times, the major subprogram was University Science Development (USD), under which thirty-one universities received over $177 million. These institutions had to give evidence of having an overall development scheme that included extensive plans for the sciences. Technically, matching funds were not required, but the institution was expected to make a significant financial contribution as part of the program. The NSF excluded from consideration not only existing centers of excellence but also institutions that it felt lacked sufficient strength to develop rapidly into such centers. There were two other subprograms relating to graduate science education under which limited grants were given for less ambitious development plans: Department Science Development (DSD) and Special Science Development (SSD).

A federal precedent for institutional support of higher education was provided by the 1887 Hatch Act, administered by the Department of Agriculture. This act established experimental stations at land-grant colleges to advance the agricultural sciences and to disseminate information, particularly among rural communities, about discoveries in the field.

The impact and the image of Science Development is reflected in the following statement from a 1971 article about the NSF: "Institutional support and fellowship grants . . . elevated . . . graduate schools and departments to top rank. Privately, NSF was given much of the credit for the development of the highly regarded astronomy department at the University of Arizona, the mathematics department of Louisiana State University, and the physics departments at Rutgers and the University of Oregon, among others. Arizona alone received $7.2 million from NSF over the past five years."[38]

At the University of Arizona, Science Development funds were used to bolster several physical science departments, notably astronomy. A major portion of the award to Arizona was used for the construction of a 90-inch reflector telescope on neighboring Kitt Peak. The Arizona astronomy department was not considered for ranking in a national evaluation in the mid-1960s; however, by the time the next report was published, in 1970, it was ranked fifth in the country. Subsequently, physicists at the University of Arizona created quite a stir in the scientific community when they published findings that called into question portions of Einstein's theory of relativity. Whether this scientific success should be directly attributed to the Science Development program is debatable, but it certainly provides a dramatic example of the potential for science building at institutions that previously had mediocre or weak research programs.

Science Development was a massive experiment in capacity building at the selected universities. The funds allocated under the program totaled $231 million, awarded between 1965 and 1971. The midpoint of the program, then, was 1968. Adjusting for inflation, $231 million in 1968 would be roughly equivalent to $1 billion in 1994. As noted above, $177 million, the largest portion of the Science Development program funds, was awarded to thirty-one universities. In 1994 dollars, this translates to $765 million, or about $25 million per university.

In the mid-1970s I directed an evaluation of Science Development conducted at the National Academy of Sciences/National Research Council. The evaluation study yielded many interesting observations about capacity building and the management of science funding toward geographical dispersion.

One could easily see a number of tangible positive effects of the program: brilliant new faculty acquired, graduate enrollment increased, buildings constructed, a telescope built, an exciting interdisciplinary institute established, and so forth. In some institutions the progress was dramatic, particularly given the short time span involved, and some might argue that the progress of these schools alone would justify the program, particularly when compared with the results of most federally funded activities.

We heard numerous complaints from university officials about the erratic pattern of federal funding. One way to head off such dissatisfaction would be to establish programs on the basis of federal commitments for longer periods; for instance, a program aimed at a ten-year funding period would have ensured greater acceleration in the sciences and would simultaneously have avoided some of the programs that occurred when a financial crunch hit higher education.

When we compare extremely successful grants with less successful ones, certain distinguishing characteristics stand out. Perhaps the key characteristic is the strength of the central administration: *grants tended to be most successful at universities that had a strong and dynamic leader before, during, and after the grant.* This was particularly true of USD grants. While this factor may be less important, even unimportant, in the case of project support, it is vital with respect to institutional aid.

The importance of continuity in office should be underscored. Some upheavals were observed when an institutional leader who had been instrumental in acquiring the grant left prematurely (from the point of view of Science Development). Thus, not only a strong leader but one who is committed to the university as well is vital to the grant's success.

Even though all concerned tried to use multiple objective criteria in awarding grants, it is clear in retrospect that one cannot underestimate the impact of a powerful personality. Whether a grant proposal originated with a department or with the central administration, one person usually played a driving role. For example, at one public institution the chairman of the physics department prodded other department heads to write their sections of the proposal. Thus, both in the preparation of proposal and in the success (and occasional failures) of the grant the presence of a strong individual was central.

It may be that the person who receives project support from the federal government becomes more committed to his research and less dependent on or committed to the institution but the person who successfully administers a Science Development grant has a stronger vision of what the institution or department might become. The chief lesson to be learned from this comparison of successes and failures is that in future funding programs the person who has demonstrated *commitment to the institution,* and not a person who will leave or who will favor a pet area, should be relied upon.

Another component of success, and one that is associated with strong central leadership, is the existence at the outset of an overall development plan for the university. For many of the successful schools, the creation of a Science Development proposal amounted to carving out a section of an existing plan prepared as the result of extensive self-study; the Science Development funds contributed to an overall balanced effort. In addition, these schools tended to be the ones that were best managed overall and relatively strong financially as a result. Perhaps it is not surprising that it was from successful institutions with these characteristics that we most frequently heard comments about how the program had helped to strengthen nonfunded departments, to improve undergraduate education, and so forth.

The College Science Improvement Program

A parallel NSF funding program, the College Science Improvement Program (COSIP), previously had been evaluated by me at the American Council on Education. During the 1960s, COSIP awarded approximately $10 million per year to improve the quality of undergraduate science education. The evaluation included a comparison of the changes over time (again longitudinal data were used) in undergraduate plans and activities in recipient colleges with those in colleges that did not receive NSF funds. In the first phase of this study, the characteristics of institutions that received COSIP grants were examined. These institutions were found to be more selective and more affluent and to have a higher percentage of Ph.D.'s on their faculties than nonrecipients. In the second phase, the relationships between COSIP support and a variety of student outcomes were analyzed, controlling for initial, potentially biasing differences. Among the findings: students in schools that had received COSIP grants were more likely to aspire toward the Ph.D. and to plan on doing research and less likely to transfer out of that school.

NSF officials reported that the administration of COSIP was modified, partially in response to the implications of one finding. COSIP grants had been given for five categories of purpose; the one that the evaluation indicated yielded the greatest number of positive relationships involved grants for undergraduate student activities. On the other hand, grants intended to benefit the undergraduate indirectly seemed to have mixed effects. It was suggested that some grants were used by the faculty to develop and extend their own research activities rather than to improve their teaching. That inference was supported by the finding that students in COSIP schools were significantly more likely to be dissatisfied with the quality of classroom instruction. Previously, the experience in some schools had been that when a faculty member received a grant for research and scholarly activity, students who would have been taught by that faculty member were assigned to classes taught by other professors. The new NSF policy was to administer such grants only after the institutions had made provisions to replace the faculty member in question so that the faculty-student ratio would not be altered.

The Experimental Program to Stimulate Competitive Research

The NSF launched the Experimental Program to Stimulate Competitive Research (EPSCOR) to rectify what some perceived to be a continuing inequitable distribution of NSF monies.[39] States, rather than regions, were chosen as the basis for the experiment, largely because the regional governmental structure of the country is less developed than state structures. States were deemed more capable of supporting and carrying on the development projects after the cessation of NSF support; regions have no comparable mechanisms for doing this.

NSF's Experimental Program is designed to facilitate self-improvement in selected states. The program's goal is to improve the ability of scientists in participating states to compete successfully for NSF and other competitive federal research programs:

—to improve the quality of research being conducted in participant states;

—to increase the number of nationally competitive scientists and thereby the federal funding in participant states;

—to effect long-term gains in the research environment in participant states.

EPSCOR places responsibility for program development and execution with state ad hoc committees selected in part by the NSF. To initiate the program, the NSF selected the states eligible for participation and assembled the initial members of the ad hoc committees. The program was divided into two phases: phase A, planning awards; and phase B, implementation awards.

The process of selecting the original states to participate in the program was based largely on prior federal funding activity to these states. The NSF wanted to build the scientific research capabilities of states whose scientists had fared very poorly in previous grant and contract competitions. Seven states were eligible for participation: Arkansas, Maine, Montana, North Dakota, South Carolina, South Dakota, and West Virginia.

During the planning phase the state committees were responsible for assessing the quality of science within their state; identifying the state's scientific problems, resources, and options for improvement; and developing an implementation plan to improve the quality, strength, and competitive status of science within the state. These nine-month planning grants resulted in full implementation proposals with which the seven states competed with each other for funding under phase B. Each state could participate in the program for five years and receive up to $3 million over that period, depending on the plan it developed. NSF support would decrease gradually from approximately 90 percent in the first year to 40 percent in the fifth year, and the states were expected to provide matching funds.

As envisioned and encouraged by the NSF, the seven implementation proposals resulting from the planning grants represented a concentrated effort to increase the ability of scientists in those states to compete successfully for federal research funds. The program descriptions reflected each state's response in light of its scientific socioeconomic, geopolitical, and academic environments. They also represented various philosophical viewpoints on how best to achieve that objective.

Monitoring and evaluation plans were to be included in each state's proposal. Those assessment activities would begin when the implementation award was made and would continue for the duration of the program. The ad hoc state committee plays a key role in local oversight of the program's functioning. After two years of implementation, the state committee was to conduct a review of the program. The purpose of this local review was to enable the state and the NSF to evaluate progress and to provide an opportunity to modify the plan, even to close the program if progress was not satisfactory. Upon agreement of the participating scientists, the state committee, and the NSF, the program would be continued for the remainder of the five years.

In the early 1980s I directed a policy analysis review of EPSCOR, with a focus on the early planning and implementation activities in these seven states. The results were reported in *Strengthening Academic Science.*[40] The progress made by the five initial recipient states—Maine, South Carolina, West Virginia, Arkansas, and Montana— was substantial, and the Congress subsequently has authorized EPSCOR funding in fourteen additional states, including Puerto Rico. Moreover, the success of EPSCOR spawned parallel programs in other federal agencies, including, for example, the Department of Energy. (In the federal government, imitation is the sincerest form of innovation.) Furthermore, the European Economic Community has conducted a planning study to see whether and how the EPSCOR model could be applied in the less scientifically developed countries of Europe.

Some dramatic breakthroughs were associated with EPSCOR funding, which is all the more surprising considering that the amounts invested— $3 million per state over a five-year period—were modest. One example is pioneering superconductivity research that, according to experts, may well be the most important discovery in physics in decades. The researcher responsible for the major discovery was employed at an EPSCOR institution, the University of Alabama at Huntsville.

Current Talent Development Programs

The spectrum of current NSF talent development programs includes several programs that target precollege education and several for colleges and universities. They are being implemented under the leadership of Luther Williams, the NSF's deputy director, who consistently has insisted on evaluation and accountability.

Precollege programs include the Comprehensive Regional Centers for Minorities (CRCMs), Partnerships for Minority Student Achievement (where school districts take the lead and in-class activities are emphasized), and summer camp programs. The CRCMs typically link a number of organizations in an urban center with the school systems to improve the educational opportunities available to minority students through such activities as tutorial programs, parent support groups, mathematics and science clubs, science and mathematics academies, teacher workshops, Saturday academies, science fairs, and industry-based mentorship programs. CRCMs can receive up to $1 million a year for up to five years. Typically CRCMs are anchored at a university or college. For example, a prototype CRCM was established in the Baltimore area, anchored at Morgan State University.

Higher education programs include the Research Career for Minority Scholars program, which focuses on awards at the departmental level, and a much larger program, the Alliance for Minority Participation (AMP). In the AMP program statewide efforts link universities and colleges, and curriculum change is a key feature. Each participating state receives $1 million annually from the NSF, which is matched by $1 million to $2 million from other sources each year. The funding for each state lasts five years. To date, eleven AMP programs have been implemented. The NSF's national objective is to increase the number of underrepresented minorities receiving bachelor's degrees from 13,000 to 50,000 by the year 2000. According to Dr. Joseph Danek, who has had substantial responsibility for managing this array of programs, "These funds should not be considered add-ons. These activities are central to what the educational system in this country is all about."[41]

An impressive number of individuals and organizations have been developing creative programs to improve the mathematics and science education presented to our youth. Happily, these efforts continue. There will be new creative teachers, new curricula, and new programmatic efforts to develop human resourses. But even more is needed. We need a national commitment to improve mathematics and science education that will ripple through the many thousands of school districts in the United States. And we need to set aside, once and for all, the erroneous idea that most students really cannot understand this material. They can understand it, and we need them in the work force.

CONCLUSION

Greater Expectations

> What one human being does, other human beings can do, too. It's a law of human affairs that today's record becomes tomorrow's commonplace. . . . My eighteen-year-old grandson, who was a high school miler, ran the mile in 3.57—and he was not even considered very good. I was better. I just didn't run as fast because nobody else had run as fast. That's normal for human beings. Raise the standards, and everyone runs faster.
>
> Peter Drucker, "Performance, Accountability, and Results"

This is a book about science education. But I argue that mathematics education is more closely connected to the other educational and occupational achievements of young people. Ultimately, this is a book about power in U.S. society.

The inequality in our economy is staggering. Throughout history, those with power have controlled access to vehicles or instruments that would enable the weak and disenfranchised to improve their positions. The vehicles and instruments of power in the emerging global economy will be technical skills and knowledge. The major opportunity our young people have to acquire those skills is through mathematics and science education.

Women, poor people, and disadvantaged minority students consistently are discouraged from studying science and mathematics, the very subjects that would give them access to power, influence, and wealth. Sometimes this discouragement takes the form of overt racism or sexism. More frequently it takes the form of good intentions combined with pernicious expectations that these disenfranchised groups will not be able to master mathematics and science. The cycle is completed when the students themselves incorporate this false expectation, lower their own self-assessments, and limit their aspirations.

The curriculum reform efforts, teaching strategies, and the like reviewed in part II of this book represent some potential improvement in mathematics and science education. But the most important change involves expectations. Teachers must realize that virtually every student, regardless of gender, ethnicity, or economic status, can master mathematics and science. The parents of today's students must realize this. Most importantly, the students themselves must understand this.

Examples throughout this book underscore how expectations about a group's mental capabilities can bar that group's access to power in education. Other examples show how some individuals' extraordinary achievements have forced the elite group to reconsider these prejudices. For example, the towering mathematical achievements of Ramanujan were enough to silence many English scholars and others who believed that East Indians possessed only limited intellectual capabilities. Similarly, the eminent statistician Karl Pearson discussed at length how Jewish people should be barred from immigrating to the United Kingdom because they were not smart. Pearson analyzed data from intelligence testing of children. The subsequent intellectual contributions of Jewish scholars, as reflected, for example, by the number of Jewish Nobel prize winners, provide an easy refutation of Pearson's thesis. But his thesis was taken seriously at one time—he was, after all, a leading scholar—and the damage done when such statements are taken seriously cannot easily be undone. According to Elazar Barkan, Peason's study concluded that

Jewish girls were distinctly less intelligent than Gentile girls, whereas Jewish boys scored worse than Gentiles in good schools but better than those in poor schools. Faced with statistics which could be variously interpreted, Pearson quickly concluded: "our alien Jewish boys do not form from the standpoint of intelligence a group markedly superior to the natives. But that is the sole condition under which we are prepared to admit that immigration should be allowed." Aggregate average placed the Jewish population rather low physically and mentally, besides which no one could say how adaptable their progeny would become. Despite the risk that Britain may "exclude a future Spinoza," any future immigration would violate "the law of patriotism."[1]

Aptitude is a useful but limited concept. Moreover, the misuse of this concept has yielded at least as many destructive effects as its correct use has yielded positive effects. A person's aptitude as indicated, for example, by an intelligence test (which gives us only an approximate measure of aptitude) tells us very little about what a person will learn or will achieve in the work force. In part this is because aptitude is not a pure, inherited trait that exists in a vacuum; rather, intelligence and ability occur in a context. This is one reason why modern psychometricians have developed the notion "multiple intelligences."

Unquestionably, there are rare circumstances in which aptitude is the overriding factor. The unquestioned genius of a Mozart, or Ramanujan, or Einstein transcends normal boundaries. At the other extreme, there are profoundly handicapped children and adults whose ability to learn is severely limited. But for the great majority of the human population—the other 99.9 percent—aptitude is only one small factor affecting what they learn and achieve. Hard work counts for more. Effective delivery of instruction by the teacher is important. Structuring an effective environment for learning and studying is important.

It is time that we stopped excluding students from educational opportunities because of outmoded ideas about aptitude and who can learn. A student should not be denied the opportunity to study higher mathematics and science solely because his or her parents are poor. Nor should teachers, parents, or other persons of authority write off the learning potential of young women or minority students. The major theme of this book is that these unjustified negative expectations have the effect of creating much wasted talent in this country. Rather, we should expect virtually all students to be able to learn and master science and mathematics. In fact, we should expect students to excel in these subjects. To do this, they may have to work harder than they are used to or harder than they would like, but the benefits will be incalculable. We can no longer afford to write off these students based on the assumption that only a tiny percentage of the population really can do mathematics and science. It is empirically unjustified, it is unfair to the students, and it has been wreaking havoc with our economy.

In attempts to diagnose why so many people avoid or are discouraged from pursuing technical fields, mathematics was increasingly revealed to be the fulcrum, or filter. Many scientists, mathematicians, and teachers believe that only a certain kind of person—someone who looks just like them—can learn mathematics. As a result, by junior high school many students have turned away from mathematics as a boring, irrelevant, and difficult subject. It does not help matters that those teachers who are good at mathematics often are not good at communicating with people.

In our society it is considered acceptable for a person to brag about their abilities but to acknowledge that they cannot do mathematics. (Perhaps the most dramatic recent example is the admission by Hillary Clinton that she never was very good at mathematics.) In some circles it may even be desirable. But such an attitude can be lethal for educational and career development. Too many college students choose their majors and careers based upon a careful avoidance of mathematics courses. This avoidance cripples such students and is linked to our misuse of the concept of aptitude or intelligence.

Even those students whose future occupation will minimally involve technology will need to make important decisions in their personal lives, and as voters, that do involve mathematics, science, and technology.

Science and Technology in Society

As discussed in chapter 2, one reason why today's students must acquire scientific literacy is to ensure that new technologies benefit, rather than threaten, society. The "appropriate technology" (AT) movement provides a fascinating case study.

As is the case with many social or scientific movements, differing streams of influence were integrated and galvanized by one charismatic visionary. E. F. Schumacher was a German-born, Oxford-trained economist who left academia to gain experience in business, farming, and journalism. In 1965 he established the Intermediate Technology Group in England. In 1977 he published *Small Is Beautiful: Economics As If People Mattered*,[2] which, according to one reviewer, is "a work of stunning brilliance that seems certain to become a modern classic. It is one of those books that can wipe clean the windows through which we look at the world so that we can see many things that formerly were either vague or invisible."[3] In this marvelous book, Schumacher argues:

If we ask where the tempestuous developments of world industry during the last quarter-century have taken us, the answer is somewhat discouraging. Everywhere the problems seem to be growing faster than the solutions. This seems to apply to the rich countries just as much as to the poor. There is nothing in the experience of the last twenty-five years to suggest that modern technology, as we know it, can help us to alleviate world poverty, not to mention the problem of unemployment which already reaches levels like 30 percent in many so-called developing countries, and now threatens to become endemic also in many of the rich countries. In any case, the apparent yet illusory successes of the last twenty-five years cannot be repeated. . . . So we had better face the question of technology—what does it do and what should it do? Can we develop a technology which really helps us to solve our problems—a technology with a human face? (139–40)

Schumacher labeled his work "Buddhist economics" and said that "the very start of Buddhist economic planning would be a planning for full employment, and the primary purpose of this would in fact be employment for everyone who needs an 'outside' job: it would not be the maximization of employment nor the maximization of production" (53).

To illustrate the idea that small is beautiful, Schumacher argues, for example, that the maximum desirable size for a city is about half a million people. Beyond that, nothing is added but problems and human degradation. A counterexample has been cited by AT proponents: In the nineteenth century the Russians built the world's largest bell, weighing 250 tons. It broke the first time it was rung. Even though it is useless, it is still proudly displayed in the Kremlin. After all, it is the world's largest bell.

While appropriate technology usually is small technology, AT proponents emphasize technology *appropriate* to the environment, which does not always mean small. AT conserves energy and resources. According to John Todd, one of a group who call themselves "the new alchemists," many biologists and agricultural experts fear that defamation of the environment will offset any agricultural gains before the year 2000. "Among some of them there is a disquieting feeling that we are witnessing the agricultural equivalent of the launching of the Titanic, only this time there are several billion passengers."[4]

Sometimes appropriate technologists simply urge society to be more efficient. For example, Schumacher observed in an interview with *The Futurist* magazine that

our society has an immensity of transport: if I travel from London to Glasgow on one of the big motorways, I find myself surrounded by huge lorries carrying biscuits from London to Glasgow and I look across the other lane and I find an equal number of lorries carrying biscuits from Glasgow to London. Any impartial observer from another planet would come to the conclusion that biscuits, in order to achieve proper quality, must be transported at least 500 miles.[5]

Concern for the User—and the Worker

Concern for both the user and the worker is the cornerstone of the AT philosophy. AT proponents, like Schumacher, point to technology-induced unemployment and favor production activities that are labor-intensive, as opposed to capital-intensive. Thus, they are concerned not just about the inventor and the investor but also about the worker. And the user. The total overall costs of industrial innovation, including the costs of acquisition and maintenance to the user, must be minimized.

There is a growing literature within the policy sciences about how to implement organizational change. Much of that literature can be summarized in one observation: incorporation of technology and other externally introduced innovations proceeds most effectively when there is correspondence with the needs of users at the lower levels of the organization. Implementation fails when it is developed and mandated "on high" with little concern for the needs or interests of those who will be the actual users. Appropriate technology pushes this observation one step further and suggests that those concerns and aspirations actually be incorporated in the design of the hardware.

This component of the appropriate technology movement emerges from, or at least is consistent with, the human engineering subfield in applied psychology, which originated during World War II. Managers and scientists have realized for years that the designers of airplane cockpits must consider not only the wings and engine but also the pilot and copilot.

Anthropologists coined the term *cultural lag* to describe the delay between the technical development of an innovation and its effective application. Cultural lags can be observed in many spheres of human activity. One study examined the delays between basic biomedical research and subsequent clinical applications and noted some amusing and intriguing causes. For example, the first person to classify human blood groups, Jansky, wrote in Czech and gave his article a vague, inappropriate title. Copernicus, Harvey, and Darwin collectively waited forty-eight years to publish their crucial findings.[6]

Similarly, corporate executives cite the importance of "market demand," as contrasted with "technology push," in determining the success of an innovation. Edwin Mansfield traced the lengthy, complex series of events between the invention of power steering and its acceptance by the automobile industry thirty years later.[7] And a study of industrial innovation by a prestigious Cambridge, Massachusetts, research firm concluded that "being ahead of [one's] time is the biggest barrier to success."[8] The appropriate technology movement has been fueled by the realization of scientists and policymakers that vast numbers of technically superb inventions were not being sought, bought, or used.

Self-reliance

Appropriate technology, then, encourages the innovator to incorporate the user in product development; similarly, AT proponents encourage the user to become increasingly self-reliant, less dependent on machinery. Self-reliance, a traditional American value best articulated by Ralph Waldo Emerson, can be seen in back-to-the-land communities. Also, citizens are becoming increasingly self-reliant in confronting the medical system, which has evolved into a bewildering array of specialists, hospitals, clinics, and machinery. Many believe that these expensive systems and hardware dehumanize the patient in one of the most vital spheres of his or her life. The prominent social critic Ivan Illich, in his penetrating analysis *The Medical Nemesis*, discussed two destructive characteristics of the medical system today.[9] First, he identified "iatrogenic illnesses," those diseases caused by the medical system. Some patients enter a hospital with one illness and emerge cured of that disease but having acquired a new one. Second, he believed that a more pernicious effect of the bureaucratized medical establishment was the dehumanizing manner in which basic existential decisions about health, life, and death are routinely made by technicians, not patients. Illich argues that each person, even though he or she may be totally ignorant of modern medical knowledge, ultimately has both the right and the responsibility to participate in fundamental decisions about his or her own life.

Solutions

The most important solution to the problems discussed in this book, and the main purpose of this book, is a national consciousness raising about expectations. All of us—teachers, parents, students, and others—must recognize the intellectual potential for mastering science and mathematics that virtually every child possesses. I would like to tell two stories about young people who achieved despite the negative expectations of friends with good intentions (in one case) or a negative self-image (in the second case).

First Story. An old friend of mine grew up on the South Side of Chicago and entered Grinnell College in the 1950s. He was the only African American in the freshman class. The toughest course that fall was biology, and the professor's first examination was very difficult. After he had corrected the papers, the professor announced to the class that he was going to turn them back "in order." My friend was sitting in the back of the large lecture hall, and the first name the professor called was his. As he made his way to the front of the hall to receive his paper, classmate after classmate condescendingly told him, "Don't worry. We'll tutor you and help you pass this course." When the professor handed him his exam, my friend discovered that he had had the top grade in the class.

This man subsequently has been a college president and a member of the Grinnell board of trustees, and he is currently president of the College Board, the organization responsible for the demanding SATs. To this day, when he tells the story of his first exam at Grinnell there is emotion in his voice. His classmates meant well, but the damaging effects of their assumption that he must be at the bottom of the class could have been devastating to someone with less self-esteem.

Second Story. Among those whom I acknowledge in the preface for advising me during the preparation of this book is Lisa Wolf. Wolf worked as head of housing and residence halls at Scripps College, one of the Claremont Colleges, while enrolled in graduate school. In September 1993 a new Scripps student happened to mention to her that she planned to take as little mathematics as possible and that she most definitely would avoid calculus (Scripps only requires students to take a one-semester precalculus course). She explained that she had never had any aptitude for mathematics. Lisa mentioned that she had been working with a Claremont Graduate School professor who had just completed a draft of a book that showed how young women come to believe that they cannot master mathematics. The student said she would like to see the book, and Lisa lent her the draft volume. Three days later the student returned the book. After reading it from cover to cover she now planned to enroll in a second semester of precalculus. It turned out that she did well in that course and subsequently enrolled in calculus, where she also did well. This student's experience is an example of what I hope this book might accomplish. This is the kind of consciousness raising we desperately need in this country.

While the main point of this volume obviously is about making science and mathematics more inclusive, the improvements in mathematics and science education must be made even for affluent, White, male students. The recommendations for change that will benefit the excluded groups also will benefit majority students, and vice versa.

Throughout this book, particularly in part 2, I identify reform efforts and ideas that have worked or that offer the potential for success. These include workshop groups for college students studying calculus, science courses in junior high school that address practical problems, mechanisms to attract the most qualified people into teaching, and the massive human resources efforts of the National Science Foundation. All of these are secondary to the primary notion of consciousness raising and increased expectations. None of them is a single, universal, "magic bullet" solution to our mathematics and science education quagmire.

In a 1992 article Sheila Tobias made the following comments:

Materials development remains the darling of the science education community. Why the nearly exclusive focus on instructional materials? Is it because these are products that give educational reformers and their paymasters something to show? Or is it that science education reformers, with some notable exceptions, don't know what else to do? . . . The temptation is to solve a problem with a product (or . . . a project) because, for innovators and funders alike, the messy, intensely local alternatives are harder to conceptualize.[10]

She goes on to cite Gerald Holton, who has argued that we need a commitment to ongoing change as opposed to a series of one-shot cure-alls.

Above, I presented two stories about college students who overcame negative expectations and succeeded.Let us now examine some success stories about schools, programs, and teachers.

George Leonard has reported on Albert Shanker's description of the enormous success achieved by the Koln-Holweide School in Cologne, Germany.[11] In that innovative secondary school, lower- and middle-class students learn in a nontraditional environment characterized by team teaching, cooperative learning, and peer tutoring. Throughout the day, the students sit around tables, rather than in rows of chairs facing an instructor, in groups of five or six. "The table group is the basic unit of learning, the key to the school's success. Students are in constant interaction, helping one another learn. 'If a student has a problem,' the headmistress, Anne Ratzki, explained . . . , 'he doesn't have to wait for a teacher; he can ask his table group for help. If the group can't help, then the teacher will—but the first responsibility lies with the group.'"[12]

All reports are that the students thrive on this approach and actually enjoy attending school. And while the dropout rate in (West) Germany is 14 percent and 27 percent go on to college, the dropout rate for this school is 1 percent and 60 percent go on to college.

Ronald Bonnstetter and Robert Yager identified and studied many exemplary programs in elementary science education.[13] In 1977 they conducted a survey of 114 teachers involved in these programs and compared their responses with those from a national sample of all U.S. elementary science teachers. They observed the following differences between the two groups of teachers:

—Exemplary teachers had been working in the same school district for a longer period of time.

—Exemplary teachers had much more confidence in their qualifications as science teachers. There was virtually unanimous agreement about this confidence even though only 11 percent of them had majored in science.

—Exemplary teachers were more involved in professional activities, such as attending national conferences.

—Exemplary teachers were more likely to be aware of innovative materials from new national programs and also were more likely to be using them.

—Exemplary teachers were more enthusiastic about in-service training sessions in their own schools.

—Exemplary teachers were more likely to use hands-on activities in their teaching. "Almost 60 percent of the teachers from exemplary programs report daily activities involving students; a comparative figure for the general national sample is seven percent" (46).

Bonnstetter and Yager concluded that "better science instruction in elementary school needs teachers who are involved in science—and are having fun with it—perhaps in ways that are entirely new to them. It means teachers who are curious and who can't rest until they satisfy their curiosity. But it does not necessarily mean teachers who have had extensive formal preparation in science" (46).

A team of researchers from the California Institute of Technology under the direction of physicist Jerry Pine have been working with the Pasadena school system to develop and implement an inquiry-based hands-on elementary school science curriculum. Over five hundred elementary school teachers have received in-service training in this new curriculum. In collaboration with faculty from the Claremont Graduate School Education Program, a special course focusing on the physics of sound and the biology of plant growth and development has been provided to preservice elementary school teachers. The course is now being implemented with larger programs, for example, at California State University in Los Angeles. One assumption underlying the program is that "we teach the way we were taught. Therefore, if teachers are to teach for understanding using hands-on, inquiry-based methods in their classrooms, then they must themselves learn science in a similar fashion. Principles of constructivist teaching and learning apply—teachers can not learn effectively through either telling or modeling, but rather must experience for themselves, first hand, the kind of science education they are expected to pass on to their students."[14]

Noting that for many participants this innovative course was the "last and final chance" to develop a positive association with science, evaluation researchers quoted the negative attitudes with which some teachers entered the course. For example: "I am afraid of science. It stems back to biology when I had to do the frog dissection. I saw all those frogs opened up on the table with pins and living parts, and I just couldn't do it. I failed with flying colors. I tried, but I just couldn't do it" (6).

After the course, one teacher talked about her fear at the beginning of the course and "the utter relief" she felt when she realized that "I was going to be able to do this! I really did get a lot out of it . . . [the course] opened me up to science more, and especially the physics part conquered a lot of fears about what I can and can't do with the right person facilitating" (16).

The potential for achievement among students of color, even impoverished students of color, when a community and a school work together is illustrated by the experience of Ysleta High School in El Paso, Texas. In 1992 five seniors from this school, which serves a poor, almost exclusively Latino community, were admitted to the Massachusetts Institute of Technology. Joe Jasso, the assistant director of admissions at MIT, said that it was "extraordinary for five students from a general attendance high school to be admitted to the same entering class at MIT (although this has happened occasionally with private or specialized public schools). This is all the more impressive because Ysleta High is housed in an old building and has a very limited supply of scientific equipment and computers." The principal at Ysleta added, "We are part of a community that has drugs, violence and gangs. . . . We have our share of students who scorn intellectual achievement. Our dropout rate is as high as any in this area."

One of the students could not speak English two years before he was admitted to MIT; another worked part-time as a janitor. While it's hard to identify the causal factors with certainty, much of the credit must go to Paul Cain, who teaches computer mathematics. All five of the students worked with Cain, who considers himself "a catalyst for bright students, (and) credits strong parental support for the students' academic success." Cain says that "their parents give them direction and care about them. . . . I provide them with an opportunity to display their wares."[15]

Duane Nichols teaches mathematics at California's Alhambra High School. In addition to chairing the science department and teaching regular classes, he teaches a special class about biomedical research three times a week at 7:00 A.M. Thanks largely to his efforts, Alhambra High ranks first among schools west of the Mississippi River in the production of finalists in the Westinghouse science talent search. And Richard Plass of New York's Stuyvesant High School has taught and developed 181 semifinalists in the Westinghouse competition. Both Nichols and Plass make themselves available to their students and work at knowing their students. Both have multiple responsibilities and demands on their time and are constantly busy.

In hearings before the Subcommittee on Postsecondary Education of the U.S. House of Representatives I was asked to testify about mathematics and science education. Throughout the day a number of other scientists, policy analysts, and experts testified. However, the most memorable statement that day was made by Kent Kavanaugh, a high school teacher in the Park Hill school district, outside Kansas City, Missouri, who earlier that year had received a national award in recognition of his outstanding work as a science teacher from the president at the White House. This is part of what he said to the committee:

The month before I left for Washington, D.C. to receive the Presidential Award, I averaged forty hours a week at my job—not my teaching job, my second job as an analytical chemist for the Mobay Corporation of Kansas City. I must work at two or more jobs to make ends meet and to try to pay for college tuition for my son who graduates this spring. Because of this, I often come to school physically and mentally worn out. I am not the exception, I am the rule.[16]

In 1989 the Georgia Institute of Technology in Atlanta developed a special program for disadvantaged minority students in science and engineering with a rigorous five-week summer program as a cornerstone. According to an article about the program, its goals, and its premises, "No longer are minority students held by the hand and essentially told that they are the victims of an uncaring and bigoted society. Instead, the students are informed that with hard work and determination there is nothing to stop them from excelling." These Georgia Tech students who are taking part in the program are excelling in their undergraduate studies, and many of them now aspire toward advanced degrees in engineering. According to former president John Patrick Crecine, under whom the programs were developed, "The change was in us and what we told them we expected of them. . . . In the past we told them they were dumb, that they needed fixing, and we had them in remedial programs"[17]

Implications for Parents and Students

What do the many studies, statistics, theoretical formulations, and policy debates reviewed in this book mean for the high school or college student trying to decide what courses to take? What do my conclusions imply for the parent who wants the most for his or her child?

First, taking courses in mathematics and science, particularly mathematics, enhances the student's preparation for further education, the work world, and personal decision making. Obviously, taking one college course in physics does not make one a nuclear physicist. Nor do mathematics and science courses in high school or college guarantee that the student will get a better job upon graduating. But achieving in these courses will increase the student's sophistication. They will increase his or her literacy with respect to the languages being spoken in the information age. Furthermore, the mere act of mastering an advanced mathematics course develops habits of organization and work that will sustain the student in courses in entirely different subject areas and in the professional work world.

More to the point, the student will be keeping his or her career options open. That is, the student will not be ruled out of possible majors or careers, for example, becoming a physician, because he or she does not have the prerequisites. Perhaps most important of all, teachers, faculty, and administrators who review the student's record will have increased respect for his or her academic capabilities. If a college admissions committee had to choose between two high school seniors one of whom achieved a B in calculus, while the other had stopped taking mathematics after geometry, other things being equal, wouldn't the first candidate be more attractive?

Second, the student should not let fear, anxiety, or a negative self-image undermine his or her performance in a course. Perseverance and hard work, not intelligence or aptitude, are the key factors. The student should find out who the best teacher is for a given subject is and then do everything possible to get into that teacher's class. Most people will learn more from an excellent teacher who is using a poor textbook than from a poor or boring teacher who is using an outstanding textbook. Of course, the best teachers tend to use the best textbooks. Students should not hesitate to ask questions in class when they don't understand something. In all my years of teaching, I have heard many questions that begin with "This is a dumb question but . . . ," but I have yet to hear a dumb question. Students don't have to let a teacher or faculty member get away with reciting a carefully prepared lecture that sounds impressive but doesn't clearly communicate the concepts to them.

It might be a good idea to begin with one (or at most two) mathematics and science courses the first semester. The student should beware of taking too many challenging new courses at once. First impressions are also important. The student should prepare very well for the first examination in a course. As demonstrated above in the section on teacher expectations, if a student earns an A on the first test, the instructor will begin to think of that student as an A student. This will more than likely be a subconscious assessment on the teacher's part, but it may directly influence how he or she interprets the student's questions, grades the student's essay questions, or, in fact, assesses the student's responses in any ambiguous situation. The same classroom question, or essay response, can be seen as either a stupid question from a thick student or a subtle question from a probing mind, depending on how the instructor perceives the student in the first place.

If at all possible, students should visit their instructors after class to discuss the course content and ask questions and should try to establish a professional connection with them. This will probably be more effective if a student has already achieved an A or B on the first test. However, most instructors will react positively to C or D students who try to improve their grade and who take the trouble to see them.

Chapter 6 clearly demonstrates the advantages of students' forming cooperative study groups with several other students. Students interested in forming such a group should try to identify other students who are hardworking and serious about the course and with whom they have some personal chemistry. If possible, students should participate in group study several times a week, in addition to the individual time they put in studying for the course. Simply put, the more time the student spend working on the course outside of class, the more likely he or she is to succeed. Everyone in the study group should see it as a mechanism to excel, not a desperate or remedial activity. The members of a study group should not be concerned with how well they perform in comparison with the other members of the group. The goal of each student should be to do better on each test than he or she would have done had there not been a study group.

It is a good idea to set a goal for the course and then reward oneself for achieving it. For example, a night on the town, including dinner and a movie, might be the reward for a B in calculus. Or one might set up a more elaborate reward structure, for example, a night on the town for a B and a special weekend for an A. But, such external rewards, while nice, are icing. The real rewards are intrinsic. The B, or the A-, will be its own reward!

Following these recommendations will not guarantee an excellent job upon graduation. But it will yield a number of benefits, some of them intangible, and it will keep the student's options open with respect to future education and career development.

What about the parents of a preschool child? How can they prepare their child for success in school? I would emphasize two things: answering questions and reading. Children should be encouraged to ask questions about everything and to try to understand the world around them. Parents, for their part, should try not to perceive your children's questions as a bother. Children should be taught that trying to understand things is a valuable activity that is rewarded. Parents should not worry if they can't always answer their children's questions. And they should not be afraid to admit it. They can suggest that they work together to try to find the answer, even if it takes a few days. In any event, they can say to the child, "That's a good question." Ultimately, this simple statement may be the most important response of all.

Parents should try to spend some time each day reading to their child. He or she should see books as a natural part of the environment. Even very young children can play with, and appreciate, picture books. Parents should not obsess about when the child will begin reading. The important thing is that the child view reading as a pleasurable activity and enjoy playing with books.

It would be nice to have some kind of computer in the house so that the child could become comfortable with it. At first, this may simply take the form of playing games. Even minimal familiarity with computer software can give children a head start. But not every family can afford a computer, and this isn't absolutely necessary. For about ten dollars parents can purchase a blackboard and chalk. Together, parents and children can use the blackboard to explore writing letters and words and to count and play with numbers. This should not be done in an organized, rigorous, uptight manner. Instead, the blackboard should simply be another toy that the child enjoys and through which he or she may gain greater familiarity with reading, writing, and language.

The Joy of Science

In addition to the social relevance of scientific work, it is important for young people to appreciate the joy that many scientists derive from research. In an article about politics and the academy, Elie Kedourie cites the following lines from Yeats's poem "An Irish Airman Foresees his Death":

> Nor law, nor duty bade me fight,
> Nor public men, nor cheering crowds,
> A lonely impulse of delight
> Drove to the tumult in the clouds.

"Through the power of the poet's genius," says Kedourie, "these lines illumine, by analogy, the life of scholarship, and the particular fulfillment which is its reward.[18]

There is a striking parallel between the sentiments expressed in Yeats's poem and those expressed by Laura Andersson, an Oregon biochemist.

In retrospect, I cannot honestly say that I became a scientist solely because of my teachers. I had marvelous and dedicated teachers—and others who were less so. However, any motive force came primarily from within—an inescapable compulsion to ask questions and explore their answers. . . . The societal pressures against scientific careers for women still exist—and were even more prevalent when I was an undergraduate. But they never mattered, or were never a factor sufficient to deflect me from the sheer joy and unequalled exhilaration that are the rewards of working in the discipline.

Scientists, too, are human. I contend we are more, not less, likely to share our precious resource of inner joy with those kindred spirits—including students— who can see beyond the surface drudgery and hurdles to the beautiful rewards.[19]

Inclusive Science

In his book *In the Mind's Eye* John West argues that the physiological brain differences associated with learning disabilities may also provide greater abilities, particularly in the areas of spatial conceptualization and reasoning, to those with learning disabilities.[20] Moreover, he argues, it is precisely these kinds of spatial representation skills that will be needed in a computer-based economy. Thus, according to West, many students with learning disabilities may in fact possess other talents that will give them an advantage in the information age.

West bolsters his argument about the potential creativity of people with learning disabilities by discussing at length historical figures. Among the scientists and government leaders he profiles are Winston Churchill, Thomas Edison, James Maxwell, Michael Faraday, and Albert Einstein. Each of these men had a learning disability. It is hard to imagine where contemporary science would be without the contributions of Maxwell, Faraday, Edison, and Einstein. Yet, a highly structured and excessively selective education system would have weeded them out before they had an opportunity to demonstrate their tremendous creativity. In fact, most of these giants had to persist stubbornly in their education and career development despite official failures in the educational system and the work world.

A myopic system predicated on the assumption that only one kind of person can do mathematics and science foolishly excludes people who may provide the greatest contributions and innovations. Furthermore, as West illustrates, the "differences" that led to their exclusion in the past may be precisely the factors that make them more creative. For example, young people from a different cultural background will bring a different frame of reference to the solution of scientific problems, which may mean more creativity, innovation, and dramatic advances on the frontiers of research.

In a high-tech society, the ability to manipulate abstract symbols, particularly mathematical symbols, is essential for the individual who wants to succeed and prosper in the workplace. Mastery of science and mathematics is a path that people from disadvantaged groups can take to achieve social mobility. Other nations have moved more rapidly than the United States to develop a high-tech, information-based economy, in part because of their superior educational systems.

We cannot guarantee that every student who enters college to study science or engineering will find a job. Nor can we guarantee that the high school graduate who has mastered science and mathematics will be employed more rapidly or at higher pay than one who has not. But the odds are in their favor. Furthermore, the high school mathematics curriculum should be revised to include an introduction to statistics and other analytical techniques that will link more directly with the workplace and with the decision making required of citizens in a high-tech society.

The focus in this book upon mathematics and science education should not be interpreted to mean that other subjects are unimportant. For example, students need to learn history to better understand the world around them. Also, the technical fields cannot be examined in isolation. Unti we improve each aspect of elementary and secondary education, especially the teaching of reading and writing skills, it will be difficult to "jump-start" high school students into advanced mathematics. Finally, even in a high-tech society, some will succeed and prosper on the basis of reading, writing, and communication skills, without technical training. But the potential benefits of mathematics and science education continue to increase.

The research reported in chapter 5 clearly indicates the detrimental effects tracking has on student achievement. I believe we have been making a grave error in segmenting our high school curricula into heavy doses of mathematics and science for those who plan to go to college and "vocational education" courses containing very little mathematics and science for those who do not. First, the initial criteria for sorting students are far from perfect. Second, the vocational education students who later change their mind and want to pursue a college career (and one hopes that the number of such cases will be substantial) are placed at a distinct disadvantage. Third, even those students who never go to college will benefit from learning mathematics and science when they enter the work force. Fourth, college-bound students would have a much greater appreciation for their mathematics and science courses if the practical applications that presently are taught only to the vocational education students were incorporated in their courses. In short, we should have a uniform curriculum in which mathematics and science courses are offered to all high school students. Furthermore, high school mathematics and science courses should include a much greater emphasis on the practical applications of the technical concepts being presented.

In addition, mastering advanced mathematics, in particular, has an additional benefit: the student learns that he or she can achieve. This self-confidence may translate into success in other areas of the work world. The legendary coach of the 1960s Green Bay Packers, Vince Lombardi, demanded the best from each player and instilled in him a drive to win. It is instructive to read, year after year, about the extraordinary business achievements of these former players in work that has nothing to do with football.

Much can be learned from the international studies described in chapter 3. We have seen that the finding that U.S. students do poorly in the nineties does not mean that our schools have deteriorated, because the data also show that U.S. students did poorly twenty years ago. The authors of these studies state repeatedly that they were not trying to run an international horse race. Instead, these research projects were developed to learn about successful educational strategies by comparing the unique educational approaches of different countries.

In chapter 3, I underscore some of the lessons we in the United States can draw from those studies. For example, the strong performance of U.S. students on general information items learned outside of school identifies schooling, especially the curriculum, as what needs to be changed. The most important change involves presenting mathematics and science, especially mathematics, in a way that each student can see how these subjects relate to his or her future real-world experience. Other countries present advanced mathematics and science to a greater proportion of their students. As the evidence I have presented clearly indicates, virtually every American student would benefit from three or four years of mathematics and science in high school.

In this book I discuss many projects—teacher training programs, Saturday academies, curriculum revisions, and the like—each of which can contribute to a better education for our students. The first step is the realization that mathematics and science education is important for our participation in the global economy. Ultimately, success in these fields is based on expectations. It is extraordinary what human beings can accomplish when it is expected of them.

Notes

Introduction

1. P. Kennedy, *The Rise and Fall of the Great Powers: Economic Change and Military Conflict from 1500 to 2000* (New York: Vintage Books, 1989).

2. D. Goodstein, "The Science Literacy Gap: A Karplus Lecture," *Journal of Science Education and Technology* 1, no. 3 (1992), 151.

3. S. S. Penner, "Tapping the Wave of Talented Immigrants," *Issues in Science and Technology* 4, no. 3 (1988), 76–80.

4. S. Glashow, quoted in *Burning Questions: Losing the Future* (ABC News Special, 18 Dec. 1988).

5. International Association for the Evaluation of Educational Achievement, *Science Education in Seventeen Countries: A Preliminary Report* (New York: Pergamon, 1988).

6. R. M. Wolf, *Achievement in America: National Report of the United States for the International Educational Achievement Project* (New York: Teachers College Press, 1977), 9.

7. R. E. Yager and J. E. Penick, "Perceptions of Four Age Groups towards Science Classes, Teachers, and the Value of Science," *Science Education* 70 (1986), 355–63.

8. J. Eichinger, conversation with author, 1989.

9. I. Mullis and L. Jenkins, *The Science Report Card: Elements of Risk and Recovery*, report 17-S-01 (Princeton, N.J.: Educational Testing Service, 1988), 14.

10. I. Weiss, quoted in J. Raloff, "U.S. Education: Failing in Science?" *Science News* 133 (12 Mar. 1988), 165–66.

11. Penner, "Tapping the Wave of Talented Immigrants," 78.

12. D. Drew, *Strengthening Academic Science* (New York: Praeger, 1985).

13. J. A. Paulos, *Innumeracy: Mathematical Illiteracy and Its Consequences* (New York: Hill & Wang, 1988).

14. S. Tobias, *Overcoming Math Anxiety*, rev., exp. ed. (New York: Norton, 1993).

15. C. Cerf and V. Navasky, *The Experts Speak: The Definitive Compendium of Authoritative Misinformation* (New York: Pantheon Books, 1984), 173.

16. National Commission on Excellence in Education, *A Nation at Risk: The Imperative for Educational Reform* (Washington, D.C.: U.S. Department of Education, Apr. 1983).

17. American Association for the Advancement of Science, *Science for All Americans: A Project 2061 Report on Literacy Goals in Science, Mathematics, and Technology* (Washington, D.C., 1989).

18. P. U. Treisman, "A Study of the Mathematics Performance of Black Students at the University of California, Berkeley" (Ph.D. diss., University of California, Berkeley, 1985).

19. M. V. Bonsangue and D. E. Drew, "Long-Term Effectiveness of the Calculus Workshop Model" (report to the National Science Foundation, Apr. 1992).

20. R. J. Light, "The Harvard Assessment Seminars, Second Report, 1992: Explorations with Students and Faculty about Teaching, Learning, and Student Life" (Cambridge: Harvard University Graduate School of Education and Kennedy School of Government, 1992).

21. R. B. Reich, *The Work of Nations: Preparing Ourselves for Twenty-first Century Capitalism* (New York: Alfred A. Knopf, 1991), 233.

22. J. S. Coleman, E. Q. Campbell, C. J. Hobson, J. McPartland, A. M. Mood, F. D. Weinfeld, and R. L. York, *Equality of Educational Opportunity* (Washington, D.C.: U.S. Government Printing Office, 1966).

23. The College Board, "College Board Issues First Report Card on College Preparation Project for Minorities" (press release, 5 June 1992).

24. R. Rosenthal and L. Jacobson, *Pygmalion in the Classroom* (New York: Holt, Rinehart, & Winston, 1968).

1 · Technological Training and Economic Competitiveness

Epigraph: U.S. Departments of Labor, Education, and Commerce, *Building a Quality Workforce* (Washington, D.C., 1988), 23.

1. P. Drucker, *The New Realities* (New York: Harper & Row, 1989), 3–4.

2. P. Drucker, "Performance, Accountability, and Results," in *Educating for Results,* suppl. to *American School Board Journal* and *The Executive Educator* (Alexandria, Va., 1992), A8.

3. R. B. Reich, *The Work of Nations: Preparing Ourselves for Twenty-first Century Capitalism* (New York: Alfred A. Knopf, 1991), 172.

4. R. B. Reich, "Harnessing Human Capital," *U.S. News & World Report,* 22 Apr. 1991.

5. P. Lyman, "The Library of the (Not-So-Distant) Future," *Change* 23 (Jan.–Feb. 1991), 40.

6. D. Halberstam, *The Reckoning* (New York: William Morrow, 1986).

7. Critics complained that this technological-vocational emphasis on engineering education and the associated deemphasis on the liberal arts would distort Japanese society.

8. P. D. Hurd, "State of Precollege Education in Mathematics and Science," *Science Education* 67 (1983), 64, emphasis added.

9. S. E. Berryman, quoted in U.S. Departments of Labor, Education, and Commerce, *Building a Quality Workforce,* 11.

10. C. Piller, "Separate Realities," *Macworld,* Sept. 1992, 218, 221.

11. A. Smith, *Goodbye Gutenberg: The Newspaper Revolution of the 1980s* (New York: Oxford University Press, 1980); M. McLuhan, *Gutenberg Galaxy: The Making of Typographic Man* (Toronto: University of Toronto Press, 1962).

12. S. E. Berryman, "Learning for the Workplace," in *Review of Research in Education,* ed. L. Darling-Hammond (Washington, D.C.: American Educational Research Association, 1993), 367.

13. S. Davis, "The 1990–91 Job Outlook in Brief," *Occupational Outlook Quarterly,* spring 1990, 12.

14. U.S. Departments of Labor, Education, and Commerce, *Building a Quality Workforce,* 13.

15. "Training Today: More Signs of Skills Shortage," *Training,* July 1991, 14.

16. J. Hood, "When Business 'Adopts' Schools: Spare the Rod, Spoil the Child," *Policy Analysis* (Cato Institute, 5 June 1991), 3, quoted in *Inside American Education,* by T. Sowell (New York: Free Press, 1993), 6–7.

17. Commission on the Skills of the American Work Force, *America's Choice: High Skills or Low Wages* (Rochester, N.Y.: National Center on Education and the Economy, 1990).

18. T. Gonzales, "Commission on the Skills of the American Work Force," *AACJC Journal,* Feb.–Mar. 1991, 28.

19. Berryman, "Learning for the Workplace," 366. For a more extensive presentation of Berryman's ideas, see S. E. Berryman and T. Bailey, *The Double Helix of Education and the Economy* (New York: Institute on Education and the Economy, Teachers College, Columbia University, 1992).

20. G. Mee, "Ethnomathematics" (paper, Teachers College, Columbia University, 7 May 1991).

21. A. P. Carnevale, L. J. Gainer, and A. S. Meltzer, *Workplace Basics* (San Francisco: Jossey-Bass, 1991), 22–23.

22. J. S. Rigden, "High Schools Don't Prepare Youths for New Workplace," *San Francisco Chronicle,* 29 Dec. 1992.

23. C. Mitchell, "Real-World Basics," *Training,* Feb. 1991, 60–64.

24. B. Joyner, quoted in M. Schrage, "Statistics Skills Would Help U.S. Compete," *Los Angeles Times,* 14 Mar. 1991, D3.

25. Carnevale, Gainer, and Meltzer, *Workplace Basics,* 112–13.

26. W. Kolberg, *Los Angeles Times,* 16 July 1990, D2.

27. W. Clinton, "A Technology Policy for America," *EFFector Online* (Electronic Frontier Foundation) 3.08 (1992), 2.

28. Drucker, *The New Realities,* 232.

2 • Scientific Literacy

Epigraph: J. A. Paulos, *Innumeracy: Mathematical Illiteracy and Its Consequences* (New York: Hill & Wang, 1988). Copyright © 1988 by John Allen Paulos. Reprinted by permission of Hill & Wang, a division of Farrar, Straus & Giroux, Inc.

1. S. Krimsky, "A Citizen Court in the Recombinant DNA Debate," *The Bulletin* (Oct. 1978), 37.

2. D. Price, *The Scientific Estate* (London: Oxford University Press, 1965).

3. J. Dickson, *Think Tanks* (New York: Atheneum, 1971).

4. D. Guttman and B. Willner, *The Shadow Government* (New York: Pantheon Books, 1976).

5. H. R. Bernard, "Scientists and Policymakers: An Ethnography of Communication," *Human Organization* 33 (1974), 262.

6. See L. Rainwater and W. Yancey, *The Moynihan Report and the Politics of Controversy* (Cambridge: MIT Press, 1967).

7. H. Orlans, quoted in D. Drew, "Problems and Prospects in Using Research to Improve the Undergraduate Experience," *New Directions for Education and Work* 4 (1978), 92–93.

8. G. Fourez, "Scientific Literacy, Societal Choices, and Ideologies," in *Scientific Literacy*, ed. A. Champagne, B. Levitts, and B. Calinger (Washington, D.C.: AAAS, 1989).

9. B. Whorf, *Language, Thought, and Reality: Selected Writings,* ed. J. B. Carroll (Cambridge: Technology Press of MIT, 1956).

10. T. S. Kuhn, *The Structure of Scientific Revolutions* (Chicago: University of Chicago Press, 1970).

11. E. Shahn, "On Science Literacy," *Educational Philosophy and Theory* 20, no. 2 (1988), 42–51.

12. J. Trefil and R. Hazen, *Science Matters: Achieving Science Literacy* (New York: Doubleday, 1991).

13. R. Pool, "Science Literacy: The Enemy Is Us," *Science* 251 (Jan. 1991), 266.

14. Ibid., 267.

15. E. Culotta, "Science's 20 Greatest Hits Take Their Lumps," ibid. 251 (Mar. 1991), 1308–9.

16. R. M. Hazen, "Why My Kids Hate Science," *Newsweek,* Feb. 1991, 7.

17. H. H. Bauer, *Scientific Literacy and the Myth of the Scientific Method* (Chicago: University of Illinois Press, 1992), 17, emphasis added.

18. Paulos, *Innumeracy,* 3–4.

19. P. D. Hurd, *New Directions in Teaching Secondary School Science* (Chicago: Rand McNally, 1969), 1.

20. F. J. Rutherford, "Lessons from Five Countries," in *Science Education in Global Perspective: Lessons From Five Countries,* ed. M. S. Klein and F. J. Rutherford (Boulder, Colo.: Westview Press for the AAAS, 1985), 207.

21. Hurd, *New Directions in Teaching Secondary School Science,* 3.

22. K. A. Hart, *Teaching Thinking in College* (Ann Arbor, Mich.: National Center for Research to Improve Postsecondary Teaching and Learning, 1990).

23. J. D. Miller, "Who Is Scientifically Literate?" (paper presented to the AAAS Science Education Forum, Washington, D.C., Oct. 1989), 3.

24. L. Lederman, quoted in W. Booth, "Physicist Tackles Math, Science Illiteracy," *Washington Post,* 30 Dec. 1990, A14.

3 • "Don't Know Much about Science Books": Elementary and Secondary Education

1. S. Terkel, *Working* (New York: Pantheon Books, 1974).
2. A. E. Lapointe, N. A. Mead, and J. M. Askew, *Learning Mathematics,* report no. 22-CAEP-01 (Princeton, N.J.: Educational Testing Service, 1992), 4.
3. A. E. Lapointe, N. A. Mead, and J. M. Askew, *Learning Science,* report no. 22-CAEP-02 (Princeton, N.J.: Educational Testing Service, 1992), 13.
4. Some other countries excluded so many students from eligibility for the study that their results have been analyzed separately and are not included here.
5. A new worldwide study of mathematics and science achievement is being directed by David Robitaille of the University of British Columbia. The study, which will sample about 500,000 students from forty countries, will take ten years and will cost $3–4 million. According to Robitaille, prior international surveys have had a direct impact on educational policy in some countries. For example, in Sweden the study results became a national election issue; and in British Columbia, policymakers decided to offer calculus in the twelfth grade after they learned about European and Asian countries that did so (J. Gray-Grant, "UBC to Launch Educational Survey," *Vancouver Sun,* 14 Aug. 1991, B12).
6. M. D. Musick, quoted in C. S. Manegold, "U.S. Students Are Found Gaining Only in Science," *New York Times,* 18 Aug. 1994, A14.
7. International Association for the Evaluation of Educational Achievement (IEA), *Science Achievement in Seventeen Countries: A Preliminary Report* (New York: Pergamon, 1988).
8. This statistic refers to the percentage of students in academic secondary schools where science was taught; it excludes those, for example, who were attending vocational schools.
9. IEA, *Science Achievement in Seventeen Countries,* 20.
10. Here are some results from an international assessment of achievement in mathematics carried out by the Educational Testing Service, *World of Differences: An International Assessment of Mathematics and Science* (Washington, D.C.: Educational Testing Service, Jan. 1989). The figures represent an index of proficiency in mathematical computations.

Country/Province	Level
Korea	567.8
Quebec (French-speaking)	543.0
British Columbia	539.8
Quebec (English)	535.8
New Brunswick (English-speaking)	529.0
Ontario (English)	516.1
New Brunswick (French-speaking)	514.2
Spain	511.7
United Kingdom	509.9
Ireland	504.3
Ontario (French-speaking)	481.5
United States	473.9

11. C. McKnight et al., *The Underachieving Curriculum: Assessing School Mathematics from an International Perspective, a National Report on the Second International Mathematics Study* (Champaign, Ill.: Stipes, 1987), vii.

12. T. Husen, ed., *International Study of Achievement in Mathematics* (New York: John Wiley & Sons, 1967).

13. D. Walker, *The IEA Six Subject Survey: An Empirical Study of Education in Twenty-One Countries* (New York: John Wiley & Sons, 1976).

14. R. M. Wolf, *Achievement in America: National Report of the United States for the International Educational Achievement Project* (New York: Teachers College Press, 1977).

15. Walker, *The IEA Six Subject Survey,* 100.

16. Note that the United States had one of the lowest opportunity-to-learn scores in population 4, indicating that fewer students had been exposed to the full range of information being tested. However, both Belgium (Flemish-speaking) and England had lower opportunity-to-learn scores and higher science achievement scores.

17. T. Husen, in *Science Education in Nineteen Countries: An Empirical Study,* ed. L. C. Comber and J. P. Keeves (New York: John Wiley & Sons, 1973), 10.

18. Wolf, *Achievement in America,* 188, emphasis added.

19. J. Eichinger, "Science Education in the United States: Are Things as Bad as the Recent IEA Report Suggests?" *School Science and Mathematics* 90 (Jan. 1990), 35.

20. R. Leestma, R. L. August, B. George, and L. Peak, *Japanese Education Today: A Report from the U.S. Study of Education in Japan* (Washington, D.C.: U.S. Department of Education, 1987); R. Leestma and H. J. Walberg, eds., *Japanese Educational Productivity,* Michigan Papers in Japanese Studies, 22 (Ann Arbor: Center for Japanese Studies, University of Michigan, 1992).

21. N. K. Shimahara, "Overview of Japanese Education: Policy, Structure, and Current Issues," in Leestma and Walberg, *Japanese Educational Productivity.*

22. H. W. Stevenson and K. Bartsch, "An Analysis of Japanese and American Textbooks in Mathematics," in Leestma and Walberg, *Japanese Educational Productivity,* 109.

23. W. J. Jacobson et al., "Science Education in Japan," in ibid., 135–72.

24. H. Stevenson, C. Chen, and S. Lee, "Mathematics Achievement of Chinese, Japanese, and American Children: Ten Years Later," *Science* 259 (Jan. 1993), 53–58.

25. L. Thurow, *Head to Head: The Coming Economic Battle among Japan, Europe, and America* (New York: William Morrow, 1992), 278.

26. R. J. Samuelson, "Hollow School Reform," *Washington Post,* 28 Apr. 1993.

27. Stevenson, Chen, and Lee, "Mathematics Achievement of Chinese, Japanese, and American Children," 53.

28. H. W. Stevenson and J. W. Stigler, *The Learning Gap: Why Our Schools Are Failing and What We Can Learn from Japanese and Chinese Education* (New York: Summit Books, 1992).

29. R. Askey, quoted in B. Cipra, "An Awesome Look at Japan's Math SAT," *Science* 259 (Jan. 1993), 22.

30. S. W. Kim, letter to the editor of *Science* 260 (16 Apr. 1993), 278.

31. I. Westbury, "Comparing American and Japanese Achievement: Is the United States Really a Low Achiever?" *Educational Researcher* 21 (June–July 1992).

32. S. Lee and T. A. Graham, "Starting Preschool in Japan: The Beginning of Future Academic Achievement without the Academics," ibid. 21 (Nov. 1992), 34.

33. D. Laurie, *Yankee Samurai: American Managers Speak Out about What It's Like to Work for Japanese Companies in the U.S.A.* (New York: Harper Business, 1992).

34. F. J. Rutherford, "Lessons from Five Countries," in *Science Education in Global Perspective: Lessons From Five Countries,* ed. M. S. Klein and F. J. Rutherford (Boulder, Colo.: Westview Press for the AAAS, 1985), 212.

35. D. C. Berliner, "Educational Reform in an Era of Disinformation" (paper presented at the annual meeting of the American Association of Colleges for Teacher Education, San Antonio, Tex., Feb. 1992), 28.

36. Educational Testing Service, *What Americans Study: Revisited* (Princeton, N.J, 1994), 11.

37. C. Sagan, "Why We Need to Understand Science," *Parade Magazine,* 10 Sept. 1989, 10.

38. R. K. James and S. Smith, "Alienation of Students from Science in Grades 4–12," *Science Education* 69 (1985), 39–45.

39. F. J. Rutherford, quoted in AAAS, *Science for All Americans: A Project 2061 Report on Literacy Goals in Science, Mathematics, and Technology* (Washington, D.C., 1989).

40. L. Gogolin and F. Swartz, "A Quantitative and Qualitative Inquiry into the Attitudes toward Science of Nonscience College Students," *Journal of Research in Science Teaching* 29, no. 5 (1992), 500.

41. J. P. Keeves, "The Home, the School, and Achievement in Mathematics and Science," *Science Education* 59 (1975), 439–60.

42. E. L. Talton and R. D. Simpson, "Relationship of Attitudes toward Self, Family, and School Attitude toward Science among Adolescents," ibid. 70 (1986), 365–74.

43. R. A. Schibeci, "Home, School, and Peer Group Influences on Student Attitudes and Achievement in Science," ibid. 73 (1989), 13–24.

44. Gogolin and Swartz, "A Quantitative and Qualitative Inquiry," 501.

45. J. Eichinger, "High Ability College Students' Perceptions of Secondary School Science" (Ph.D. diss., Claremont Graduate School, 1990).

46. R. E. Yager and J. E. Penick, "Perceptions of Four Age Groups toward Science Classes, Teachers, and the Value of Science," *Science Education* 70 (1986), 355–63.

47. Rutherford, "Lessons from Five Countries," 208.

4 • Science and Mathematics in College

Epigraph: M. B. Zuckerman, "The Lost Generation," *U.S. News & World Report,* 21 Aug. 1989, 68.

1. R. C. Atkinson, "Supply and Demand for Scientists and Engineers: A National Crisis in the Making," *Science* 248 (Apr. 1990), 431.

2. A. Astin and H. S. Astin, *Undergraduate Science Education: The Impact of Different College Environments on the Educational Pipeline in the Sciences* (Los Angeles: Higher Education Research Institute, UCLA, 1992).

3. K. Green, "A Profile of Undergraduates in the Sciences," *American Scientist* 77 (Sept.–Oct. 1989), 475.

4. S. A. Maple and F. K. Stage, "Influences on the Choice of Math/Science Major by Gender and Ethnicity," *American Educational Research Journal* 28, no. 1 (spring 1991), 37–60.

5. E. Seymour and N. M. Hewitt, *Talking about Leaving: Factors Contributing to High Attrition Rates among Science, Mathematics, and Engineering Undergraduate Majors: Report to the Alfred P. Sloan Foundation on an Ethnographic Inquiry at Seven Institutions* (Boulder: Bureau of Sociological Research, University of Colorado, 1994).

6. S. Tobias, "Science Education Reform: What's Wrong with the Process?" *Change* 24 (May–June 1992).

7. Green, "A Profile of Undergraduates in the Sciences," 478.

8. Quoted in E. Seymour, " 'The Problem Iceberg,' Science, Mathematics, and Engineering Education: Student Explanations for High Attrition Rates," *Journal of College Science Teaching*, Feb. 1992, 236, reprinted in G. A. Hartz, "For Discussion, Why Not Lecture?" *Teaching Professor*, Apr. 1993, 6.

9. W. E. Massey, "A Success Story amid Decades of Disappointment," *Science* 258 (Nov. 1992), 1178–79.

10. J. E. Ware, Jr., and R. G. Williams, *Discriminating Analysis and Classification of Teaching Effectiveness Using Student Ratings: The Search for Doctor Fox* (Santa Monica: Rand Corporation, 1976); idem, "Validity of Student Ratings under Different Incentive Conditions: A Further Study of the Dr. Fox Effect," *Journal of Educational Psychology* 68, no. 1 (1976), 48–56.

11. D. S. Webster, *Academic Quality Rankings of American Colleges and Universities* (Springfield, Ill.: C. C. Thomas, 1986).

12. D. Drew, *Science Development: An Evaluation Study* (Washington, D.C.: National Academy of Sciences, 1975).

13. D. Drew and R. Karpf, "Ranking Academic Departments: Empirical Findings and a Theoretical Perspective," *Research in Higher Education* 14, no. 4 (1981), 305–19.

14. W. Hagstrom, "Inputs, Outputs, and the Prestige of Science Departments," *Sociology of Education* 44 (1971), 375–97.

15. L. J. Zimbler, *Faculty and Instructional Staff: Who Are They and What Do They Do?* (Washington, D.C.: U.S. Department of Education, 1994).

16. H. R. Allen, "Workload and Productivity in an Accountability Era," in *The NEA 1994 Almanac of Higher Education* (Washington, D.C.: NEA, 1994), 25–38.

17. J. Tronvig, "Conflict between Teaching and Research among University Professors" (Ph.D. diss., Claremont Graduate School, 1987), ii.

18. K. A. Feldman, "Research Productivity and Scholarly Accomplishment of

College Teachers as Related to Their Instructional Effectiveness: A Review and Exploration," *Research in Higher Education* 26, no. 3 (1987), 227–98.

19. R. Zoellner, "Are Teaching Professors Automatically 'Losers'?" *Chronicle of Higher Education,* 28 June 1976, 40.

20. S. Asch, *Opinions and Social Pressure* (San Francisco: Freeman, 1955); idem, *Studies of Independence and Conformity* (Washington, D.C.: American Psychological Association, 1956).

21. J. A. Davis, "The Campus as a Frog Pond: An Application of the Theory of Relative Deprivation to Career Decisions of College Men," *American Journal of Sociology* 72 (July 1966), 17–31; S. Stouffer, F. Suchman, L. De Vinney, S. Star, and R. Williams, *The American Soldier: Adjustments during Army Life* (Princeton, N.J.: Princeton University Press, 1949).

22. C. E. Werts and D. J. Watley, "A Student's Dilemma: Big Fish–Little Pond or Little Fish–Big Pond," *Journal of Counseling Psychology* 16 (1969), 14–19.

23. D. E. Drew and A. W. Astin, "Undergraduate Aspirations: A Test of Several Theories," *American Journal of Sociology* 77 (1972), 1151–64.

24. See, e.g., D. Drew, "The Impact of Reference Groups on the Several Dimensions of Competence in the Undergraduate Experience" (Ph.D. diss., Harvard University, 1969).

25. A. W. Astin, "Undergraduate Achievement and Institutional 'Excellence.'" *Science* 161 (1968), 661–68.

26. D. E. Drew and M. Patterson, "Noah's Ark in the Frog Pond: The Educational Aspirations of Male and Female Undergraduates" (paper presented at the annual meeting of the American Sociological Association, New York, Aug. 1973).

27. See M. Horner, "Femininity and Successful Achievement: A Basic Inconsistency," in *Roles Women Play,* ed. M. Garskof (Belmont, Calif.: Brooks/Cole, 1971).

28. J. Reitz, "Undergraduate Aspirations and Career Choice: Effects of College Selectivity," *Sociology of Education* 48 (1975), 308–23.

29. K. Alexander and B. Eckland, "Contextual Effects in the High School Attainment Process," *American Sociological Review* 40 (1975), 402–16.

30. M. J. Bassis, "The Campus as a Frog Pond: A Theoretical and Empirical Reassessment," *American Journal of Sociology* 82 (1977), 1318–26.

31. I recognize that both "Latino" and "Asian American" are broad categories. For example, the category "Asian American" used here and elsewhere by researchers would encompass students of Japanese, Chinese, Korean, Thai, and other backgrounds. Each of those cultures is distinctly different, and each presumably would have a different effect on the values, orientation, and aspirations of college students. Unfortunately, even with the relatively huge sample represented in the HERI data bank, there still are not enough students from each of these subgroups to justify statistically desegregating the analysis at that fine level. In preliminary analyses I desegregated and analyzed separately Puerto Rican students, but the numbers were so small as to call into question the statistical validity of estimates based on those subsamples. Consequently, Puerto Rican students were included in the "Latino" category.

32. In light of the sample size, the probability criterion for variable entry was set at .001, and the tolerance threshold was set at .30. Mean substitution was employed for missing data on the independent variables.

33. L. J. Sax, "Mathematical Self-Concept: How College Reinforces the Gender Gap" (paper, Higher Education Research Institute, UCLA, Los Angeles, 1992), 10.

34. Atkinson, "Supply and Demand for Scientists and Engineers," 427.

35. E. L. Collins, "Meeting the Scientific and Technical Staffing Requirements of the American Economy," *Science and Public Policy* 15, no. 5 (1988), 336–37.

36. R. Pool, "Who Will Do Science in the 1990s?" *Science* 248 (Apr. 1990), 434.

37. Collins, "Meeting the Scientific and Technical Staffing Requirements of the American Economy," 339.

38. B. L. Madison and T. A. Hart, *A Challenge of Numbers: People in the Mathematical Sciences,* report for the National Research Council Committee on the Mathematical Sciences in the Year 2000 (Washington, D.C.: NRC, 1990).

39. "Tough Times for Scientists: Ph.D.s Find Once-Plentiful Jobs Are Scarce," *San Francisco Chronicle,* 7 Sept. 1992, A17–18.

40. J. Mervis, "Analysts Debunk Idea of Scientist Shortage, Citing Defects in Current Economic Models," *The Scientist,* 29 Apr. 1991, 1, 4.

41. R. Schoenberg, "Strategies for Meaningful Comparison," in *Sociological Methodology,* ed. H. L. Cosiner (San Francisco: Jossey-Bass, 1972).

42. D. Drew, *Science Development: An Evaluation Study* (Washington, D.C.: National Academy of Sciences, 1975).

43. D. Drew and J. Wirt, *The Effects of Federal Funds upon Selected Health Related Disciplines,* R-1944-PBRP (Santa Monica: Rand Corporation, 1976).

44. B. Long, "Confessions of a Non-Scientist," *Visions from Oregon Graduate Institute* 5, no. 3 (1989), 30–31.

5 • Hidden Talent: Underrepresented Groups as a Resource

1. J. Lantos, "Farewell to a Classroom of Young Heroes," *Los Angeles Times,* 15 June 1991, B4.

2. P. Jacobs, "Keeping the Poor Poor," in *Crisis in American Institutions,* ed. J. H. Skolnick and E. Currie, 6th ed. (Boston: Little, Brown, 1985), 113–23.

3. D. C. Berliner, "Educational Reform in an Era of Disinformation" (paper presented at the annual meeting of the American Association of Colleges for Teacher Education, San Antonio, Tex., Feb. 1992), 10.

4. J. Hurst, "Invisible Poor Whites," *Los Angeles Times,* 11 July 1992, 1.

5. H. L. Hodgkinson, "California: The State and Its Educational System" (Washington, D.C.: Institute for Educational Leadership, 1986), 1.

6. Quality Education for Minorities Project, *Education That Works: An Action Plan for the Education of Minorities* (Cambridge: MIT, Jan. 1990), 13.

7. J. Kotkin, "U.S. Kids Are Doing Better Than You Think," *Los Angeles Times,* 28 July 1991, M1.

8. J. S. Coleman, E. Q. Campbell, C. J. Hobson, J. McPartland, A. M. Mood,

F. D. Weinfeld, and R. L. York, *Equality of Educational Opportunity* (Washington, D.C.: U.S. Government Printing Office, 1966).

9. R. Rosenthal and L. Jacobson, *Pygmalion in the Classroom* (New York: Holt, Rinehart, & Winston, 1968).

10. T. Sowell, *Inside American Education* (New York: Free Press, 1993), 97.

11. C. Sims, "From Inner-City L.A. to Yale Engineering," *Science* 258 (13 Nov. 1992), 1234.

12. R. Logan, *Howard University: The First Hundred Years, 1867–1967* (New York: New York University Press, 1968).

13. C. M. Matthews, *Underrepresented Minorities and Women in Science, Mathematics, and Engineering: Problems and Issues for the 1990s* (Washington, D.C.: Congressional Research Service, 5 Sept. 1990), i, 4.

14. R. Pool, "Who Will do Science in the 1990s?" *Science* 248 (Apr. 1990), 435.

15. Ibid.

16. Quality Education for Minorities Project, *Education That Works*, 1.

17. J. Oakes, *Lost Talent: The Underparticipation of Women, Minorities, and Disabled Persons in Science* (Santa Monica: Rand Corporation, 1990), 15, emphasis added.

18. See J. Crouse and D. Trusheim, "The Case against the SAT," *Public Interest*, fall 1988, 97–110.

19. T. L. Hilton, J. Hsia, D. G. Solorzano, and N. L. Benton, *Persistence in Science of High-Ability Minority Students* (Princeton, N.J.: Educational Testing Service, 1988), 163.

20. N. Gray, "Academic Preparation and SAT Scores" (Ph.D. diss., Claremont Graduate School, 1990).

21. H. P. Ginsburg and R. L. Russell, *Social Class and Racial Influences on Early Thinking* (Chicago: Society for Research in Child Development, 1981).

22. J. Oakes, *Multiplying Inequalities: The Effects of Race, Social Class, and Tracking on Opportunities to Learn Mathematics and Science* (Santa Monica: Rand Corporation, 1990).

23. D. G. Solorzano, "Chicano Mobility Aspirations: A Theoretical and Empirical Note," *Latino Studies Journal,* Jan. 1992, 53.

24. W. Pearson, Jr., and H. K. Bechtel, eds., *Blacks, Science, and American Education* (New Brunswick, N.J.: Rutgers University Press, 1989).

25. G. Thomas, quoted in ibid., 37.

26. J. Gaston, quoted in ibid., 124.

27. A. Jetter, "We Shall Overcome, This Time with Algebra," *New York Times Magazine,* 21 Feb. 1993, 29.

28. N. Caplan, M. H. Choy, and J. K. Whitmore, "Indochinese Refugee Families and Academic Achievement," *Scientific American,* Feb. 1992, 36.

29. B. H. Suzuki, "Asian Americans in Higher Education: Impact of Changing Demographics and Other Social Forces" (paper presented at the National Symposium on the Changing Demographics of Higher Education, New York, 9 Apr. 1988), 13.

30. A. Yamagata-Noji, "The Educational Achievement of Japanese Americans" (Ph.D. diss., Claremont Graduate School, 1987).

31. The College Board, "News from the College Board" (press release, New York, 5 June 1992).

32. M. Maddox, "Breaking the Poverty Cycle: The Inner-City Community College Prepares to Educate Disadvantaged Re-Entry Women for Self-Sufficiency" (Ph.D. diss., Claremont Graduate School, 1988).

33. R. Kanigel, *The Man Who Knew Infinity: A Life of the Genius Ramanujan* (New York: Charles Scribner's Sons, 1991), 3. Copyright (c) 1991 Robert Kanigel. Reprinted with permission of Scribner, an imprint of Simon & Schuster, Inc.

34. W. Thackeray, quoted in ibid., 64.

35. E. H. Neville, quoted in ibid., 336.

36. J. Nehru, quoted in ibid., 354.

37. D. Bloor, *Knowledge and Social Imagery* (Chicago: University of Chicago Press, 1991). See also M. Ascher, *Ethnomathematics: A Multicultural View of Mathematical Ideas* (Belmont, Calif.: Brooks-Cole, 1991).

38. Bloor, *Knowledge and Social Imagery,* 107.

39. W. Stark, *The Sociology of Knowledge* (London: Routledge & Kegal Paul, 1958), 162.

40. O. Spengler, *The Decline of the West,* trans. C. F. Atkinson (London: Allen & Unwin, 1926), 59.

41. Bloor, *Knowledge and Social Imagery,* 121. See also L. Wittgenstein, *Remarks on the Foundations of Mathematics* (Oxford: Blackwell, 1956).

42. Bloor, *Knowledge and Social Imagery,* 129.

43. J. S. Sebrechts, "The Cultivation of Scientists at Women's Colleges," *Journal of NIH Research* 4 (June 1992), 22.

44. B. Healy, "Women in Science: From Panes to Ceilings," *Science* 255 (Mar. 1992), 1333.

45. Sebrechts, "The Cultivation of Scientists at Women's Colleges," 24.

46. Ibid. The study Sebrechts cites is Greenberg, Lake, Analysis Group, Inc., *Shortchanging Girls, Shortchanging America* (Washington, D.C.: American Association of University Women, 1991),

47. E. Falconer, quoted in ibid., 24.

48. Women's College Coalition, "Math and Science Graduates: Women's Colleges Are Answering the Call" (Washington, D.C., 1992).

49. J. R. Cole, "Women in Science," *American Scientist* 69 (1981), 385–91.

50. J. A. Turner, "More Women Are Earning Doctorates in Mathematics, but Few Are Being Hired by Top Universities," *Chronicle of Higher Education,* 6 Dec. 1989, A15.

51. Ibid.

52. M. Barinaga, "Is There a 'Female Style' in Science?" *Science* 260 (16 Apr. 1993), 384.

53. J. R. Cole and H. Zuckerman, "The Productivity Puzzle: Persistence and Change in Patterns of Publication of Men and Women Scientists," in *Advances in Motivation and Achievement,* vol. 2, *Women in Science,* ed. M. W. Steinkamp and M. L. Maehr (London: JAI Press, 1984), 217.

54. J. R. Cole and H. Zuckerman, "Marriage, Motherhood and Research Performance in Science," in ibid., 119–25.

55. H. S. Astin, "Citation Classics: Women's and Men's Perceptions of Their Contributions to Science," in *The Outer Circle: Women in the Scientific Community*, ed. H. Zuckerman, J. R. Cole, and J. T. Bruer (New York: Norton, 1991), 68.

56. M. A. Paludi and L. A. Strayer, "What's in an Author's Name? Differential Evaluations of Performance as a Function of Author's Name," *Sex Roles* 12, nos. 3–4 (1985), 359.

57. K. D. Rappaport, *Rediscovering Women Mathematicians* (Washington, D.C.: Educational Resource Information Center, 1978).

58. M. H. Rice and W. M. Stallings, *Florence Nightingale, Statistician: Implications for Teachers of Educational Research* (paper presented at the annual meeting of the American Educational Research Association, San Francisco, 16–20 Apr. 1986).

59. S. Tobias, *Overcoming Math Anxiety*, rev., exp. ed. (New York: Norton, 1993), 74. Reprinted with permission by the author and publisher, W. W. Norton & Co., Inc. Copyright (c) 1993, 1978 by Sheila Tobias.

60. M. Sadker and D. Sadker, *Failing at Fairness: How America's Schools Cheat Girls* (New York: Charles Scribner's Sons, 1994).

61. M. Sadker, D. Sadker, L. Fox, and M. Salata, "Gender Equity in the Classroom: The Unfinished Agenda," *The College Board Review* 170 (winter 1993–94), 17.

62. A. Grieb and J. Easley, "A Primary School Impediment to Mathematical Equity: Case Studies in Rule-Dependent Socialization," in Steinkamp and Maehr, *Advances in Motivation and Achievement*, vol. 2, *Women in Science*, 317–62.

63. S. G. Brush, "Women in Science and Engineering," *American Scientist* 79 (Sept.–Oct. 1991), 404.

64. See E. E. Maccoby and C. N. Jacklin, *The Psychology of Sex Differences* (Stanford: Stanford University Press, 1974); and C. Benbow and C. Stanley, "Sex Differences in Mathematical Ability," *Science* 210 (1980), 1262–64.

65. See P. F. Campbell and S. C. Geller, "Early Socialization: Causes and Cures of Mathematics Anxiety," in *Women in Scientific and Engineering Professions*, ed. V. B. Haas and C. C. Perrucci (Ann Arbor: University of Michigan Press, 1984), 173–80.

66. P. Rosser, *The SAT Gender Gap: Identifying the Causes* (Washington, D.C.: Center for Women Policy Studies, Apr. 1993), 45.

67. P. Clark Kenscaft, quoted in J. Toth, "Women's Seeming Inaptitude with Figures Doesn't Add Up," *Los Angeles Times,* 14 Aug. 1991, A5.

68. J. S. Eccles, "Bringing Young Women to Math and Science," in *Gender and Thought: Psychological Perspectives,* ed. M. Crawford and M. Gentry (New York: Springer-Verlag, 1989), 40.

69. Ibid., 53.

70. H. Markus and D. Oyserman, "Gender and Thought: The Role of the Self-Concept," in Crawford and Gentry, *Gender and Thought*, 113, 114.

71. Oakes, *Lost Talent*, 30. See also M. Linn and J. Hyde, "Gender, Mathematics, and Science," *Educational Researcher* 18 (Nov. 1989), 17–19, 22–27.

72. Oakes, *Lost Talent,* 36.

73. Tobias, *Overcoming Math Anxiety,* 82.

74. Oakes, *Lost Talent,* 52.

75. L. Friedman, "Mathematics and the Gender Gap: A Meta-Analysis of Recent Studies on Sex Differences in Mathematical Tasks," *Review of Educational Research* 59, no. 2 (1989), 185–213.

76. Maccoby and Jacklin, *Psychology of Sex Differences.*

77. C. A. Klein, "What Research Says about Girls and Science," *Science and Children,* Oct. 1989, 28–31.

78. The possible connection between biology, genes, gender differences, and achievement in mathematics, science, and other areas is examined thoroughly by A. Fausto-Sterling in *Myths of Gender: Biological Theories about Women and Men* (New York: Basic Books, 1985).

79. S. J. Gould, *The Mismeasure of Man* (New York: Norton, 1981).

80. See, e.g., H. Gardner, *Frames of Mind: The Theory of Multiple Intelligences* (New York: Basic Books, 1983).

81. Gould, *The Mismeasure of Man,* 92–95.

82. C. Jencks, *Rethinking Social Policy: Race, Poverty, and the Underclass* (Cambridge: Harvard University Press, 1992), 96.

6 · Workshop Groups and Calculus Instruction

Epigraph: E. Carpenter, F. Varley, and R. Flaherty, *Eskimo* (Toronto: University of Toronto Press, 1959).

1. P. U. Treisman, "A Study of the Mathematics Performance of Black Students at the University of California, Berkeley" (Ph.D. diss., University of California, Berkeley, 1985).

2. It might appear contradictory to argue, on the one hand, that poverty undermines the ability of most students to learn in school and, on the other hand, that innovations like the Treisman calculus workshop groups can overcome the effects of poverty. The fact is that some young inner-city students live in environments where it is a struggle to survive—environments characterized by poverty, poor health, alcoholism, drug abuse, and violence. It would be naive to argue that inspired teaching or an innovative curriculum will transform the education of these young people. Many of them have to deal with so much stress in trying to survive that they have no energy left for school.

The schools cannot solve all of society's problems. Society must find a way to help these young people to bring their lives to a minimum comfort level before they can truly benefit from education. Even under these abominable conditions, though, some students will find a way to learn. Moreover, the work of Treisman and others shows that for those who survive and stay in the educational system early poverty need not be an insurmountable barrier to subsequent learning and achievement.

3. M. V. Bonsangue and D. E. Drew, "Long-Term Effectiveness of the Calculus Workshop Model" (report to the National Science Foundation, Apr. 1992).

4. J. Marlowe and K. Culler, "How We're Adding Racial Balance to the Math Equation," *Executive Educator,* Apr. 1987, 24–25.

5. R. J. Light, "The Harvard Assessment Seminars: Explorations with Students and Faculty about Teaching, Learning, and Life" (Cambridge: Harvard University Graduate School of Education and Kennedy School of Government, 1992), 6.

6. D. Drew, "The Impact of Reference Groups on the Several Dimensions of Competence in the Undergraduate Experience" (Ph.D. diss., Harvard University, 1969).

7. Light, "The Harvard Assessment Seminars," 20.

7 • Curriculum Reform and Talent Development

Epigraph: D. Goodstein, "Needed: An Isaac Newton of Science Education," *Los Angeles Times,* 3 Dec. 1989, M8.

1. National Research Council, *Everybody Counts—A Report to the Nation on the Future of Mathematics Education* (Washington, D.C.: National Academy Press, 1989), 6.

2. J. Blum-Anderson, "Increasing Enrollment in Higher-Level Mathematics Classes through the Affective Domain," *School Science and Mathematics* 92 (Dec. 1992), 433–36.

3. S. J. Gould, "The Median Isn't the Message," *Discover* 6 (June 1985), 40–42.

4. J. Bruner, "A Look at Incongruity," *University of Cincinnati Occasional Papers,* no. 4 (1966).

5. M. Frankenstein, "Critical Mathematics Education," in *Freire for the Classroom: A Sourcebook for Liberatory Teaching,* ed. I. Shor (Portsmouth, N.H.: Boynton/Cook, 1987), 186–87.

6. J. A. Turner, "With Number of Ph.D.'s Down, Mathematicians Debate Calculus Reform and Better Teaching," *Chronicle of Higher Education,* 31 Jan. 1990, A18.

7. E. Garfield, quoted in D. J. Lewis, "Why Johnny Can't Count: An Examination of Mathematics," *LSA Magazine* 14, no. 2 (spring 1992), 14.

8. R. Cole, *The Call of Stories* (Boston: Houghton Mifflin, 1989), 11–12.

9. E. Fandreyer, "Mathematics Education: A Remark from the Practitioner's Point of View," *UME Trends,* Jan. 1990, 6.

10. P. Connolly, quoted in J. A. Turner, "Math Professors Turn to Writing to Help Students Master Concepts of Calculus and Combinatorics," *Chronicle of Higher Education,* 15 Feb. 1989, A14.

11. Mathematical Sciences Education Board, report prepared for fall meeting, 1986, as quoted in C. McKnight et al., *The Underachieving Curriculum: Assessing School Mathematics from an International Perspective, a National Report on the Second International Mathematics Study* (Champaign, Ill.: Stipes, 1987).

12. T. Carpenter et al., "Results from the National Assessment of Educational Progress," in *Results from the Second Mathematics Assessment of the National Assessment of Educational Progress,* ed. M. K. Corbitt (Reston, Va.: National Council of Teachers of Mathematics, 1981), as quoted in McKnight et al., *The Underachieving Curriculum.*

13. T. Romberg, quoted in E. Levitan Spaice, "At Last, Math Curricula Enter the Real World," *Christian Science Monitor,* 19 Nov. 1992.

14. L. A. Steen, "Celebrating Mathematics" (retiring presidential address at the annual meeting of the Mathematical Association of American, Atlanta, 8 Jan. 1988).

15. R. S. Cole, "Why Should We Care About the Teaching of Calculus?" *Washington Center News* 7, no. 2 (1993), 5.

16. J. Poland, "A Modern Fairy Tale?" *The American Mathematical Monthly* 94, no. 3 (1987).

17. E. Effros, quoted in G. White, "Japanese Company Tutors U.S. in Math," *Los Angeles Times,* 19 Nov. 1990, D9.

18. G. W. Tressel, "Thirty Years of 'Improvement' in Precollege Math and Science Education," *Journal of Science Education and Technology* 3, no. 2 (1994), 80.

19. L. Williams, quoted in E. Culotta, "Can Science Education Be Saved?" *Science* 250 (Dec. 1990), 1327.

20. R. Yager, quoted in ibid., 1329.

21. B. Aldridge, quoted in M. Barinaga, "Bottom-Up Revolution in Science Teaching," *Science* 249 (Aug. 1990), 978.

22. E. Culotta, "The Reform Agenda: Emerging Consensus," *Science* 250 (Dec. 1990), 1328.

23. R. Roy, letter to the editor, *Science* 251 (Jan. 1991).

24. E. Culo, "Science Standards Near Finish Line," *Science* 265 (Sept. 1994), 1648.

25. R. E. Yager, "A Rationale for Using Personal Relevance as a Science Curriculum Focus in Schools," *School Science and Mathematics* 89 (Feb. 1989), 144–56.

26. *Los Angeles Times,* 16 Aug. 1992.

27. W. G. Wraga and P. S. Hlebowitsh, "STS Education and the Curriculum Field," *School Science and Mathematics* 91 (Feb. 1991), 54–59.

28. J. Dewey, *Democracy and Education* (1916; New York: Free Press, 1966), 127, quoted in ibid., 127.

29. Wraga and Hlebowitsh, "STS Education and the Curriculum Field," 51.

30. J. D. Miller, "Who Is Scientifically Literate?" (paper presented to the AAAS Science Education Forum, Washington, D.C., Oct. 1989), 25.

31. R. Pool, "Teaching Science Appreciation," *Science* 248 (Apr. 1990), 157–58, quotations on 157.

32. B. C. Clewell, B. T. Anderson, and M. E. Thorpe, *Breaking the Barriers: Helping Female and Minority Students Succeed in Mathematics and Science* (San Francisco: Jossey-Bass, 1992).

33. L. B. Hayden and M. W. Gray, "A Successful Intervention Program for High Ability Minority Students," *School Science and Mathematics* 90 (Apr. 1990), 323–33.

34. Ibid., 326–29.

35. D. Hamilton, "Formula for Success," *Los Angeles Times,* 7 Aug. 1992, B1.

36. L. Hoopes, quoted in ibid., 16 Aug. 1992.

37. H. M. Levin, "Structuring Schools for Greater Effectiveness with Educationally Disadvantaged or At-Risk Students" (paper presented to the American Educational Research Association annual meeting, New Orleans 7 Apr. 1988), 4.

38. R. Abramson, "Patron on the Potomac: The National Science Foundation," *Change* 3 (May–June 1971), 38.

39. The following descriptive information about the Experimental Program is based on NSF program documents, 1978–79.

40. D. E. Drew, *Strengthening Academic Science* (New York: Praeger, 1985).

41. J. Danek, personal communication, 1992.

Conclusion

Epigraph: P. Drucker, "Performance, Accountability, and Results," in *Educating for Results,* suppl. to *American School Board Journal* and *The Executive Educator* (Alexandria, Va., 1992), A4–A11.

1. E. Barkan, *The Retreat of Scientific Racism* (New York: Cambridge University Press, 1992), 157.

2. E. F. Schumacher, *Small Is Beautiful: Economics As If People Mattered* (New York: Harper & Row, 1973).

3. E. Cornish, "Think small," *The Futurist,* Dec. 1974, 276.

4. J. Todd, *An Ecological Economic Order* (Great Barrington, Mass.: E. F. Schumacher Society, 1985).

5. S. Love, "We Must Make Things Smaller and Simpler: An Interview with E. F. Schumacher," *The Futurist,* Dec. 1974, 282.

6. J. H. Comroe, Jr., and R. D. Dripps, "Scientific Basis for the Support of Biomedical Science," *Science* 192 (Apr. 1976), 105–11.

7. E. Mansfield, *Industrial Research and Technological Innovation: An Econometric Analysis* (New York: Norton, 1968).

8. A. D. Little, Inc., *Patterns and Problems of Technical Innovation in American Industry* (Washington, D.C.: U.S. Department of Commerce, 1973).

9. I. Illich, *The Medical Nemesis* (New York: Pantheon Books, 1976).

10. S. Tobias, "Science Education Reform: What's Wrong with the Process?" *Change* 24 (May–June 1992), 16–17.

11. G. Leonard, "The End of School," *Atlantic,* May 1992, 24–28.

12. A. Ratzki, quoted in ibid., 28.

13. R. J. Bonnstetter and R. E. Yager, "A Profile of Excellence: Teachers of Exemplary Programs in Elementary Science," *Science and Children,* May 1985, 45–46.

14. M. St. John and B. Heenan, "The Hands-on Interdisciplinary Preservice Science Course: An Interim Report from the Evaluation Team" (Pasadena: Inverness Research Associates, May 1994), 2.

15. L. Abram, "5 at Impoverished School in El Paso Gain Entry to MIT," *Los Angeles Times,* 1 Apr. 1992, A5.

16. K. Kavanaugh, testimony, in *Math, Science, and Engineering Education: A National Need: Hearing before the Subcommittee on Postsecondary Education of*

the Committee on Education and Labor, One Hundred First Congress, First Session, Hearing Held in Kansas City, MO, May 1, 1989 (Washington, D.C.: U.S. Government Printing Office, 1989).

17. "Academic Oasis at Georgia Tech," *Santa Monica Outlook,* 14 July 1994, A8.

18. E. Kedourie, "Politics and the Academy," *Commentary* 94, no. 2 (1992), 55.

19. L. Andersson, "But Why?" *Visions* 5, no. 3 (1989), 31.

20. T. West, *In the Mind's Eye: Visual Thinkers, Gifted People with Learning Difficulties, Computer Images, and the Ironies of Creativity* (Buffalo, N.Y.: Prometheus Books, 1991).

Index

Library of Congress Cataloging-in-Publication Data

Drew, David E.
  Aptitude revisited : rethinking math and science education
for America's next century / David E. Drew.
    p.   cm.
  Includes bibliographical references (p. –) and index.
  ISBN 0-8018-5143-2 (alk. paper)
    1. Mathematics—Study and teaching—United States.
2. Science—Study and teaching—United States. I. Title.
QA13.D74   1996
510'.71'073—dc20   95-35256